**'I love you
but I'm not in love with you'**

'I love you
but I'm not in love with you'

What happens when the passion goes?

Andrew G. Marshall

BLOOMSBURY

Bloomsbury Publishing Plc
36 Soho Square
London W1D 3QY

A CIP catalogue record for this book
is available from the British Library

ISBN 0 7475 7817 6
ISBN-13 9780747578178

10 9 8 7 6 5 4 3 2 1

Typeset by Palimpsest Book Production Limited, Polmont, Stirlingshire
Printed in Great Britain by Clays Ltd, St Ives plc

Bloomsbury Publishing, London,
New York and Berlin

The paper this book is printed on is certified by the
© Forest Stewardship Council 1996 A.C. (FSC). It is ancient–forest
friendly. The printer holds FSC chain of custody SGS-COC-2061

To Polly Vernon and Ed Jaspers

Thank you for helping get this book off the ground.

Contents

Introduction

Five years ago the occasional couple would present themselves at my therapy office after one partner had confessed, 'I love you but I'm not in love with you.' At first I was surprised; the phrase seemed to belong to a character in a smart New York sitcom. Yet real people were using it to describe something profound that was happening to their relationship. How could someone love but not be *in* love?

These couples would describe each other as best friends, or say that their relationship was more like that of a brother and sister, except most were still having sex. In essence, the partnership had become defined by companionship rather than passion, and that was no longer enough. Over time more and more couples complained of the same problem. Not everyone spontaneously used the phrase, 'I love you but I'm not in love with you', but all recognised the sentiments. For these couples the dilemma was especially painful: the person who had fallen out of love still cared deeply about his or her partner, and certainly did not wish to hurt them, but they wanted to end the relationship.

A typical couple would be Nick, a forty-two-year-old sales manager, and Anna, a thirty-nine-year-old teacher. Nick and Anna had been married for fifteen years and, despite some difficult patches, such as Nick's redundancy, their relationship had flourished. So when Nick dropped the 'I love you but . . .' bombshell Anna was devastated: 'I thought we had a happy relationship, I really did. Not perfect, of course, but then who can claim that? I've tried to get him to explain why he doesn't love me any more but he keeps saying he doesn't know. The best he has managed is that I don't listen. Except he's never told me before that he was unhappy.' Nick explained that the feeling had been building for several years and that he needed to tell their two teenage children and have a trial separation. 'He has no honour, no loyalty,' Anna complained. 'He is completely selfish. I feel he's leaving me for someone he hasn't even met yet.'

Faced with couples like Nick and Anna, I turned to the professional literature but found it dominated by couples who dislike, or even hate, each other, whereas I needed to know about couples who did not love enough. Worse still, I could find no research into how prevalent the problem had become, no theories about why it should be happening now or any suggested treatment programme. There was only one solution: I would have to fill the gap myself.

I initiated a research project in which all couples seeking help were asked to fill in a questionnaire after their first session. They were given a list of common problems that might have brought them into counselling. The results were startling: 47 per cent complained that the 'passion had gone', and 43 per cent said, 'I love my partner but I'm no longer in love/My partner no longer loves me.' Many of the traditional reasons for seeking help polled much lower: money issues were noted by 24 per cent, an affair by 21 per cent; differing opinions on how to bring up children were cited by 19 per cent, and out-of-control fights by 15 per cent. When couples were asked to choose the problem causing the *most* distress, 'I love my partner but I'm no longer in love/My partner no longer loves me' came third, with 24 per cent, close behind 'difficulty understanding each other's viewpoint' with 26 per cent and 'argue too much' with 25 per cent.

The research also backed up something that I had observed in my therapy office: people who ticked the 'I love you but . . .' option were less likely also to tick 'we argue too much' and more likely to pick the neutral 'we find it difficult to understand each other's viewpoints'. Anna certainly did not like arguments: 'My parents would scream at each other the whole day long, and I swore I'd never put my kids through the same thing.' If the worst came to the worst, she would simply walk away. Meanwhile Nick was so considerate, and so good at seeing her side, that he talked himself out of any disagreement: 'I wish that Anna didn't go up to bed so early. I don't get in until late and I'm left tiptoeing round the house alone, but it's not her fault really because after ten she can hardly stay awake.' In fact, they were both so thoughtful that the only open source of friction was that both enjoyed and therefore wanted to do the ironing. This might sound like heaven, but when someone cannot truly voice their feelings – even if only about minor issues – the relationship cools. Slowly over the years, degree by degree, all the emotions are dulled. Ultimately it is as harmful to row seldom, as it is to row all the time.

My second observation from my 'I love you but . . .' (ILYB) clients was that this lack of argument exacerbates the tendency for two partners to grow more like each other. The modern trend to be friends as well as lovers is another pressure, as we normally choose friends who are like us. This may seem wonderful but relationships need friction too. It is the grit in the oyster that makes the pearl and the difference that provides the love interest. More importantly, when there is so much pressure to be everything to each other, to share friends and even tastes, there is little room to be an individual as well as one half of a couple. 'I started to feel that I couldn't be myself,' explained Nick, 'I was trapped by what people expected of me.'

The third key observation was that most partners who had fallen out of love had recently had a life-changing experience. In Nick's case it was the death of his father: 'I remember standing at the foot of his bed and thinking, "Shouldn't I be doing something with my life?" Worse still, I could see how little time I had.' While Nick was struggling with abstract questions about the meaning of life, Anna retreated into herself too: 'I was close to Nick's dad – he'd almost been a second father – but I thought I'd be of most help offering support. So I held back my tears and didn't burden him with my grief too.' While she thought she was being strong for Nick, he read her response to his father's death as unfeeling and felt very alone. Instead of sharing their different reactions, neither said anything for fear of upsetting the other. It was not until later in counselling that all Nick's resentment came tumbling out. Other events, like reaching a milestone birthday, the birth of a child or a parental divorce, can also trigger a crisis of self-examination which, in turn, can tip over into questioning the relationship.

Over an initial twelve-month period I tried out some tentative treatment programmes with these early ILYB clients and started to read a wider cross-section of literature. I looked at books written by businessmen, philosophers, social biologists and marketing gurus; I looked into alternative relationships and found a small amount of research on successful couples. Some of these ideas could be taken directly into my counselling room and others had to be adapted. Slowly I found something that not only saved relationships but also helped ILYB couples achieve a much deeper intimacy and a truly satisfying bond.

I decided to write this book for three reasons. Firstly, I wanted to share a programme that works both with people in crisis and with other therapists. Secondly, I felt that a lot of information which can significantly improve a relationship is difficult to pass on in a therapy session. Counselling is about listening to people's problems, not teaching. With this book, couples and individuals can digest the ideas at their own rate. Thirdly, and most importantly, I wanted to spread the word that falling out of love does not mean the end of a relationship.

How Does the Programme Work?

This book is not a lecture about trying harder or not expecting too much from love – there are plenty of those already. My mission is to help people understand love and to point out the everyday habits that we think protect relationships but which in fact undermine them. When people hear about my work their most common reaction is to sidle up and ask, 'Is it really possible to fall back in love?' My answer is always the same: an emphatic 'Yes.' What's more, couples can emerge with a better understanding of themselves and each other and a stronger bond. This book will explain why and how.

The Seven Steps to Putting the Passion Back into Your Relationship will help you to: communicate better; have more productive arguments; take your sex life to a deeper level of intimacy; find a balance between being fulfilled as an individual and being one half of a couple. *If Your Relationship Has Reached Crisis Point* will provide a strategy for talking through the issues and dealing with the immediate fallout. *After the Crisis* shows how to bond again and rediscover love. Alternatively, if you have already separated, this section will help you to understand what happened, outline your options and help you to move on to a more rewarding future. Throughout the book you will find illustrations from my casebook, although I have changed names and details, and sometimes I have merged two or three cases to protect the couples' identity and their confidentiality. At the end of each chapter are a series of exercises. These can be done alone or, if you are working through this book with your partner, together.

The seven steps to putting the passion back into your relationship

Step One

Understand

'You know we've been having problems.'
'I thought things had got better.'
'I've been feeling like this for a long time;
* I hoped things would change.'*
'What? You didn't say anything.'
'It's just that . . . I love you, but I'm not in
* love with you.'*

When a relationship hits a crisis point the natural response is to try
to fix it as quickly as possible. But, in the panic, it is very easy to
get confused about the true nature of the problems and head off in
the wrong direction. So the first step is truly to UNDERSTAND.

Chapter One

What Is 'Love' Anyway?

In the past couples split up because they hated each other; today it is just as likely to be because they don't love each other enough. Love has changed from being just one of the ingredients for a successful relationship into everything: it is the glue that binds us together. Previous generations might have stayed together for economic need, because of what the neighbours might say or for the sake of the children, but we are no longer prepared to live in anything other than a passionate and fulfilling relationship. In some ways this is wonderful. Within a society fixated on working longer hours, being more productive and aiming higher, love remains a small beacon of happiness. But consequently these new demands put a lot of strain on our relationships.

If our relationships are to live or die by love, we need to have a pretty good idea of what love is and what sustains it. But when everything is going well we tend to relax; we let love smooth over everyday problems and don't ask questions, as though letting in too much daylight will destroy the magic. This is fine, until the love disappears and a couple is left wondering what happened: one partner cannot explain why they might still care but are no longer *in* love, while the other wants to know what they have done wrong. Sometimes the 'I love you but . . .' (ILYB) partner will arrive in my counselling office with a list of complaints: 'He is disrespectful', 'She shouts at the children', 'He's rude to my parents', and other similar gripes. But, however comprehensive, it never explains what happened to all the promises: 'I will love you, no matter what, until the end of time, for better or for worse.' What happened to the days when just hearing your beloved's name could quicken your pulse, or all that walking on air? What about that feeling that the two of you could take on the world? More than anything else these couples long to know how their passion turned from something special into just something OK – and finally into something disappointing – because without understanding the causes how can they fix anything?

A typical example is Michael and Fiona, both in their late thirties and together since their late teens. 'I no longer feel I'm special to Fiona,' complained Michael. 'I know we have responsibilities but we used to be everything to each other. Now I seem to come way down on the list. I might joke that I come after the kids' guinea pigs, but it's really not very funny.' Michael had been feeling like this for several years and had withdrawn into himself. At first Fiona thought there might have been someone else, but finally Michael confessed that he loved her but was no longer in love and was considering leaving. 'We're not a couple of kids sharing chips in a bus shelter any more,' she moaned. 'It can't be how it used to be. Just think of all the things I do for you: cooking, cleaning, ironing. Do you think I feel special every day? Life isn't like that.' Michael and Fiona were both talking about love but they had very different definitions. With no agreement about what constitutes love, their conversation went round in circles.

Almost every popular song is about love, as well as half of all novels and films; we read about it or see it on the TV every day. Surely we should understand love and, at the very least, be able to define it. But this is where the confusion starts. We can love our mothers, our children and our friends – even chocolate. When it comes to our partners, love can describe both the crazy, heady days at the beginning of a relationship and ten years later, taking his or her hand, squeezing it and feeling sure of each other. Can one little word really cover so many different emotions? Dictionaries are not much help. They list almost two dozen definitions, including affection, fondness, caring, liking, concern, attraction, desire and infatuation, and we all instinctively agree that there is a huge gap between liking and complete infatuation. The problem is that we have one word for three very different emotions: the early days or so-called 'honeymoon' passion; the day-to-day intimacy with a long-term partner; and the protective instinct for a child or the bond with a parent. To clarify the differences between these three emotions we need a new vocabulary, partly to remove the confusion between two partners with different takes – like Fiona and Michael – but mainly because by naming and explaining the differences we will understand love better.

A New Vocabulary

In the 1970s the experimental psychologist Dorothy Tennov set out to understand what happens when someone falls in love but was surprised how few of the founding fathers of her discipline had examined the phenomenon. Freud dismissed romantic love as merely the sexual urge blocked, while pioneering sexologist Havelock Ellis reduced these complicated emotions down to an equation: love = sex + friendship. So Tennov interviewed some 500 people in depth and – despite differences in age, sexuality and background – found a startling similarity in how each respondent described their feelings during the early days of love. These are some of the most common descriptions of being in love:

- Intrusive thinking – you can't stop daydreaming about your beloved.
- An aching in the heart when an outcome is especially uncertain.
- Buoyancy – as if walking on air – if there is a chance of reciprocation.
- An acute sensitivity to any acts or thoughts that could be interpreted

favourably – 'She wore that dress because she knows I like it'; 'He hung back after the meeting so he could talk to me.'

- A total inability to be interested in more than one person at a time.
- A fear of rejection and unsettling shyness in the presence of the beloved.
- Intensification of feelings through adversity (at least up to a point).
- All other concerns fall into the background – as a respondent told Tennov: 'Problems, troubles, inconveniences that normally occupied my thoughts became unimportant.'
- A remarkable ability to emphasise what is truly admirable in the beloved and avoid dwelling on the negative, even to respond with a compassion for negative qualities and render them into another positive attribute – 'It doesn't matter that he is shy because I can enjoy bringing him out of his shell'; 'She might have a temper but that shows how deeply she feels everything.'
- A feeling that, despite all the potential for pain, love is a 'supreme delight' and 'what makes life worth living'.

Not only do people all over the world experience almost exactly the same feelings in this early romantic phase, but also both men and women report the same intensity. To distinguish between these overwhelming emotions and the more settled ones of a long-term couple, Tennov coined a new word to describe this early phase of falling in love: LIMERENCE.

The obsessive, intrusive nature of **limerence** would immediately be recognised by Martin, a twenty-eight-year-old whom I counselled: 'I met her at a salsa class, the attraction was instant and we ended up exchanging telephone numbers – even though I knew she was married. It was against everything I believed in but I couldn't stop myself. It was impossible to work until we'd had our morning talk; I'd ache if she didn't call and even found myself "just happening" to walk down her road to stare through the window so I could picture where she made those surreptitious calls.' Twelve months later, when the affair had ended, Martin admitted that they came from totally different backgrounds and had little in common. He put the attraction down to lust, but most of the time the affair had been non-sexual. Tennov agrees: 'Sexual attraction is not "enough", to be sure. Selection standards for **limerence** are, according to my informants, not identical to those by which "mere" sexual partners are evaluated, and sex is seldom its main focus. The potential for sexual mating is felt to be there, however, or the state described is not **limerence**.'

Limerence can come, as it did for Martin, when a spark of interest is returned and becomes what the French call a *coup de foudre* – a thunderbolt. Alternatively it can sneak up and in retrospect the moment is recognised as something very special. Anthony, a thirty-nine-year-old web designer, had been dating Tasha for several months. They were enjoying each other's company but Anthony had not seen her as 'the one' until a visit to an art exhibition: 'She was so wrapped up in the painting that she didn't realise I was watching. In that detached split second I was overcome with tenderness. The vibrant greens and blues spilt from the painting on to Tasha. She had somehow joined the suntanned naked bodies from the canvas, the cool water and the reflections from the trees and the grass. All the natural colours of the scene had been heightened and exaggerated by the artist and I found myself being sucked into the painting too. My feelings were bolder and more colourful too – could that tenderness really be love?'

For other couples, a friendship can turn into something passionate when one half finally sees the other in a different light. Juliette and Edward, now in their forties, were at school together and shared an interest in music but nothing more – until Edward's eighteenth birthday party: 'I don't know how, but all of a sudden I noticed Juliette as a woman. It sort of sneaked up on me – maybe it was her long dark hair – but suddenly a light switched on: love at first sight, but several months later. I plucked up my courage and decided to kiss her, but I was very aware that she was a friend and worried about how she would take it. It felt odd and I remember a very quizzical look on Juliette's face as I leaned closer. Almost like she was saying, "Do you know what you're doing?" No words – it was all in the eyes but I hoped she understood. "Yes, I do."'

As hinted before, **limerence** can be the source of as much unhappiness as pleasure. It is possible for the object to remain a complete stranger, or be someone we know but who is unaware of our feelings. Even under these barren circumstances **limerence** can still grow and develop. Samantha was taking a language class and became obsessed with her teacher: 'The way his tanned muscles would ripple as he reached up to write on the flip chart; the pattern of the springy black hairs on the back of his arms as he'd lean across my desk to mark an exercise; how he'd push his fingers through his thick black hair. Even if he lived to be a hundred, you knew his hairline would never recede.' Samantha began to develop a set of complicated scenarios for how a relationship could develop: 'My favourite involved my car breaking down after class and the recovery services being unable to come for at least five hours, so he'd offer to take me home. Except his car would break down in the middle of a forest – a strange detail as I lived in the city – and neither of us would have a mobile. Our only hope of rescue would be a passing car, but nobody comes along that deserted road. So we have to snuggle together for warmth.' In reality Samantha was too shy to express her feelings and, in any case, her lecturer was married. Yet years later the smell of a school corridor – 'a strange combination of bleach, unwashed gym kit and chalk' – can bring back vivid memories for Samantha which are just as potent as those associated with real long-term relationships.

It is important that we have this new word for these intense feelings. Firstly, **limerence** recognises the normality of borderline crazy behaviour in the first stages of love; in other circumstances hanging around waiting for your beloved would probably be considered stalking. Secondly, when **limerence** wears off some people fear they are falling out of love, when in fact it is a natural phenomenon that happens to everyone; romantics can become addicted to the high and spend their whole lives moving on to the next affair, in the hope of finding that special someone with whom the buzz will last for ever. Thirdly, when someone talks about loving but not being *in* love, part of their definition of love is tied up with the magic of **limerence.**

Tennov describes five stages of **limerence** in her book, *Love and Limerence* (Stein & Day, 1980):

1 Eyes meet. Although the sexual attraction is not necessarily immediate, there is some 'admiration' of the beloved's physical qualities.
2 **Limerence** kicks in. Someone under **limerence** will feel buoyant, elated and, ironically, free – not just from gravity but also emotionally unburdened. All these beautiful feelings are attributed to the beloved's fine qualities. Tennov's respondents identified this as probably the last opportunity to walk away.
3 **Limerence** crystallises. With evidence of reciprocation from the beloved, either real or interpreted as such, someone under **limerence** experiences extreme pleasure, even euphoria. Tennov writes: 'Your thoughts are mainly occupied with considering and reconsidering what you may find attractive in the LO (limerent object), replaying events that have transpired between you and the LO *and* appreciating qualities in yourself. It is at this point in *West Side Story* that Maria sings "I Feel Pretty".'
4 Obstacles occur and the degree of involvement increases. 'You reach the stage at which the reaction is almost impossible to dislodge,' says Tennov, 'either by your own act of will or by further evidence of the LO's undesirable qualities. The doubt and increased intensity of **limerence** undermine your former satisfaction with yourself. You acquire new clothes, change your hairstyle and are

receptive to any suggestion to increase your own desirability in the LO's eyes. You are inordinately fearful of rejection.'

5 Mooning about, either in a joyful or a depressed state. (Tennov's respondents were surprisingly willing to describe themselves as depressed: 42 per cent had been severely depressed about a love affair and 17 per cent had even thought of committing suicide.) 'You prefer your fantasies to virtually any other activity,' writes Tennov, 'unless it is a) acting in ways that you believe will help you attain your LO or b) actually being in the presence of the LO.' A third option is talking endlessly about your beloved to friends. As all the popular songs about the broken-hearted attest, even being rejected or ignored does not dampen down the madness.

Tennov's respondents mentioned eye contact so often – 'the way she looked at me, or rather the way she rarely did' – that she believed the eyes to be the true organ of **limerence** rather than the heart. Indeed, research by social psychologists Michael Argyle and Mark Cook confirms the importance of eyes meeting across a crowded room. They found that when humans experience intensely pleasurable emotions our pupils dilate and become larger, which unconsciously and involuntarily betrays our feelings. What is more, a small increase in the secretion of the tear-ducts causes the eyes to glisten, producing what Argyle and Cook call the 'shining eyes of love'.

So how long does true **limerence** last? Tennov found few full-blown cases that calmed down before six months had passed. However, the most frequent – as well as average – duration for **limerence** was between eighteen months and three years. This fits with the findings of social biologist Cindy Hayman, of Cornell University, who tracked three brain chemicals (dopamine, phenylethylamine and oxytocin) in 5,000 subjects in thirty-seven different cultures and also found that the intense phase of attraction lasted somewhere between eighteen months and three years.

But once **limerence** has faded does it have to disappear completely?

18

Certainly the crazy, obsessive, possessed side of **limerence** cannot be recaptured, but the intense joy, walking on air and supreme delight can return, though most commonly as flashbacks rather than the all-engrossing early stages of **limerence**. Often these flashes come after periods of adversity, such as after being separated from your partner while she was away on a course or during the reconciliation phase after he had an affair. According to Stendhal, a nineteenth-century French writer famous for his essays on love, 'The pleasures of love are always in proportion to the fear.' Many couples feel a burst of **limerence** after an argument, especially during the 'making-up' phase. Phil and Edina experienced this after Phil crashed Edina's laptop, destroying a report she'd been writing. 'We both hate arguing but this row went round and round; even the next morning we weren't really talking. I saw things my way and she saw them her way – and that was that,' says Phil. 'We were completely stuck. At lunchtime we had to go off to a rendezvous. On the way to the car she brushed her fingers gently across the back of my arm. It felt electric, a huge surge of joy, as I knew she didn't want to fight either. We could work this out. My heart leapt and I floated down the street.'

Although resolving a conflict or returning from a long trip away are the most effective ways of re-experiencing **limerence**, there are other less dramatic ideas in the exercise section at the end of this chapter. However, it is important to remember that neither the intense form of **limerence** nor its associated biological attraction lasts for ever, and therefore we should not castigate ourselves if we no longer feel the same as we did at the beginning of the relationship. And maybe it is just as well. Would it really be practical to be forever thinking about our beloved to the exclusion of everything else, or to be always shy around them and fearful of rejection? When people make serious errors of judgement and engage in reckless affairs or inappropriate relationships, later claiming to have been 'blinded by love', they are nearly always describing the effects of **limerence**. In many ways it can be a curse as well as a pleasure.

*

So what happens to love after **limerence**? Once again the problem is how to define terms. Sometimes books and articles refer to 'mature love', which sounds very boring, or 'deeper feelings', which seems condescending to **limerence**, as although it is not deep-rooted it is strongly felt. Again we need a new expression to explain this second kind of love, therefore I have coined the term LOVING ATTACHMENT. This kind of love is not as flashy as **limerence** but it is just as beautiful: your partner stepping out of the bath on a Sunday morning and you suddenly seeing him or her from a new angle and being reminded of their beauty; watching your children together in the school play and sharing a look of complete pride; spontaneously buying a bowl of hyacinths for your partner when you had only gone out for a paper. Understanding **loving attachment** is vital because it offers an important clue for ILYB couples. When someone talks of not being *in* love, he or she is complaining about a lack of **loving attachment**.

Limerence versus Loving Attachment

Our culture's romantic myths of 'True love conquers all' and 'I'll love you no matter what' are all built on poets' and songwriters' experiences of **limerence**. Although the magic brings us together and helps us over the first few obstacles, to achieve and sustain a relationship something more is needed: LOVING ATTACHMENT. One of the easiest ways to understand this type of love is to compare it with **limerence**. Someone under the spell of **limerence** is bound tightly to his or her beloved, however well or badly he or she behaves. In the case of Samantha and her lecturer, he virtually ignored her as he was unaware of her feelings but her attraction to him remained strong. By contrast, **loving attachment** needs to be fed or it will wither and die. While **limerence** makes someone turn even their beloved's weaknesses into strengths, long-term couples – **loving attachment** couples – are only too aware of their partner's weaknesses. Finally, a couple under the spell of **limerence** do not care about practical matters such as earning a living because they have their love 'to keep them warm', whereas partners in a **loving attachment** couple tackle the complexities of life and its practical demands together.

Unfortunately the myths about romantic love – and lack of knowledge about **limerence** – make us believe that once we have found our partner we can relax, that love will automatically bridge any problems. Even when overworked or preoccupied with children, we imagine that our partner will understand if he comes bottom of the list of priorities, or that she will forgive us if we fail to complete that task for her. In the short term, **loving attachment** will survive this kind of neglect. But, if consistently abused, a relationship will deteriorate. 'I feel taken for granted,' explained Antonia, while her husband, Jerry, shifted in his chair until he'd almost turned his back on her. 'As long as the house runs smoothly and the kids don't make too much noise, he ignores me. He comes home and turns on the TV or plays on the Xbox with the boys. He doesn't actually talk to me, not about anything important.' This was too much for Jerry; he finally turned round and took her hand: 'But I love you. Isn't that enough?' He had assumed that their relationship worked in the same way as when they first met, when **limerence** was at its height and their bond could survive no matter what. Most couples end up in my office because one partner feels that their love is not returned and has, over time, become detached. This was the case with Antonia. It is easy to think that love ends because of some monstrous piece of bad behaviour, but more often it decays gradually through a million minor hurts. In fact, **loving attachment** can never be taken for granted and, like anything precious, it needs to be carefully tended.

What Feeds Loving Attachment?

For most people the following list will be second nature. However, couples under stress will skimp or disregard these relationship necessities.

- **Listening.** With full attention, nodding and asking questions so the speaker knows he or she is truly being heard.
- **Sharing.** Feelings, snippets from your day or chores.
- **Generosity.** It can be with your time, doing a job for your partner that he or she does not like, or a small gift.
- **Body contact.** A cuddle on the sofa, stroking the back of your partner's arms in the car or full sexual contact.
- **Supporting.** Watching your partner play sport, paying a compliment, babysitting while he or she takes an adult education course, buying into their dreams.
- **A shared sense of humour.** Private jokes, messing about and general silliness is a great way of bonding.
- **The extra mile.** We most appreciate the gestures that are really tough for our partner, like humouring our difficult mother or agreeing to that joint bank account.

If **loving attachment** has been lost, is it possible to reattach? I firmly believe it is and at the end of the chapter there is an exercise to get you started.

Next we come to the third kind of love, which offers more clues to understanding ILYB. If **loving attachment** has been neglected and the couple have detached, their 'love' turns into AFFECTIONATE REGARD, which is very similar to what we feel for our parents, children, siblings and best friends. **Affectionate regard** will make us care for someone, want the best for them and certainly not want to hurt them, but that person's destiny does not feel intertwined with ours in the way it does with **loving attachment**. In ILYB the 'I love you' invariably means 'I have **affectionate regard** for you'.

Loving Attachment versus Affectionate Regard

While **loving attachment** needs to be nurtured to thrive, this third kind of love is seldom conditional. I call it AFFECTIONATE REGARD because affection largely exists independently of how the recipient behaves. This is why the bond between parent and child can survive more dislocation and even neglect than the bond between partners. It is a sad truism that many children who have been abused by their parents can still want a relationship with them, and generally even the parents of murderers passionately defend their sons or daughters. Of course most parent–child relationships do not have to survive such extremes. But even within the happiest families parents can put their children through grief that would not be acceptable from anybody else. Conversely, no matter how often our children disappoint or exasperate us, our **affectionate regard** for them endures. The love for a close friend is also **affectionate regard**, as once again we 'let pass' behaviour from a friend that would be difficult to accept from a partner. A petty but telling example would be the friend who slurps his or her tea: this behaviour is mildly annoying when someone pops round, but living with her or him would quickly set your teeth on edge. More serious character defects can be overlooked in friends; our lives are not tightly intertwined and we can either close our eyes to bad behaviour or simply see less of someone. This is why friendships ebb and flow but the **affectionate regard** remains.

Confusing **affectionate regard** with **loving attachment** can cause a lot of misery. This is what happened in the case of Nick and Anna, the sales manager and teacher. Nick's relationship needs had not been met and he had become detached. 'We always go out with other couples,' he complained, almost in despair, asking his wife, 'When was the last time we went out just the two of us?' Anna saw things differently: 'But we still had fun, that time we all rented the cottage down in Devon – all those endless games of Monopoly. That game of strip Monopoly!' Nick couldn't disagree but in his eyes their marriage had become like a warm bath: comfortable but not very exciting. Anna had not realised how bad things had become because she had misread the **affectionate regard** – left over from fifteen years of shared memories – as **loving attachment**. Indeed Nick described their relationship as being like one between a brother and sister. For him, the loss of the passion from early **limerence** was a particular let-down.

So why can **loving attachment** slip into **affectionate regard**? I will go into this further over the next few chapters, but there are two main culprits: neglecting physical intimacy and not allowing each other to be different enough. Instead of being two individuals in a relationship, the partners become one amorphous couple and either one or both will complain about losing their identity – a common symptom of ILYB. Here is one of the most difficult paradoxes about sustaining **loving attachment**: for a long-term relationship we need to find enough similarities with our partner – either culturally, socially or emotionally – to make a connection, yet we need enough difference to stop the relationship stagnating. Often it is the friction of rubbing off each other's rough edges that provides the spark of passion. Look at all the great fictional characters we fall in love with at the cinema, theatre and in books: Rhett Butler and Scarlett O'Hara, Cathy and Heathcliff, Elizabeth Bennett and Mr Darcy, Romeo and Juliet. Not only are they all passionate in their relationships but also each half is very different from the other. You might not want such a charged relationship but look at the alternative: the only famous fictional conflict-free couple are Darby and Joan – and who wants to be like them?

Summary

- Popular romance feeds us the ideal of unconditional love; during the **limerence** phase something approaching this is often achieved. However, once a couple has moved into **loving attachment,** truly unconditional love becomes a distant memory.
- Unlike **limerence, loving attachment** dies if it is not reciprocated – especially sexually. However, **loving attachment** can last for ever.
- When a relationship has been ticking along happily enough it is possible to confuse the warm feeling as **loving attachment,** when in reality it has become **affectionate regard** – caring for and wanting the best for someone but with no underpinning romantic passion.
- When someone says, 'I love you but I'm not in love with you', they probably mean: 'I have **affectionate regard** for you but I have lost the **loving attachment.**' In the worst cases there is an additional layer to this: 'I miss the **loving attachment** so much that I now feel nostalgic for the excitement of **limerence.**'
- We consider falling in love and sustaining love as something magical and deliberately choose to shroud the process in mystery. While understanding how a magician saws a lady in half might spoil the illusion, understanding love is the first step in discovering how to revitalise it.

Exercises

Limerence Exercise – Eye Contact

To quote the writers of popular songs, in the early days of **limerence** 'I only have eyes for you' or 'Can't take my eyes off you'. However, once we have settled down and moved in together there are countless other distractions from our partner's beautiful eyes: the television, the newspaper and our watches. In fact, when Harvard psychologist Zich Rubin conducted an experiment using sophisticated recording apparatus, he discovered that couples whose questionnaires indicated a greater intensity of love looked into each other's eyes for significantly longer than couples less in love. In fact, couples in love spend 75 per cent of the time looking at each other when they are talking, rather than the usual 30–60 per cent.

We could debate for ever: do we stop really looking at our partner and the love fades, or does the love fade and we stop looking? Certainly Rubin believes that staring into each other's eyes can trick the brain into releasing phenylethylamine – a natural amphetamine and one of the brain chemicals that makes people fall in love. Try the following eye-contact exercise:

1 Attract your partner's attention, either by calling his or her name or putting your hand on their shoulder. The second part is particularly effective as you can use gentle pressure to bring her or his head away from the computer screen, for example, and to look at you.
2 Wait until you have your partner's full attention and he or she is looking into your eyes and wondering what is happening.
3 Look into their eyes. It does not need to be for more than a second – just long enough so you really see each other.
4 Give them a kiss on the lips.
5 Your partner will probably be suspicious and may ask something like, 'What do you want?'

6 Just smile and walk away.

7 Repeat the next day.

If your partner asks about the kiss, don't be defensive ('Can't I even ask for a kiss?') or go on the attack ('I have to ask for a kiss because you never give me one.'). Just explain how you used to enjoy eye contact when you were first dating. Although at first this exercise will seem forced, before long it will be incorporated into your routines and will become second nature.

Limerence Exercise – Connections

In the early stages of **limerence** Tennov noted how people are desperate to make links between themselves and their beloved. 'If a certain thought has no previous connection with the limerent object,' she writes, 'you immediately make one. You wonder or imagine what the LO would think of the book in your hand, the scene you are witnessing, the fortune or misfortune that is befalling you. You find yourself visualising how you will tell them about it, how the LO will respond, what will be said between you and what actions will – or might – take place in relation to it.' How different this seems from the dull evening routine of many long-term couples: 'How was your day?' 'Fine.' End of conversation.

To reintegrate this element of **limerence** back into your relationship, look for events that can be stored up and shared in the evening with your partner. You could even write them down in a notebook so as not to forget. There are two secrets to making these snippets interesting: firstly, look for the details that bring a story to life; secondly, seek out events, opinions and characters that play to your partner's particular interests.

Often with ILYB couples one partner has been editing their daily news. It can be for a variety of reasons: fear of boring their partner; to protect them from the unpleasantness of the daily business grind; simply to forget about minor irritations. All these reasons may be valid, but holding back will create a gulf between you and your partner. So try not to edit and instead, just like in the early stages of **limerence**, make a full and frank disclosure.

Ultimately everyone needs a witness to their life – without one we feel invisible, misunderstood and, in the worst cases, unloved. So listen attentively to your partner's news, ask questions to draw him or her out and show you are truly interested.

Loving Attachment Exercise

Try auditing everything that happened yesterday between you and your partner:

1 Starting from when you woke up, make a list down one side of a piece of paper. A typical list would be: breakfast; got ready for work; kissed goodbye; phoned from work; ate supper together; talked about day; watched TV. At the weekend it would be longer and more involved.

2 Now look back over the list and ask what, if anything, fed your **loving attachment**.

3 Give yourself a tick beside anything positive on the list, but be certain that the event has truly strengthened your bond. For example, a phone call for a chat could be included but not one asking your partner to pick something up.

4 Are there any items that could be changed so that tomorrow they might feed your **loving attachment**? For example, you could massage her feet while you watch TV or leave some freshly squeezed orange juice on the kitchen worktop for when he comes down later.

5 Could you add in an act of kindness tomorrow, like running her a bath or sending him a sexy text?

6 Is there anything on the list that you wish you had not done? Often we conveniently forget our less loving acts, but write these down too. This will encourage you to be more patient tomorrow.

Here are some of the questions my clients ask about the **loving attachment** audit:

Q. How long does it take to make a difference?

A. Changes do not happen overnight. Generally it takes couples three or four weeks to make a significant difference to their feelings about each other.

Q. If I have fallen out of love with my partner shouldn't it be up to them to change?

A. When we're upset with someone our natural instinct is to treat them less well. Guess what? They normally sink down to our level and the relationship becomes trapped in a negative circle. Why not lead by example and do something nice instead? Your partner might not respond in kind immediately but before long she or he will feel better disposed and ready to return the favour. Miracle of miracles, you have set up a positive circle. It just takes somebody to make the first move – why not you?

Chapter Two

The Six Stages of a Relationship

In classic love stories eyes meet across a crowded room. Two people fall in love, get married and set up home together. But what comes after 'happily ever after'? Our culture offers a few landmark events – engagement, wedding, christening – but not every couple can or wants to fit this pattern. Without a proper template of what to expect, how can we tell whether problems are a natural part of a maturing and changing relationship or a fundamental flaw? Unfortunately psychologists and social scientists are not much help: they have put their energy into studying failing relationships and have virtually ignored happy ones. So most couples are left fumbling in the dark, comparing themselves with friends but with little true understanding.

In the early 1990s, when I started seeing gay couples, there were even fewer ideas about what happened after their first exchanged glances than for heterosexuals. So I started researching the literature and came across a study by David McWhirter and Andrew Mattison – *The Male Couple* (Prentice Hall, 1984) – who over five years had tracked 156 gay couples in California between the ages of twenty and sixty-nine. None of these couples were in therapy and they were therefore more representative of the general population. McWhirter and Mattison soon found patterns and went on to identify a series of key stages that these gay couples went through, each with specific issues and problems. Using my own experience from counselling I adapted this model and found it so useful that I presented my findings to colleagues. Before I was even halfway through it became obvious to all of us that these stages were equally applicable to heterosexual couples. By taking away all of society's expectations about how relationships should progress we had revealed the underlying patterns for how all partnerships actually develop.

My road map from the first tentative 'I love you' to a whole lifetime together has six stages, each of which has particular hurdles and lessons for keeping love alive. In some cases couples will interpret issues that arise naturally when crossing from one stage to another as personal failure, or even as 'falling out of love'. But in reality the **loving attachment** has moved into another phase and has subtly changed. Other couples are simply stuck at one point on the journey or one partner has moved on to the next stage more quickly than the other, opening up a gap of different attitudes and expectations. This chapter explores each stage and when it happens, looking at skills to be acquired.

Blending

FIRST YEAR TO EIGHTEEN MONTHS INTO THE RELATIONSHIP

The new lovers want nothing more than to be together. Dorothy Tennov, who named this phenomenon, writes, 'The goal for **limerence** is not possession, but a kind of merging, a "oneness", the ecstatic bliss of mutual reciprocation.' This is nowhere more tangible than in the bedroom, with couples at this stage reporting high sexual activity. Paula and Mark had been dating for three months when Paula admitted, 'We took to brushing each other's teeth and using the same toothbrush. I know it sounds disgusting but I think it's really sexy and has brought us even closer.' All differences are overlooked or ignored as two people blend into one.

Blending provides new experiences and an opportunity for self-improvement. If one half of the couple has a passion – for opera, for example, or mountaineering, Egyptology or dog-breeding –

the other partner will immerse himself or herself in the hobby even if they previously had no interest in it. This might start off as part of the process of sharing everything with the beloved but it can be built into a lifetime of enjoyment. 'Dating Paula I actually felt cleverer,' explained Mark, a twenty-nine-year-old in IT. 'I hadn't been to university, I just learnt on the job. Although Paula had a degree, she was so interested in everything about me that I gained enough confidence to speak up more at work.' Mark's experiences are typical: during **blending** partners appropriate desired qualities from each other and integrate them into their own personality.

The intensity of togetherness means that both halves feel they understand their partner and are completely understood in return. When couples look back at this period it seems full of magic and madness. In fact humans need a bit of both, otherwise how could anyone trust a stranger enough to let her or him into their life?

Most common problems:
- Each partner is frightened of upsetting the other and of love being withdrawn, so everything possible is done to avoid arguments.
- If there is a row it feels like the end of the world. Unlike couples who have been together for years, **blending** couples have no experience of falling out with each other, disagreeing and making up again. Intellectually, **blending** couples know it is possible to survive a fight, but with no actual proof of living through one they worry that any disagreement could be fatal.
- One partner holds back for fear of losing their identity.

Skill: Letting go
It is important to surrender to the feelings during **blending**. On the one hand **limerence** helps couples to let down their barriers, but at the same time the rational voice is forever warning, 'Be careful.' Relationships put two fundamental human instincts at war with each other: we all long to be close – to be understood, to hold or

be held by another person – yet we also want to be in control, to be masters of our own destiny. Successful relationships strike a balance between these two needs. However, to start on the journey – especially as we grow older and more cynical – we need to trust and believe that this time it will be different.

Nesting

SECOND AND POSSIBLY THIRD YEAR

The couple become more committed and decide to move in together. Sexual desire moves from a frenetic level to something more manageable. Finally the couple become aware of things beyond the bedroom and creating a home together becomes their new way of expressing their love. This is where **loving attachment** begins. But living together and decreasing levels of **limerence** mean that issues suppressed during **blending** come up to the surface. Previously, when visiting each other's places, it was easy to avoid arguments over 'who does what' but now these practical issues take centre stage. 'It just wasn't the same any more,' said Nina, who had been together with Nigel for just under two years. 'I got really frightened that I was falling out of love. In some ways that wasn't a bad thing: I was concentrating better at work – goodness knows what my colleagues must have thought when I'd spend half the day on the phone to Nigel.' While the previous stage capitalised on attraction and minimised distractions, moving in together can highlight the differences. 'I thought Nina also wanted us to buy a place of our own, our own little corner,' said Nigel, 'but she thought paying off her student loan was more important. For the first time I looked at her and thought: Do I really know this woman?' Fortunately, instead of denying their different opinions or ignoring them, Nina and Nigel talked things through and resolved their argument. 'We've agreed to buy a few pieces of really good furniture that we can take with us,' said Nigel. 'We're just putting a lick of paint over the worst bits of this rented flat,' added Nina. 'Nina's got a really good eye,' said Nigel. 'I know it's not much, but when we show our friends I really feel we've achieved something: this is us,' Nina said, finishing off his thought. Unfortunately some **nesting** couples worry about their emerging differences, especially those with ILYB – 'What's wrong with us?' is a typical cry. These couples in particular need reassurance that their relationship is not dying but moving into another phase.

Most common problems:
- Familiarity can breed annoyance – eccentricities have transformed themselves into nasty habits.
- Rows often centre round 'male' and 'female' roles in the house. No matter how modern a couple might be, moving in together can reawaken old role models from childhood.
- Arguments go round in circles without getting resolved.
- Long-term tracking by researchers at the University of Texas suggests eighteen months' to three years' courtship as the optimum period for a happy marriage. But some couples find commitment hard and deciding to live together is a big decision.
- During **blending** the couple only had eyes for each other, but now friends and family become important again. The return of these outside forces can cause tensions between the couple.

Skill: Arguing
Often the rows seem to be about petty things – like whose responsibility it is to clean the bath or which colour to paint the bedroom – and couples, especially ILYB couples, often feel it is pointless to make a scene. This type of argument should not be avoided, however, partly because the issues will fester but mainly because **arguing** provides an opportunity to practise settling disagreements. It is far better to learn on minor issues, where the stakes are low, than wait until something major and unavoidable crops up.

Self-affirming

THIRD OR FOURTH YEAR

Up to this point couples have always stressed their similarities, perhaps encouraging a partner to join in with a favourite hobby or even giving something up to spend more time together. However, during **self-affirming** a couple has to feel confident enough to enjoy separate activities, to remember that there exists an 'I' as well as a 'we'. After all, it does not take two people to go to the DIY superstore and choose a hammer. It is only natural for a couple's individual traits, habits and characteristics to re-emerge and relationships actually need each partner's individuality to ensure growth.

An example of a couple who successfully negotiated the self-actualising skill of being independent and interdependent are Maya and Robin, who both have children from previous relationships. 'At the beginning we'd only do stuff as a whole family,' explains Robin, 'but after a while I missed playing tennis, and as my son and both Maya's boys were interested too I started coaching them on Saturday mornings. I felt guilty when I suggested it because I didn't want to exclude Maya, but actually she was happy to take my daughter shopping. And it doesn't stop us all meeting up for lunch.' On the first week of the new arrangement Maya was not so sure, but she was soon won over: 'It was stupid really to expect to be everything to each other. Robin doesn't like going to the theatre and there's really nothing to stop me going at the beginning of the week with one of my friends – and it's cheaper then.' Robin and Maya found other benefits too. 'Being apart gave us something to talk about when we met up later,' explained Robin.

During this stage each partner has to balance what is in his or her best interests with those of the relationship. This can come as quite a shock, especially after **blending** and **nesting**, where the needs of the relationship have always come first. Some couples pretend their personal needs are not important, but this builds up long-term resentment and potential identity issues – a hallmark of ILYB. Another problem during **self-affirming** is one partner asserting their individual

needs sooner than the other. This is often read as personal criticism
– 'Why don't you want to spend time with me any more?' – rather
than a natural phenomenon of this stage of the relationship.

Most common problems:
- If one half has no clear idea of who they are, or has low self-
  esteem, it can seem more comfortable to them to hide in a couple
  than to re-establish a separate, parallel identity.
- With ILYB couples, one partner will often think the other's time
  alone is a threat to the partnership, or one partner will be unable
  to voice their independent personal needs.
- One partner tries to stop the other having personal time, for fear
  it will signal the end of the relationship.
- Power struggles emerge centre stage.

Skill: Compromise
If the squabbles during **nesting** have been resolved the couple find
it easier to deal with the bigger issues lurking behind the petty ones.
During the first two stages the basic human need to be close has
been at the forefront. Now, with **self-affirming,** the need to be in
control of our destiny reasserts itself. So the couple remember their
individual needs and begin negotiating on how much personal time
is permissible. Often this can take hours and hours of discussion,
and with smaller issues in particular this can be exhausting.
Compromise is important, otherwise the balance will fall too much
in one person's favour and ultimately undermine the relationship.

Collaborating

APPROXIMATELY FIFTH TO FOURTEENTH YEAR
Couples use the security gained from within the relationship – and
the greater sense of themselves gained from **self-affirming** – to
launch successful outside projects. It could be a career change, a
further-education course or simply new interests. This stage is called

collaborating because of the high degree of support the other partner gives. The excitement and freshness generated is brought back into the relationship and shared. Alternatively the project can be a joint one, using complementary skills – the most common choice is having children together. Couples who meet later in life may decide to launch a business or travel together. Whatever the joint or individual goal, it imports new things into the relationship and avoids stagnation.

During **collaborating** reliability and dependability replace the insecurity and fear of possible loss from the previous stages. Couples have earned their easy familiarity and have developed complementary skills around the house; they know how the other thinks and feels but without the illusions of the first year. A shared shorthand is used for sorting out differences, rather than the previous stage's hours of negotiation. Although this type of communication is time-effective it can cause misunderstandings. If a couple are tired and stressed by children one partner often needs extra reassurance. 'I sort of know that Miranda loves me,' said Don, 'but it wouldn't hurt her to show me on a couple of occasions.' 'When we first met he had this funny business where he'd kiss different parts of my body and tell me that he loved them,' Miranda responded. 'It seems stupid to ask but it would be so nice.' If this type of thinking is not dealt with one half will feel isolated – a housemate rather than a lover – and become a ripe candidate for ILYB.

Most common problems:
- Taking each other for granted, or one partner growing quicker and therefore risking leaving the other behind – this is especially common for couples who met in their late teens and early twenties.
- If there is poor communication one partner can become too wrapped up in an outside project and neglect the other.
- There is a fine line between separate activities that enrich a relationship and those that cause a couple to grow apart.

- This is probably the hardest stage of the six stages. It is therefore no surprise that the average duration for a failed marriage in the United Kingdom is 11.3 years. (Source: Office for National Statistics, 2004.)

Skill: Generosity

Previously, compatibility and common goals were the ingredients for a successful relationship. In these later stages a lack of possessiveness is the key. It can be a difficult transition and is especially hard when one partner launches into something new when the other is either not ready or has not found their own path. ILYB couples have often found independence within the relationship difficult; this is unfortunate because couples who successfully negotiate the issues of **collaborating** stop living in each other's pockets. The extra distance helps keep the interest in each other alive and minimises the potential for boredom. Couples at this stage have to be generous enough to bless each other's projects and believe they will ultimately improve and not undermine the relationship.

Adapting

FIFTEEN TO TWENTY-FIVE YEARS

These couples are busy **adapting** to the changes thrown at them rather than dealing with internal changes within the relationship. These can be everything from children leaving home to ageing parents. By now each partner has given up the fantasy of what the other person might be and tends to think, 'He's always been like this and probably always will be' or 'What's the point of going on about her bad habits? They're actually quite endearing.' Perversely, when someone stops trying to change us and accepts us as we are, this is when we are most likely to bend. Couples at this stage feel contented; friendship and companionship are important. With increased self-confidence and less concern about what other people think, this is often a period of sexual reawakening. The frequency might not be as high as during the first stage but the quality is much better.

Nick and Anna provide an example of how outside pressures can impact on a couple: Nick felt extra responsibility for his mother following his father's death, while Anna talked about what would happen when their two teenage boys went off to university and how empty the house would seem. For Anna and Nick, looking at how their relationship had changed during the first five stages of love provided not just a fresh perspective but also a breakthrough in their counselling. Previously Anna had been always upbeat, always focusing on the positive aspects of the relationship. Concentrating on the challenges of the **adapting** stage – in her case the boys leaving home – Anna said, 'It's not just their physical presence, because they're always out, but the thought that it will be just the two of us. I feel all empty.' She turned to Nick: 'Just you and me for Sunday lunch.' Now Nick felt she understood that real changes needed to be made in order to save their relationship.

Although **collaborating** might be the hardest stage, **adapting** is the one most likely to throw up ILYB. The downside of accepting partners, warts and all, is that it makes change seem impossible. With this viewpoint, 'she/he has always been like this' quickly shifts from reassuring to depressing. Both men and women tell me, 'I want to feel special again.' And they can. By taking a fresh look and putting in a little work, what seemed stale and empty soon becomes warm with life again.

Most common problems:
- Couples can take each other for granted and become less express- ive and less likely to show emotion.
- Although there are advantages to accepting each other's foibles there is also a darker side. ILYB couples in particular often assume that their partner is incapable of change and so ending the rela- tionship seems to be the only option.
- Sometimes during a crisis one partner may wish to retreat back to the safety of an earlier stage: men who have been made redun- dant are compelled to start home improvements, as during the

nesting stage, or want a return to the closeness of **blending;** women who previously shouldered the majority of the caring – for children and elderly relatives – can return to **self-affirming**.

- One partner will assume that the other has enough to worry about and not confide their own problems.
- Sleeper problems begin to burst to the surface, reawakened by family events. For example, the death or serious illness of a parent can make someone reassess their childhood, with a knock-on effect for their relationship today. A couple's children reach the same age as when the couple first met and thereby unwittingly bring back issues long since buried. These connections are difficult to spot, however, so couples need to keep talking rather than retreat into separate corners.

Skill: Listening

By this stage couples feel they know each other very well, but major life changes – bereavement, milestone birthdays and teenagers' traumas – can hit in entirely unpredictable ways. **Adapting** couples make assumptions about their partners' reactions and needs based on the past – not always the best predictor for the future. Therefore it is important to listen – really listen – both to what is being said and what is being left unsaid. Some people try to solve their partner's problems but listening is more important, especially when someone is still absorbing the shock of change.

Renewing

TWENTY-FIVE YEARS TO FIFTY PLUS

Older couples are often the most romantic and the closest. This is much more than an echo of the **limerence** during **blending**. Closeness at stage one was based on the promise of a future together. Now the bond is based on the reality of a lifetime together. **Renewing** partners stop looking outside the relationship and focus all their attention inwardly. In effect they have come full circle and begin reaping the benefits of investment in their relationship. Shared memories and private jokes are very important for **renewing** couples: 'Every night before I put the light out I tell Martha that I love her,' says Iain, 'but she has to chip in that she loves me more than I love her. Maybe she's right; we've been through a lot together but I've always known that I can count on her.' This sort of security makes these the couples least likely to have ILYB.

Most common problems:
- Sometimes, as at the **blending** stage, these partners can be afraid to voice differences, especially when other people start encroaching on their time together – for example, when children expect too much help minding grandchildren.
- Health worries can isolate and turn closeness into claustrophobia. However, these are minor difficulties for the relationship and this stage can truly be called the best of times.

Skill: Patience
As we grow older we seem to become a caricature of ourselves. For example, someone who might previously only have worried about being late starts doing dry runs of journeys to make sure they know exactly how long they will take. Not surprisingly, this can make us more difficult to live with. Therefore patience and understanding can be useful skills for negotiating a way through idiosyncrasies and keeping the worst in check.

What if I don't fit these stages?
The first three stages generally apply at whatever age someone meets their partner, whether it is first love or love number ninety-nine. Stages four and five are of shorter duration for couples who meet later in life and for second marriages, while stage six is another universal experience. Remember that *The Six Stages of a Relationship* are a guide, not a prescription. So don't worry if you have not done everything in the right order. For example, some couples have a child together (stage four: **collaborating**) before moving in together

(stage two: **nesting**). Although this makes it harder to balance the independence and interdependence of a successful relationship (a crucial skill in stage three: **self-affirming**), most couples find a way round. It makes for a bumpier ride but then the potential for growth is even greater. Alternatively, when times are tough, you might find yourself retreating back to an earlier stage. A classic example is a couple who recommit to the relationship after one of them has an affair – they will spend several intense months **blending** again, although this stage will be much shorter the second time round.

Summary

- Relationships have a natural rhythm and each stage has a natural season.
- Although every partnership is different and subject to its own particular circumstances, following the general pattern makes for an easier journey.
- During times of stress, one or both partners will sometimes retreat back to an earlier stage. Once secure again, however, the couple will boomerang back to their natural stage.
- Problems arise because people assume their partner will always have the same needs as at the start of the relationship, but life changes us and our expectations.
- Getting stuck at one stage through not learning the key lessons can seriously undermine a relationship.
- ILYB couples often find the **self-affirming** stage hard because they prefer to stress 'couple' needs rather than individual needs.
- Understanding *The Six Stages of a Relationship* is the first step to diagnosing some of the problems behind an ILYB crisis. It can also be the first step on the fast track to a fulfilling partnership.

Exercises

Although each exercise has been designed for its relevant stage of love these skills can be useful at any time, so it is worth browsing through all the exercises and finding other ideas for tackling your issues.

Blending: Get in Touch with Your Inner Adult

New love can turn even the most self-assured into frightened teenagers. This exercise aims to help you find the competent adult side of your personality again.

1 Down one side of a piece of paper make a list of the things you argued about in the first year of previous relationships.
2 Down the other side fill in how you solved them. This will get you back in touch with your hard-earned life skills.
3 If you find it difficult to remember problems, here are a few suggested headings: money, washing-up, time apart, friends, child-care, tidiness, how often each of you initiates telephone calls.
4 Finally, think about how you can use these skills to solve today's problems.

Rows are vital to clear the air and learn about each other's needs. When your head has seen that these issues can be resolved it will be easier to let go and trust your heart.

Nesting: Hot-seating a Decision

Moving in together is a big decision and many couples try to put it off for as long as possible. If you are having trouble taking the plunge, remember that relationships cannot stand still – they need to develop. The best way to deal with ambivalence is to 'hot-seat' the feelings. I use this phrase because you become like a television interviewer, placing your partner in the hot seat and gathering as much information as possible without making value judgements.

Normally we try to talk down our partner's fears. For every potential problem we have an immediate answer. This might be a practical solution, reassurance ('Don't worry, I would never do that') or dismissal ('Don't be so stupid'). With this exercise you not only listen to your partner's fears but also ask him or her to expand on them and discuss all the 'what if's. Try these questions: What will be the consequences of moving in together? What other disadvantages are you worried about? What is the worst that could happen? What else?

Don't be afraid of silence while your partner thinks. As a counsellor I find nodding my head encourages people to open up further. This actively shows that you are listening but does not interrupt someone's thought patterns. Don't be tempted to talk down their problems; just keep going with a fear until all the possibilities have been exhausted. Jot down a heading that encapsulates the fears (for example, 'lack of space') and move on to the next area. If the fears come out in a rush, write them all down and then tackle the 'what if' scenarios one by one.

Once all the fears have been given a heading you will begin to see which are the most important. After a fear has been named and put down on paper my clients will often say, 'Actually I'm not that bothered about that one.' So I cross it off the list. After listening to your partner's fears, identify the ones which you share and add any different fears of your own.

Once everything is out in the open and we feel listened to our fears are much more manageable. Now you are ready to look for possible solutions.

Self-affirming: Relationship Board Meeting

The following exercise will help not only to separate individual responsibilities from shared ones but also to provide an opportunity for compromise, the main asset for this stage.

1 On separate cards write down the major tasks and responsibilities that your life together generates. The list could include

the following: money, social life, car, garden, cooking, food shopping, decorating, insurance, paying bills, families, making large purchases, holidays, pets, household chores, laundry. Some couples like to include abstract ideas such as fun, spontaneity and cuddles. The choice is up to you, but the more cards and the more detail the better.

2 Take a piece of paper each and divide it into three columns: me, you and us.

3 Write down where you feel each task should go; afterwards share your responses and the thinking behind them. Often you will agree on who does what but there may be a proviso. For example, one partner might look after the car but deciding on a replacement will be a joint responsibility. These provisos offer an opportunity to clarify how far one partner's power extends.

4 Remember that compromises only work when there is something in it for both parties. So go back and check: does the division feel fair? Did one of you back down too quickly? Was one of you too ready to please? With genuine compromise there are no winners or losers.

Here is an example of the 'Relationship Board Meeting' in action:

Samantha instantly took the 'social life' card but subsequently admitted, 'I've never been very good with money and have no idea how to budget. Bob is very good, so I let him take over the standing orders and working out how much we spend in different areas. It was rather a relief to stop worrying about it.' Bob was happy to take the card with these particular responsibilities. It soon became clear where each partner's strengths lay. The problems arose when either Bob or Samantha felt they were not properly consulted in the other's areas of expertise. So we found a compromise: Samantha consulted Bob about whether he wanted to go to a particular concert, but she made the bookings and checked if other friends wanted to join them; Bob consulted Samantha about budgets but he made the arrangements, such as consolidating their loans. The secret is to find a balance that plays to individual strengths but without undermining the loving bond.

Collaborating: Finding Your Dream

If you have yet to find a project to embark on, either together or separately, this exercise should help. Before starting it is important to understand the blocks to reaching your potential. Instead of fantasising about a potential project or interest and properly investigating the possibilities, many people immediately tell themselves one of the following:

- 'It's not practical.' Forget about the practicalities; anything is possible in dreams.
- 'It won't bring in any money.' Dreams feed your soul and express who you are, providing an interest so all-consuming that time just disappears. It could be taking an art course, building a model railway in the garden or getting your golf handicap down. Money does not come into it.
- 'I'm not talented enough.' Dreams are about enjoying yourself, so whether you do something well, indifferently or badly is completely unimportant. If you enjoy it, keep on doing it. Also, researchers have found that anybody can reach professional standards in anything, no matter what their original aptitude. It just takes about 10,000 hours' practice. So who knows?

Having temporarily silenced your internal critic, you are now ready to:

1 Find somewhere quiet so you won't be disturbed.
2 Close your eyes and imagine where you would like to live, then what work you would like to do, what kind of relationship you would like to have, what social life, what hobbies?
3 Imagine all the details so the fantasy seems as real as possible – don't rule anything out as impossible until you've finished creating your perfect life.

4 Fill in the pictures properly. What colours? What smells? What sounds?

5 Imagine a door to your dream world, open it and enter into the dream. What more can you learn as you really immerse yourself?

6 Open your eyes and work out how to start realising your dream.

7 Make a start the next day: book the golf lessons, buy a book about water-colour painting or start measuring up your garden for a model railway track.

Adapting: Listening Skills

Couples at this relationship stage think they know so much about their partners that they can even predict what they are going to say, but they may have stopped actually listening.

Everybody thinks they are good at listening – after all, it just involves a bit of concentration and not saying anything. Simple. Or is it? In 1984 Howard Beckman and Richard Frankel recorded how long doctors let patients talk for without interruption. The average time was just *eighteen* seconds. Remember, these doctors knew they were being studied so one would imagine they were trying to show off their listening skills. When the doctors were presented with the research two things happened: firstly, they insisted that they had let their patients talk for much more than eighteen seconds; secondly, they claimed that if they listened without interruption they would never get anything done, as patients would talk endlessly. So Beckman and Frankel did some follow-up research. This time the patients were allowed to talk for as long as they wished, without interruption. Most talked for only thirty seconds and no patient talked for more than ninety seconds.

This listening exercise is very simple but is one of the most effective.

1 Flip a coin to decide who goes first.

2 Partner number one can talk for as long as he or she likes about a current issue, without interruption.

3 To prove that partner number two is really listening, rather than rehearsing their answer, he or she has to summarise the main points when partner number one has finished. Three examples of what your partner talked about will normally suffice.

4 Swap roles. Partner two talks while partner one listens.

5 Partner one summarises number two's views.

6 Repeat the above as many times as necessary.

Renewing: Sculpting Your Relationship

Couples at this stage have known each other for so long that it is good to have a fresh perspective. This exercise brings complex feelings up to the surface and helps put them into words. It can be done alone but is better if completed with a partner.

1 Take a box of buttons or a pile of coins and spread them out on a table.

2 If you are doing this with your partner, divide the tokens so you have half each.

3 Without conferring, each person chooses one token to represent themselves, one for their partner and one for each member of the family.

4 Now you are going to create a picture of your family with the buttons/coins.

5 Start with you and your partner. How close or how far apart should you put these tokens?

6 Don't think too much about where to put everything. Go with your instincts for the time being.

7 Next move on to your family. Is your daughter closer to your partner than to you? Does she get in between you sometimes and therefore should be placed in the middle? Does your son seem outside the family? What is the best way to show that?

8 Next add in hobbies, pets, interests or jobs that make up part of your world. Where should these tokens be placed?

9   When you have finished adding everything, take a second look at your picture and check everything is in the right place.

10 Share your thinking with your partner. Did you choose the token to represent yourself and your partner for any special reason? Explain what all the tokens symbolise and your reasons for placing them where you did.

11 Finally, if you could change one thing in both your own picture and your partner's, what would it be? How could you make this happen in reality?

Remember that an open mind and new ideas will allow your relationship to continue to grow.

Step Two

ARGUE

'You never talk to me, not properly.'
'I do.'
'I never know what you're thinking.'
'I go along with what you suggest, don't I?
Nobody loses their temper; it's better that way.'
'But nothing ever gets sorted out.'

Most people would rather avoid rows; they are unpleasant and
sometimes make the problems worse. However, too few rows are
as bad for a relationship as too many. One or both partners will
swallow their opinions and end up feeling resentful, or the couple
will just drift apart. Nothing gets the issues out in the open better
than starting to ARGUE.

Chapter Three

Why Arguing Is Good for Your Relationship

When clients facing the 'I love you but . . .' dilemma arrive in my office they have no idea how to answer the question that most obsesses their partner: Why have you fallen out of love with me? My most common diagnosis is that the couple are not arguing enough. Twenty years ago couples used to arrive at my practice complaining of terrible rows. These days they turn up and say, 'We can't communicate.' It is almost as if proper arguments have been banned from many modern relationships.

No rows, no falling out and no bitterness – it sounds wonderful but is it really possible to completely transcend the tensions and live blissfully ever after? In reality arguing is an important part of a healthy partnership; it uncovers the issues that really matter and enables partners to distinguish between minor irritations and serious problems. An argument creates the impetus to speak out, cuts through excuses and creates a sense that 'something must be done'. Although rows sometimes make us uncomfortable that discomfort can be good.

So why are we so afraid to let rip with our loved ones? The first reason for being less confrontational is the trend for couples to be each other's best friends as well as lovers. It is considered bad form for friends to scream at each other: friends should be supportive, understanding and, most importantly, accept us as we are. 'My husband has a terrible habit of interrupting people,' says Kate, a thirty-two-year-old market researcher. 'His best man even joked about it in his wedding speech. I've tried teasing him but he says I knew his failings when I married him. So now I have to bite my lip.'

Couples with children can be especially nervous of having rows. 'Not in front of the children' is the buzzword for a generation that is ultra-cautious about undermining their sons' and daughters' confidence or causing other psychological problems. And with children being allowed to stay up later as they get older, 'not in front of the children' becomes an excuse for barely arguing at all. This is a pity, because when children witness a constructive argument they learn important lessons about honesty, compromise and reconciliation.

Another reason is that couples are simply too nice to argue. In many of these partnerships one or both halves watched their parents get divorced and are only too aware of how apocalyptic a row can be. 'The day we got married I told Jim, "I'll discuss, I'll listen but I won't fight",' says Lydia, a fifty-nine-year-old dental technician. 'I watched my father and mother fight incessantly and it's no way to live.' In an insecure world, where work is forever restructured and our extended families live further apart, our relationships are more important than ever. Therefore is it any wonder that we play safe and avoid conflict?

Busy work schedules mean that couples spend less time together. On the most simplistic level, if you hardly see each other you have fewer opportunities to fight. But it goes deeper. Just as overworked parents stress the importance of 'quality time' with their children, couples want the little time they do spend together to be perfect. Not only does this expectation put pressure on a couple to get the most out of their shared leisure time; it also makes them less inclined to express their dissatisfaction. 'Our only concentrated time together is on holiday or during weekends away,' explains Kate's partner Robert, a thirty-five-year-old software salesman. 'After splashing out thousands to fly to the Maldives I was not going to let myself get jealous about the way Kate flirted with the staff.' It takes sustained time together to feel relaxed enough to let down your barriers and be open about your grievances. When does a two-career couple have that?

The changing nature of the workplace is another culprit in making us less likely to argue. New management techniques have done away with old-fashioned confrontation in favour of finding consensus, and this is making itself felt at home as well as in the office. Michael is a forty-year-old manager with London Underground whose wife, Sue, noticed a marked difference in him after a particular training course. 'He decided we could only make a point if we were holding the talking stick – a wooden spoon from the kitchen,' she explains. 'I wanted to clock him with it. But every time I lost my temper he would calmly say things like, "I hear your anger," and, "We won't get closure this way." I had to keep telling him, "I'm not one of your middle managers."' As Sue discovered, it takes two to make an argument.

Some younger, high-flying couples – particularly those in their twenties – feel an immense pressure to be perfect. These individuals may have excelled in school, attended the best universities and colleges, graduated into exciting or highly paid jobs and are now buying their own homes. The perfect relationship is another box to tick and, sadly, arguments do not fit into that profile. Michelle, a twenty-seven-year-old TV researcher, speaks for many who strive for perfection: 'I would have been mortified if any of our friends had known that Claude and I were having relationship problems.' Michelle was very concerned about achieving and worried if any of her contemporaries were promoted, in case she was falling behind. Her marriage had become part of this competition. Unfortunately this couple had played the game so well that even Michelle was not aware of any serious difficulties until her husband disappeared for two months and reappeared on the other side of the world.

Other couples do not argue because one partner is so keen to help the other grow that they almost become their personal therapist or guru. How can you complain about that? After all, it is done out of the best possible motive: 'I just want the best for you.' However, these well-intentioned partners can soon be telling their other halves how to feel. Martin, a forty-two-year-old financial consultant, found himself in this position: 'My father had died and I was in shock. I thought he'd always be there for me. How could this have happened? I just wanted to sit quietly in the car and get my head straight. However, all the way through the four-hour car journey home my wife kept on at me: "You've got to get this out."' There is a fine line between trying to help someone and controlling them.

Underlying all the above reasons for not arguing is one unifying fear: What will happen if a row gets out of control? My clients confess, 'Often I'd like to get angry but I'm frightened I'll never stop,' or, 'If I let it out, will I go completely nuts?' and 'Will he think less of me/what if she rejects me?' Of course these are all perfectly reasonable concerns, especially for someone who has seldom let go before. Another group of couples have argued in the past but have had bad experiences: 'When she loses her temper she shouts me down and I hate it,' or, 'If I get angry he blanks me for days afterwards and the atmosphere is horrible.' So how do these couples overcome their fears? In my counselling room I reassure my clients that I will stop the argument from getting abusive and remind them that our session has a time boundary (fifty-five minutes), so it cannot last for ever. (Obviously I have to keep a close eye on the clock to make sure that my clients do not leave at boiling point.) I will also ensure that there is no fallout or cold silences. In effect my clients might be performing some risky feats, but I provide a safety net.

If you too are afraid of arguments, or intensely dislike rows, how can you feel safe enough to let go at home? This is important because even if you agree with the merits of arguing and digest all the techniques for constructive rows – laid out in the next chapter – nobody is prepared to enter a dangerous arena without a safety net. After twenty years of witnessing couples' arguments I have found three key traps that turn arguments from something fruitful and ultimately healing into something unproductive. These are blaming, belittling and going round in circles. For each of these three traps there is a separate strategy to avoid falling in or to climb out quickly. To understand these strategies I need to explain the underlying philosophy: the three laws of relationship disputes. This knowledge will become your safety net. The exercise section at the end of this chapter has advice about how to incorporate them into your relationship.

The Three Laws of Relationship Disputes

1 All arguments are 'six of one and half a dozen of the other'

This wisdom was always my mother's response when my sister and I fell out and tried to get her to take sides. After more than twenty years of relationship counselling I have yet to meet a couple who do not share equal responsibility for their problems – the exception being violent and abusive relationships or when someone is an addict. From time to time I hear such a persuasive story that I'm tempted to believe I've finally found an exception to the first law. However, with a little digging I always find that the story is not so black and white. Both sides have made an equal, if different, contribution to their unhappiness.

Unfortunately our culture, and particularly the law, is determined to separate the innocent from the guilty. When we tell our friends, 'You'll never believe what he said to me' or, 'Guess what she's done now', we edit the story to make ourselves appear in the best possible light. We do not mention that we were two inches from our partner's face, screaming at the top of our voice, or we conveniently forget our own mean and inconsiderate acts. As we reconstruct the fight, either in our heads or for anyone who will listen, we become more right and our partner more wrong. This process might make it easier for us to live with ourselves but it makes it harder to live with each other.

What about adultery? Is that also **six of one and half a dozen of** the other? After an affair society certainly likes to label the 'guilty' party, who cheated, and the 'innocent' party, who was cheated on. Yet in my experience the circumstances are always much murkier. When Donna had an affair at work and her husband Martin found out she was deeply ashamed and they came into counselling. 'What Martin won't listen to is the reasons why I felt tempted,' explained Donna. 'He had been so busy that it seemed he paid me no attention whatsoever. When this man at work noticed me it was very tempting. He even seemed interested in what I was saying.' Before anything happened Donna tried to talk to Martin and plan more activities together, but Martin's most important contract was up for renewal. Tied up with his work, Martin did not even notice that Donna had embarked on an affair. Donna found this particularly upsetting: 'I'd make this extra-special effort whenever I went out, and of course I was going out more often. My moods were all over the place – excited one minute then horrified that I could do something like that. Yet still Martin didn't twig.' Eventually she confessed to the affair and it ended. What Donna did was wrong but Martin's behaviour was a contributing factor. Innocent? Guilty? Can anyone truly apportion blame? And ultimately does it matter?

When all the 'if's, 'but's and 'extenuating circumstances' have been stripped away the responsibility in every relationship dispute is roughly fifty/fifty. Some might claim it is more like forty-eight/fifty-two, but a generosity of spirit – a very good asset in a relationship – would suggest that it is pointless to quibble.

Once **six of one and half a dozen of the other** has been taken on board couples are much less likely to fall into the trap of blaming during a nasty argument. After all, both halves have contributed to the problem.

2 Emotional equals attract
When I trained as a relationship counsellor I found this idea of emotional equals attracting hard to accept. Surely in every relationship one person is better at talking about their feelings than the

other, and doesn't that make them potentially better skilled with emotions? It is certainly a widespread belief that one half of a partnership – normally a woman – is better at relationships. On many occasions one partner will bring the other to counselling with the implicit message, sometimes spelt out, 'I'm fine, it's him/her who needs sorting out.' However, twenty years of counselling have taught me to know better. I smile as it soon becomes obvious that both partners need the sessions – equally.

To explain this second law it is important to understand what makes up an emotionally healthy individual. The first factor is an ability to be honest about and engage with feelings. Every family has its own problem topics handed down from one generation to the next, subjects that the family are so uncomfortable with that each member pretends they do not exist. Common examples would be sex, anger, money, competitiveness, sibling rivalry and jealousy, but the list is endless. 'When I was growing up, my mother would get all flustered whenever there was kissing on the TV,' said Terry, a twenty-nine-year-old plumber, 'and although I'd tease her about it I've never really felt comfortable talking about sex and, unlike mates at work, would never brag about conquests or make dirty jokes. It just doesn't feel right.' Obviously, being human, it is impossible for us to cut ourselves off from complicated emotions, so we ignore them. I compare this to putting up a screen to hide an unpleasant view. As a rule of thumb, the fewer the emotions hidden behind the screen the more emotionally healthy the individual. Some people have low screens and find it easier to look behind at the difficult emotions; others have such high and thick screens that they are totally unaware of their off-limits subjects.

The second factor for emotional health is well-balanced boundaries. In some families everybody is so in and out of each other's business that it becomes hard to know which problems or emotions belong to which family member. These low boundaries can be a problem, as these children can grow into adults who do not respect their partner's need for privacy or grasp that he or she might have different viewpoints. Conversely there are some families where the boundaries are so high that the members share virtually nothing; these children can grow into adults who shut their partners out.

In many cases someone who appears to be very good at talking about relationships may turn out to be comfortable with only a narrow range of emotions. Meanwhile their partner – who talks less but thinks more deeply – may find it easier to delve into the difficult topics hidden behind the screen. Alternatively the silent partner might be better at listening. Whatever the different skills, screens and boundaries each partner brings to the relationship, both have a matching level of emotional maturity. Often these skills are complementary and the secret of relationship counselling is to get a couple to pull in the same direction.

An example of a relationship which seemed on the surface to be emotionally unbalanced is that of Carrie and Jay, in their fifties with two grown-up children. Carrie did most of the talking and whenever I asked Jay a question he would either shrug or tell me, 'I don't know.' That would be Carrie's cue for a long discussion of Jay's mother, his childhood and what he was feeling. Jay would sit there, nodding. Carrie was certainly fluent in the language of feelings but became increasingly uncomfortable when the spotlight was turned on her. Out of her mouth would come a barrage of words, but afterwards when I looked at my notes it seemed she had said nothing concrete. So instead I asked Jay to talk about Carrie's background, and slowly a few facts emerged. 'Carrie's mother was ill for much of her childhood and she used to lie on a divan in the living room,' he explained. 'I became her eyes and ears,' Carrie chipped in. Slowly they painted a picture of a little girl who would listen for hours to her mother's complaints and be her permanently on-call agony aunt. Carrie would also bring snippets of news from the family and neighbourhood and they would pore over the details together. 'It made me feel important, OK,' explained a more subdued Carrie. Conversely Jay came from a family where nobody ever talked about feelings.

No wonder Carrie and Jay were attracted to each other. Jay found someone to discuss those forbidden feelings and Carrie found a partner for her ventriloquism act. This relationship had worked well at the beginning but Carrie had become more expressive and Jay quieter, until both started hating the other – as is often the case – for the very qualities that first attracted them to each other.

It was a question from Jay that proved the breakthrough: 'Did you and your mother ever talk about your relationship?' Carrie blustered. I kept quiet. 'It can't have been fun stuck inside with your mother when the other girls were out playing,' Jay added thoughtfully. Carrie had often analysed the family but there were unspoken limits. Her relationship with her mother and the restraints it had placed on Carrie were completely taboo. Although Jay might have been more detached from his family the distance had sharpened his perception. Both Carrie and Jay had their emotional strengths and weaknesses; in effect, equals had attracted.

Emotional equals attract is a very difficult philosophy to accept. I remember explaining it to a journalist, who became very thoughtful. 'So what does it say about me that I've just had a short relationship with someone needy and paranoid?' she asked. I wished I had kept quiet. But she decided to answer her own question: 'After my divorce, I suppose needy and paranoid just about summed me up.' Many other people would have found it easier to blame the ex-partner than look at themselves. Yet blaming our partner makes us disrespectful and cruel towards them, and ultimately produces destructive and belittling arguments.

Understanding that **emotional equals attract** makes people less likely to fall into the second argument trap: belittling. After all, each partner has just as many failings – and strengths – as the other.

3 The eighty/twenty rule
The stubborn issues – the ones that are really hard to resolve – are nearly always 80 per cent about the past and only 20 per cent about today. Patterns set up in our childhood have a knock-on effect on our adult relationships but often we are completely unaware. When

Kitty passed her driving test in her mid-twenties she could not understand why her partner's inability to drive became such a big issue. 'It had never bothered me before,' she said. When introduced to the idea that arguments can have roots back in childhood, though, Kitty began to make connections: 'My dad started losing his sight when I was about three; in fact my earliest memory was of his car being towed away after a nasty accident. From then onwards my mother did all the driving and there were times when naturally she resented always being the one on soft drinks at parties.' For Kitty, her partner automatically leaping into the passenger seat had triggered past associations. Once she understood her feelings and explained them to her partner driving became less of a flashpoint.

Another example of the **eighty/twenty rule** are Brian and Andy – a gay couple for whom taste and design caused rifts. They were most likely to fight over purchasing something for their house. The 20 per cent was about a natural-fibres rug for the living-room but the 80 per cent was about their backgrounds and their families' attitudes to money. Andy had been brought up in a middle-class family where money was always plentiful until his father's drinking habits got out of control and the business failed. From this experience Andy had learnt to enjoy money while it was around. Meanwhile Brian came from a working-class family – with six brothers and sisters – where, although his father had a steady job, money was always tight. One of his strongest childhood memories was of finding a ten-shilling note on the beach, the pleasure of being able to give it to his mother and the extra food it bought that week. Brian's lesson from childhood was that money is scarce and should be hoarded. Although understanding the **eighty/twenty rule** did not settle whether Brian and Andy should have bought the rug it did stop the dispute getting out of control or going round endlessly in circles.

Understanding the **eighty/twenty rule** will stop the same issues coming up repeatedly and prevent an argument from descending into bitterness. To learn more about the three laws of relationship disputes, and to lock them in as your safety plan, look at the exercises at the end of this chapter.

Summary

- Arguments are necessary for solving the inevitable conflicts between two people in a loving relationship.
- Many couples are frightened of having rows in case they spin out of control.
- Misunderstandings, problems and rows are **six of one and half a dozen of the other;** by taking this on board couples will stop blaming each other.
- The second law of relationship disputes – **emotional equals attract** – shows not only that both halves of a couple have equal skills with which to solve a row but also that these skills are usually complementary. This knowledge stops couples from belittling each other.
- If a dispute seems insoluble look at how the 80 per cent from the past is driving the 20 per cent from today. This helps couples to understand what a dispute is really about and stops the argument going round in circles.

Exercises

Six of One and Half a Dozen of the Other

Naturally, it is easier to spot when other couples are equally to blame than to accept equal responsibility in our own relationships. So, while trying to get the hang of this idea, take a break from examining your life and look at a couple from a favourite TV show, book or film.

Take Mr Darcy and Elizabeth Bennett, the timeless couple created by Jane Austen, as an example. Austen even helps us spot their respective weaknesses by calling the book *Pride and Prejudice*. She carefully balances her characters so that the blame for misunderstandings and obstacles to their happiness can be laid equally at both their feet. What about Jane Eyre and Mr Rochester, or Rhett Butler and Scarlett O'Hara? Look at the sitcom *Friends* and examine the responsibility of Rachel and Ross or Chandler and Monica.

After a while spotting the **six of one and half a dozen of the other** for famous couples becomes easy. When this is the case start applying the same test to your own relationship.

Emotional Equals Attract

When something is hard to take on trust, it is a good idea to find evidence from your life experience. This exercise will help you explore the concept and provide a launch pad for thinking about your own relationship.

1 Choose a couple who you know very well and have a chance to watch regularly. If your parents are still together that would be ideal, but your partner's parents, a sibling and their partner or a pair of friends will work equally well.
2 Take a piece of paper, divide it in half and at the top of each half write the name of one of the partners.
3 Think of all the personal qualities that make for a good relation-

ship: expressive of feelings; keeps things in proportion; good listener; open to change; well-maintained boundaries; insightful; brave; forgiving; thoughtful; assertive; willing to compromise; affectionate; curious; good with compliments; self-aware; kind; ambitious; outgoing; reliable in a crisis.

4 Allocate each of these qualities – and any more you come up with – under each partner's name. If both partners demonstrate the quality put it down for both of them.

5 If you wish you can add character defects too, but this is not essential.

6 Compare both partners. How well-balanced are the couple? Does the partner who seems to have less on their list have any hidden qualities that are harder to spot?

The Eighty/Twenty Rule

This concept is easier to come to grips with than the other exercises, so we will start closer to home.

1 Make a list of the petty things about your partner that irritate you. For example: hanging around the house without getting dressed on their day off; winding up the dog; leaving bills lying around the hallway.

2 Now turn Sherlock Holmes on yourself and discover why these issues get your goat. What does each bad habit mean to you? What memories does each bring back? What would your mother or father say about these things? What would your previous boyfriends, girlfriends or partners have said?

3 Next think back to your childhood and come up with your earliest memory. See how many details you can remember. Where were you standing? Who else was there? What were the colours, smells, tastes? What about touching something? How did you feel? Once the memory is as vivid as possible look for other childhood moments that might link in.

4 Still playing detective, start to put together a case. Remember

how detectives first try out a theory, mentally exploring the possibilities and then looking for evidence to either support the theory or knock it down. Take the same approach with the influences of parents on your personality and your relationship issues. For example, Kitty – whose father lost his sight – could discover how frightening her first memory had been. Aged three, we are very dependent on our parents. She could then ask what impact this had on her choice of partners. Does she play safe with a very reliable man? Conversely she might need to keep confronting her fears and therefore choose the excitement of being with a dangerous man. Do not close down any line of enquiry without thinking it through and testing your gut reaction. This is hard because we are naturally loyal to our parents, but the aim is to understand ourselves, not to blame them.

5 Finally, think back to your parents' favourite sayings. They might be philosophical – for example, 'Life's not fair' or 'Do as you would be done by' or 'There's no such word as can't' – or they might be personal – 'Why can't you be more like your brother?' or 'Big boys don't cry' or 'Don't worry, you're the . . . one' (fill in the gap: pretty, clever, etc.). Look at how much the drip, drip, drip of these sayings has marked your personality or view of the world. How many of the contentious issues with your partner are built on these opinions? Are they still true?

Considering these questions will help you to pinpoint the hidden 80 per cent of a current issue with your partner to which you might previously have been oblivious.

Chapter Four

Have the Sort of Arguments that Solve Problems

Since the sexual revolution of the sixties society no longer considers sex dirty, bad or something embarrassing to be hidden away. Today's forbidden feeling is anger. But anger, like sex, is a part of being human and cannot be wished away. Whether we like to admit it or not, everybody gets angry at some time. ILYB couples are made particularly uncomfortable or frightened by anger and therefore develop strategies for keeping conflict at bay. However, all avoidance strategies not only fail to deal with the underlying anger but ultimately cause more pain than dealing with it head-on.

Anger-avoidance Strategies

The four most common avoidance strategies are: detachment, rationalising, skipping and blocking. After examining the pitfalls and dead-ends of each strategy I will show what happens to the unresolved anger. Finally – with our safety plan from the previous chapter in place – we are ready to look at the nuts and bolts of productive arguments: what to say, what not to say and when to stop.

Detachment

Couples tell themselves: 'It doesn't matter', 'We'll agree to differ' and 'Ultimately, who cares?' While putting anger into cold storage can work in the short term, this strategy risks freezing over every feeling, including the positive ones. The effect is devastating. Jennifer is a forty-year-old maritime lawyer: 'There were things I didn't agree with, important things, but I didn't want to rock the boat. So I didn't say anything; I just shut down and gradually all my emotions became dulled.' Jennifer woke up one day in a passionless marriage, drifting towards divorce without knowing what was wrong. 'The whole focus of our counselling was on teaching us how to argue productively,' Jennifer explains. 'Although nothing was solved when we were shouting at each other, later when we'd calmed down and had a civilised conversation we always found a compromise.' The round-table discussions were productive because they had been through a cathartic conflict first. However, this is tough and many couples find themselves trapped in a vicious circle. By not arguing and processing anger, partners will become withdrawn and less likely to communicate – until the only strategy left is to detach.

Rationalising

While feelings are generally located in the body – for example, love seems like an ache in the chest whilst fear is a sinking sensation in the stomach – rationalising keeps everything logical, plausible and in the head. Nick and Anna had originally preferred to describe their arguments as 'heated discussions', and instead of letting the anger out they tried to neutralise it by keeping everything very logical. A typical example would be the time Nick elbowed Anna in bed during the night. 'He attacked me,' she complained. 'I hardly think "attacked",' countered Nick. 'That suggests an element of premeditation.' Anna was straight back with, 'I'm not allowed to have an opinion now?' The underlying issues were not being addressed as the argument quickly became about language, all conducted in the most reasonable voices. By Nick and Anna's standards it was a nasty fight, but they were both still unsatisfied and quietly seething. So we started to unpack the real issues. The elbow in the back during a restless night symbolised what Anna saw as Nick's uncaring attitude. But because she wanted him to stay she was determined to be 'sweetness and light'. The feeling still had to come out somehow, and this 'heated discussion' was a subconscious attempt by Anna to deal with some of the frustration. If they had both lost their tempers Anna would probably have blurted out the truth about holding back her feelings. By keeping everything very rational, Nick and Anna were protecting themselves not only from raised voices but also from a proper understanding of their relationship's dynamics and a lasting solution.

Skipping

Couples accept that they will get angry, but because they also feel guilty or uncomfortable they push the feeling away as quickly as possible. Anger is normally a wake-up call that something is wrong, but instead of listening to the message hidden beneath the pain these couples skip straight forward to resolving the dispute. Jackie would get home later than her partner, Peter, and immediately start preparing the evening meal. If she was late she would ask him to help chop up vegetables or cube meat. Although Peter was willing to help it nearly always ended up with one or other of them getting angry. Sometimes she would skip the row by trying to second-guess what his problem might be. 'No wonder you're so slow – that knife needs sharpening,' she would tell him, or, 'You're fed up because your favourite chopping board is still in the dishwasher.' Alternatively, he would try to solve the problem on the spot: 'You've had a hard time at work; go and put your feet up.' As soon as anger appeared on the scene Peter and Jackie tried to avoid the argument by heading for the exit sign. These suggestions might have been made with love, but by skipping over the anger they had found only superficial answers. In counselling we unpacked the layers beneath chopping boards and tiredness: Jackie felt that a good wife should have a hot meal prepared by a certain time; Peter was able to reassure her that he was more flexible. There was more to their rows than this, however – ultimately the couple had very rigid ideas of what men and women do in a relationship. Nonetheless Jackie felt that she was doing the lion's share of the household chores and wanted more help, while Peter feared that she wanted to order him around – rather like his site supervisor. Although he was willing to do more at home he did not want the same dynamics as at work. By no longer skipping the anger, Jackie and Peter discovered all the layers of the argument and a proper solution.

Blocking

This anger-avoidance technique is fairly rare with ILYB couples but quite common among the rest of my clientele: one half gets angry but the other half simply refuses to engage with their anger. In these relationships the conflict is upfront and sometimes bitter. Sian and Steven could generally solve their differences but there was one topic that completely overwhelmed their coping skills: Steven had two large dogs which had been bred specially to retrieve objects from water, and at the weekend he would be off at competitions. Sian was not a dog person and certainly not a large-wet-hairy-dog person, so the dogs lived in a kennel outside. However, the potential for disagreements about Steven's hobby were endless. If Sian ever tried to tackle him about them Steven would either go silent and let her rant or walk out of the room. Sian would be left fuming, brimming over with anger. Although Steven would get angry, and perhaps slam a door, none of it would be expressed directly to Sian.

Unprocessed Anger

Some people are so determined to mask their anger – because good people don't get mad – that it has nowhere to go but inwards. Ultimately the anger turns into headaches, ulcers, nervous conditions, depression or self-harm. The other costs of masked anger are not getting what you want and low self-respect. At the other end of the scale is sudden anger. These people deny anger – because they do not like it in themselves or other people – until the pressure builds to an intolerable level and they explode. For example, Virginia would – as her partner George described it – go ballistic. She would yell, swear and even throw things – like the breakfast bowl he'd put in the sink rather than the dishwasher. Privately George would dismiss his partner as 'a moody cow'. But because Virginia had suppressed all previous irritations George was not aware of the thousand other things that had broken down her composure – just the final straw. From his viewpoint her anger had no rhyme or reason: 'I'd forgotten to put my bowl away hundreds of times before and she'd not reacted like that, totally out of all proportion to the crime.'

ILYB couples usually find less dramatic ways to cope with unresolved anger. I think of this as sneaky anger, because rather than directly confronting the issue a person plays games, either consciously or unconsciously. In cases of sneaky anger, people may seem co-operative on the surface but actually never do what they are asked. They forget to make phone calls, put off DIY projects or deliberately load the dishwasher incorrectly – so their partner does not ask again. Psychologists call this passive-aggressive behaviour. While positive anger explodes and clears the air, passive aggression hangs around, poisoning a relationship. As children these people were often told not to yell, talk back, lose their temper, argue or rebel. In effect their parents were saying, 'Let's pretend these feelings and impulses don't exist in me and I'll pretend they don't exist in you.' Passive-aggressive adults always have a million excuses which make the real issues hard to tackle.

Mark, a thirty-seven-year-old local government officer, would agree to do something for his partner but actually felt anything but co-operative: 'I'd smile to her face and agree, "Of course it was my turn to empty the laundry basket." But I'd never quite get round to doing it. I was blowed if she was going to boss me about.' Eventually his partner retaliated and stopped doing things for him too. Having reached stalemate, they started counselling, where Mark learnt to be honest about his feelings instead of sneakily hiding his anger away. Finally they could properly negotiate who did what rather than snipe at each other. Other games played by the passive-aggressive include: 'Oops, I forgot'; 'Yes, but . . .' (add your own excuse); acting dumb and helpless; and sulking. Meanwhile their partner's patience snaps and she or he loses their temper. The passive-aggressive person will then turn self-righteous and blame their partner for the upset. Although a passive-aggressive person can seem powerful, their only control is in frustrating others; they often lose track of their own wants and needs and ultimately have unsatisfactory relationships. There is more on dealing with passive aggression in the exercise section.

The alternative type of sneaky anger is low-grade resentment. People exercising this trait do not make direct criticism, just comments with a distinct edge. Jilly, a forty-five-year-old animal behaviourist, found low-grade resentment was ruining her life: 'He'd make sarcastic comments like "wonderful" and "of course, Princess" when I wanted, for example, to go out with my girlfriends. But if I challenged him he'd just say something like, "Can't I even have an opinion now?" It was impossible to pin him down. Did he object to my night on the town, what I was wearing, or was he just jealous? Who knows? We'd end up bickering all the time.' Behind each sarcastic comment are several unspoken feelings and many possible different layers of meaning – from lighthearted comment to deep hurt. Is it any wonder that neither party knows what they are really discussing or where they truly stand?

Having looked at the pain and problems caused by avoiding arguments it is time to look at constructive arguments. When I explain this concept to my clients one partner will often say, 'This is all very well but I don't want just to pick a fight.' The other will chip in, 'It all seems so artificial.' So let's be clear: I am not suggesting that you become needlessly confrontational or have arguments for their own sake. Every day we are given invitations to get angry: someone cuts in front of the car; our call is not returned; we are criticised unfairly. Next time an argument is brewing, however, try not to side-step it. Some clients who are very uncomfortable with conflict start gently, either with strangers or work colleagues. Jackie, who avoided arguments over preparing the evening meal, could feel herself getting angry with a shop assistant who was too busy talking to a colleague to serve her. 'Normally I would stand there and fume inside,' she explained, 'but this time I could feel my teeth clenching and I thought, go for it. I was surprised how calm I sounded when I said, "Excuse me, could you help me?"' The second surprise for Jackie was that there was no smart comment or comeback from the assistant. 'It turned out to be no big deal,' she told me. After practising on strangers she was ready to be honest with Peter too. Jackie might have recognised her invitation to get angry, but many couples have become so adept at avoiding issues that they forget the signs.

The Seven Signs that You Need an Argument

Couples who argue regularly can afford not to worry about the first few signs, but ILYB couples – who hate even disagreements – should use even one sign as an invitation to argue.

- One partner is more silent than usual.
- Body language: not looking each other in the eye; hunched shoulders; crossed arms; tense jaw; tapping your foot; pacing around.
- Voice pitch changes: tension in the vocal cords makes them tighter and the sounds more brittle.
- Taking offence easily: 'Why did you do that?'
- Repeatedly checking with each other – 'Are you OK?'; 'Everything all right?' – but receiving a sharp or irritated response.
- Pointless contradicting: 'No, I don't agree'; 'Are you sure?'
- Things that you have put up with for ages, without complaint, suddenly start grating.

The only way to release this anger properly is to express it. Methods can range from a pointed comment – like Jackie's icy request for assistance in the shop – through to getting angry, shouting and even releasing an exasperated scream. I call this venting. Venting not only releases anger safely but stops it building up to the uncontrollable levels that give anger such a bad name. Venting does not include throwing things, abusive language or getting physical. These extreme forms of release only happen because all previous provocation has been ignored. A note of caution: venting only works if addressed to its proper target. Indiscriminate venting – for example, shouting at an innocent junior member of staff after criticism from a senior – will just pump up the anger.

Three Steps to Conflict Resolution

1 Explore: 'I need to say . . .'

This is all about venting anger and explaining grievances and frustrations, and hopefully it will come naturally out of the row. For more information about letting go of bottled-up feelings see 'How to Be Emotionally Honest' in this chapter's exercise section.

Sometimes one partner will need to do more venting than the other. Don't try to reason: someone gripped by emotions will not have access to their rational mind. Acknowledge their feelings: 'I can see you are upset.' Make sure all feelings have been vented before moving on to the second step. Check with each other: Do you need to say anything more?

Tip: Don't get personal. Rather than criticising the person, complain about the behaviour. Instead of, 'You're so untidy,' try, 'Please don't leave your coffee cup on the side.'

2 Comprehend

Hear each other out properly. Don't use the time while your partner is talking to rehearse your defence; listen. Ask questions so that you are clear about what is meant, and ensure that there are no misunderstandings. If you pay your partner the compliment of active listening they will return the favour. If you are unable to listen it probably means that you are still angry and need to vent some more.

Part One: What is my responsibility?

Remembering that rows are **six of one and half a dozen of the other,** think about your contribution. How has your behaviour extended or deepened the problem? When you have a clear idea of your own failings, find something – however small – and apologise for it. For example, Nick and Anna fought after their son's poor mock-GCSE results. Anna had been away on a training course and blamed Nick for not having supervised his revision properly in her absence. The row went round and round in circles. Anna still felt annoyed but apologised for her contribution to the friction: 'I'm sorry that I gave you the silent treatment.' A few hours later, after more reflection, Anna had another apology: 'I was angry with our son too and I'm sorry I took some of it out on you.'

Part Two: I comprehend your problems

Try to look at matters from your partner's viewpoint. Are there any mitigating circumstances? What problems could she or he have been facing at the time? Is there anything from their past that makes this a blind spot? For example, Anna told Nick, 'It must have been hard taking on both parental roles while I was away.'

Tip: Sometimes, when couples find it difficult to apologise for their contribution or find any mitigation for their partner, I ask them to change seats and literally imagine themselves in their partner's shoes. Five minutes' arguing the other side is usually enough, but this is an effective trick for understanding your partner's case better. Some couples change chairs at home, some cross over and argue from different corners of the room and some just make the switch in their head. If you find it impossible to step into your partner's shoes you are probably still too angry. Return to exploring if this is the case.

3 Action

Until you have both vented your feelings and tried to comprehend each other's viewpoint it will be impossible to find a solution that sticks. Unfortunately some couples – particularly ILYB ones who hate rows – will try to move straight to action. As previously discussed, these short-cut solutions can work but they generally leave one partner feeling resentful and can therefore sow the seeds for future disputes.

When Nick and Anna truly understood each other's side of the row Nick agreed to make supervising their son's schoolwork a greater priority, while Anna agreed that next time work took her away she'd try to get ahead with the laundry so Nick would have more time to devote to their son. Ask yourself: 'What have we learnt from this fight?' 'Would we do anything different if these circumstances came up again?' 'How will we do things differently next time?' 'What should we do about this problem now?'

Tip: Don't be obsessed with winning. Either try to find a compromise which pleases both parties or aim for a trade-off: 'I won't read in bed if you give up the disgusting habit of dunking biscuits in your tea.' Even becoming aware of sensitive areas and agreeing to tread lightly can be a good outcome.

What If the Argument Turns Destructive?

- Remember: it is better to have a bad argument than none at all.
- When the temperature rises this is usually a sign that the real feelings are beginning to come to the surface, a sign of hope. In counselling the arguments get worse before they get better.
- Resist the temptation to say, 'And another thing,' and throw in additional gripes. These examples might strengthen your case but they also prolong and complicate the argument. Try to solve one issue at a time instead.
- Have you been criticising rather than complaining? In general,

complaints use 'I' while criticism uses 'you'. For example, a complaint would be, 'I wanted us to go to bed at the same time.' Voiced as a criticism it would be, 'You didn't come to bed on time.' The first invites a discussion about bedtimes; the second will make your partner defensive and prolong an argument.

- Shouting and getting passionate is acceptable. But if language gets abusive or there is a threat of pushing or slapping you should separate for ten to fifteen minutes and return when both of you have cooled down. Whoever feels threatened should call 'time out'. This means separating to different rooms or allowing one another to go out for a short walk/drive. The exact length of time spent apart is up to each couple but it should be negotiated beforehand. It is vital that discussion is resumed – some couples have a quick post-mortem while others enter round two – otherwise the person in the middle of venting will be unwilling to let their partner have 'time out' in future for fear of not getting an opportunity to release their anger properly.

- Remember the **eighty/twenty rule** (see Chapter Three) and look at what might be lying underneath the arguments that keep returning and returning. One couple in counselling fought about defrosting the fridge. She felt that he bought too many frozen products without using up what was already there. He did the cooking and felt that it was up to him to plan the meals. It got very nasty, especially as her parents had given them lots of chicken which he claimed took up most of the space. This battle kept recurring, with variations, for several weeks, and still the freezer had not been defrosted. Finally we looked deeper and discovered the core issue. She had bought the freezer before he moved in and felt that he did not respect her property. In her opinion, if the freezer was not properly maintained it would break down and they could ill afford a new one. He had more of a 'come what may' approach to money and generally felt that they would muddle through. When he truly understood his partner's fears the issue disappeared and the freezer was finally defrosted.

- Use the *Three Steps to Conflict Resolution* (above) to dissect your argument. A good opening gambit would be to apologise for your half of the argument. Next look at what went wrong. A good way to achieve this, without re-igniting the row, would be to say something like, 'I don't want to bring up the issues again, but why do you think it got out of hand?' or, 'How could we have approached it differently?' or, 'What can we learn?'

Sometimes my female clients claim that their husbands are so bad at communicating feelings, and anger in particular, that it is imposs-ible to argue effectively. I tend to shy away from gender stereotypes – partly because I have met plenty of emotionally articulate men and women who are not 'in touch with their feelings', but mainly because of the **six of one and half a dozen of the other** rule. Nearly every woman who complains about her partner using one of the anger-avoidance strategies turns out to be using a complementary one herself. Sometimes it is easier to criticise a partner than to recog-nise our own contribution to the problem.

Summary

- Trying to avoid anger can cause more problems than letting rip with a good argument.
- Destructive strategies for keeping anger at bay include detachment, rationalising, skipping and blocking.
- Only after a couple have vented their feelings will they be ready for a productive rather than a negative argument.
- Although rows are never nice at the time, they do provide an opportunity to resolve long-standing issues.
- If arguments go round in circles it is often because one of the *Three Steps to Conflict Resolution* – explore, understand, action – has been skipped.
- Arguing and properly making up again is the most intense form of bonding you can have. Isn't it about time to prove how much you love your partner by having a really good argument?

Exercises

How to Be Emotionally Honest

Couples like to think that they have integrity and generally tell each other the truth. One partner might pretend that the new home cinema cost a little less than it did, the other forgets to mention the stripper at their best friend's hen party, but there are few serious transgressions. Yet when it comes to our feelings the rules change. We constantly tell white lies to preserve the peace or to avoid upsetting our partner. How often have you said, 'No problem', 'Of course I don't mind' or, 'It's nothing' when actually you meant the complete opposite? Often a couple will boast, 'We can tell each other anything,' but in reality they tell each other close to nothing. Although both saying and hearing the truth can be scary, emotional honesty will set your relationship free and save it from becoming dull.

Follow these simple steps:

Learn to name your feelings

Many clients claim not to have many feelings, but the reality is that they are not always aware of their full range. Some clients look blank when I ask them to write down as many 'feelings' as possible. But I bring in a flip chart and before long we have filled a complete sheet.

- *How many feelings can you list?* Write as many as you can on a piece of paper and then try to think of some more.
- *Look at the range of your feelings.* Feelings belong in families, so circle and connect ones that you think belong together. In my opinion there are probably seven main groups: **shock** (which includes surprise, confusion, amazement), **anger** (including rage, resentment, frustration, annoyance, irritation, impatience), **sadness** (including grief, disappointment, hurt, despair), **fear** (including anxiety, worry, insecurity, panic, jealousy, guilt, shame), **love** (including acceptance, admiration, appreciation, gratitude, relief, empathy, compassion), **disgust** (including contempt, disdain, aversion, scorn, revulsion) and **happiness** (including joy, fulfilment, satisfaction, pleasure, contentment, amusement). However, you may find more families or decide that some emotions belong in different places. There are no right or wrong choices.
- *Understand the complexity of your feelings.* So many of these feelings seem negative – four whole families in fact – and the 'love' and 'happiness' family are often overlooked during our original brainstorm. On closer inspection, though, some of them are neutral, especially in the 'shock' family. The negative ones can have positive aspects: for example, there is always passion along with jealousy. Meanwhile, the positive ones have a downside: admiration, for example, can become unblinkered hero-worship.
- *Keep a feelings diary.* For a week, whenever you have a few spare

minutes, jot down any feeling that you have experienced. It could be on the train, when your next appointment is running late or as you watch your kids playing. Write all your feelings, especially the ones that are uncomfortable. This is a private diary, so be emotionally honest with yourself. You don't have to do anything with these feelings; just be aware of them and practise naming them.

- *Be bold.* Within each group the feelings range from the mild to the wild. When unsure of our emotions we try to downplay them for fear of being overwhelmed. Yet most people feel something a notch or two up the scale from what they first report. So next time you write down that you are upset, for example, try to be more honest and explore hidden emotions such as anxiety, disappointment or frustration.

  Looking back at the families of emotion, ask yourself: Am I experiencing feelings from every category? If one family is particularly under-represented it is important to understand why. Did your parents have trouble experiencing these feelings? Why should you be inhibited? Try deliberately to look out for these emotions in everyday life – even if they all come from the mild end of the spectrum. For example, if you feel very little from the 'love' or 'happiness' families, make sure you record the small pleasures. If you see a beautiful flower or smile at a cartoon in the paper write down 'happy' or 'content'.

Distinguish between feelings and thoughts

Just putting 'I feel' at the beginning of a sentence – for example, 'I feel you were wrong' or, 'I feel you were out of order' – does not make someone emotionally honest. Such sentences tell us nothing about the emotions of the person talking. We could guess: disappointment, perhaps, but maybe frustration or even contempt. What the speaker has expressed is an opinion.

- *Feelings often come from our body.* We have a physical reaction: a tightening of the chest; a sinking in the stomach; the heart beating faster; trembling.

- *Thoughts come from our head.* They are opinions, ideas, judgements and beliefs. This does not make them any less valid, but they are not feelings.

Communicate the feelings

Once you have become fluent at identifying and naming feelings in your diary, move on to expressing them to your partner.

- *Own the feeling.* 'I feel . . .' rather than, 'You make me feel . . .' For example, 'I feel angry (infuriated, frustrated or whatever) when you keep leaving plastic bottles by the back door for me to put into the recycling box.' Not, 'You make me angry with your thoughtlessness.' The more specific the complaint, the less it seems like an attack on someone's personality. After all, it is much easier to change our behaviour – putting out the plastic bottles – than our personality.
- *Often just acknowledging your feeling will make you less on edge.* In some cases you will no longer even feel the need to tell your partner, but if you do decide to tackle them be certain to follow the next suggestion.
- *Be responsible when handling negatives.* There is nothing wrong with being angry, frightened or even disgusted – it is part of being human, but these emotions get a bad press because we do not handle them well. So think what you want to say beforehand and weed out any 'you make me' statements. Try to start every sentence with, 'I feel . . .' After telling your partner about your feelings listen to what he or she has to say too.

Listen attentively

In the same way that you expect your partner to be attentive to your feelings, be prepared to offer the same respect back.

- *Do not interrupt or try to minimise your partner's feelings,* and don't tell him or her not to feel that way.
- *Acknowledge what has been said, even if it has been hard to*

hear. A responsible way to handle this without taking all the blame would be to say, 'I feel sad that you say that I . . .'

Remember: a greater awareness of feelings leads to a richer life, with not only a better understanding of yourself but also better empathy for your partner and improved people skills.

Working Through the 'Three Steps to Conflict Resolution'

ILYB couples want either to minimise disagreements or to get them over with as quickly as possible. This exercise is therefore designed to slow down your journey through the three steps.

1   Take three pieces of paper and write EXPLORE at the top of one, COMPREHEND on the second and ACTION on the third.
2   Take either a current dispute or an argument you had recently.
3   Exploring is all about feelings, so each time one of you comes up with a feeling write it down on the EXPLORE page.
4   Exploring is also about opinions and beliefs – 'A good father would look after his kids'; 'A good wife would not go out in the evening.' Write all this down too.
5   Exploring is about facts – 'I can't get home before seven-fifteen'; 'Our household generates ten loads of washing and someone needs to do it.' Write the most important ones down.
6   Check back over your EXPLORE page. Along with the facts, make sure that there are plenty of feeling words and beliefs. Can you think of anything more from either of these two categories?
7   Sometimes a potential solution (for the ACTION sheet) might come up early in the conversation. Write the discovery on the relevant sheet, so it is not lost, but return to filling up the EXPLORE sheet.
8   Next take the COMPREHEND sheet. Comprehending is about why things happen – 'I get angry because I'm stressed from work'; 'I don't feel like sex when I'm ignored.' Write these down.
9   Beliefs always come from somewhere: our upbringing, religion, general culture or the media. The particularly powerful ones are

from our childhood; how might your upbringing have affected your beliefs? Write down your findings.

10 Looking at the EXPLORE and COMPREHEND pages think about how you might use these insights to find a solution.

11 Solutions work best when there is a benefit for each party. For example, Partner A agrees to give Partner B five minutes' peace and quiet after arriving home, but in exchange Partner B agrees to give the children a bath later in the evening so A can rest. Make sure the solutions can be checked rather than being general and hard to verify, for example, to 'try harder'. Write the agreement on the ACTION page. You could even write it like a contract – 'I agree to . . . if you agree to . . .' – and both sign it.

12 Bring out the ACTION sheet a week later and see if both of you have kept your side of the bargain. If you haven't, take three new pieces of paper, write out the headings and go through the exercise again, exploring how both of you feel, comprehending what went wrong and setting a better plan of action.

How to Deal with a Passive Aggressor

1 Ask yourself, 'Why can't my partner assert him/herself directly?' Passive aggression is normally the choice of people who feel power-less. Is your partner allowed to say no?

2 Bring the hidden hostility to the surface. Challenge their too-easy agreement: 'I don't think you want to . . .' Don't feel guilty or allow yourself to be manipulated into apologising for having got angry or annoyed.

3 Avoid misunderstandings. Repeat back instructions, set precise deadlines and, at work, establish penalties for procrastination.

4 Once you've made a stand follow through. If someone is always late and you've told them you'll leave if they are more than ten minutes late and don't call, make sure you leave after those ten minutes. Failure to carry out penalties will severely weaken your position.

How to Stop Being Passively Aggressive

1 Accept that anger is normal.
2 Accept that you can still be a good person even when you feel angry.
3 Look at the benefits of using anger well. It gets things done and rights wrongs.
4 Understand your fears about being angry. What is the worst that could happen? What strategies could you use that will allow you to be angry but circumnavigate those fears?
5 Old behaviours, even if they worked for you when young, will need updating. Unlike a child, who has to go to school whether they like it or not, you have choices.
6 Practise saying no. It cuts through a lot of passive-aggressive behaviour. If there is a row at least both of you know what you are fighting about, instead of your anger being masked by sneaky behaviour.
7 Tell your partner when you feel pushed around.

Step Three

TARGET

'How do you think things are going between us?'
'Fine. Look, I don't know.'
*'I'm trying to make things better. I love you and I'll do
anything to make everything better.'*
'I know.'
*'We talk but it just goes round in circles. What do you want
from me?'*

In most long-term relationships there is no shortage of love floating
about, but somehow it just doesn't seem to get through. No wonder
one half ends up feeling unloved. Better loving communication
comes from better TARGETING.

Chapter Five

Do You Both Speak the Same Language of Love?

If you wanted to communicate with somebody from Japan you might hire an interpreter or study that person's language and culture. However, when we fall in love we assume our partner has exactly the same take on romance as we do. During the early days of a relationship – when **limerence** is at its height – these differences do not matter. Our whole focus is on our beloved and, given this level of attention, we are almost guaranteed to find a mutual love language. The problem comes after the honeymoon phase, when realities such as earning a living begin to intrude on the romance. At this point we retreat back to our main language, with perhaps a little of a second language thrown in. This is not a problem if our partner's take on love is the same as ours, but here is the catch: I have identified five different languages of love. So what happens if you speak one language and your partner mainly speaks another?

Kathleen and Philip, a couple who sought my professional help, are a good example of this kind of miscommunication. Beneath some terrible rows it was clear they had a very special bond, but neither of them felt loved. When I asked how they showed they cared, Kathleen explained about spending the months before a birthday or Christmas scouring the shops for just the right gift, hiding it in a secret place and finally decorating the parcel with fancy ribbons. By contrast, Philip demonstrated his caring side with compliments about Kathleen's looks and by saying 'I love you' every day. Both are equally good ways of expressing love. Except that here each partner secretly wanted the other to speak his or her own very particular love language. In consequence she felt devastated when he gave her just a card and money to buy her own present; he was upset because she never whispered sweet nothings. No wonder they were in trouble.

Different love languages would certainly explain the dilemma that many ILYB couples bring to my office. While one partner has fallen out of love the other is still very much in love and devastated about what has happened. The 'in love' partner is probably getting their needs met, but unwittingly he or she is not talking their partner's love language often enough for them to feel loved. Why should this happen? Sadly, we assume that our partner's love needs are exactly the same as ours. It is a natural assumption but a deadly one. Among other couples one partner will be trying a multitude of ways to express love but will still fail to get through. Alice, a forty-two-year-old wildlife conservation manager, was no longer in love with Jasper, her partner of seventeen years. Originally Jasper had pledged to do anything to rescue their relationship: he had started helping out more round the house, paid her more compliments and generally tried to be more attentive. 'I didn't know love had to be such hard work,' he complained when he started counselling. To make matters worse Alice was still not certain if she loved him. 'I think she wants me to be somebody else,' said Jasper, 'and I don't know if I can be – or even want to be.' Not only was he failing to communicate his **loving attachment**, but the effort involved was driving the couple further apart. The answer was not for Jasper to try harder – a scattergun approach – but to do less and to target better.

Love Languages

Over the past twenty years I have observed many different ways of expressing love, but they seem to fall into five broad categories, as follows:

Creating quality time together

This can range from lying in each other's arms while watching TV through to exotic foreign holidays. These people can become fed up if their partner spends too much time on friends, hobbies or at work. Their most likely complaint would be, 'We never have any fun together,' or, 'You've got time for everybody but me.' The worst thing their partner could do would be to put off a 'date' or a 'family day out' to catch up on chores, or cancel because a friend needs them.

If this is your partner:

The event is less important than spending time together, but a generous partner would choose an activity that gives their other half pleasure too. Even if the date involves something that you do not particularly enjoy, go along with good grace as this will earn you more plus points. During time together stay truly focused on your partner, sharing not just your time but your thoughts too. This could be a comment on the shared activity or something personal that has come up during the week.

Caring actions

Sometimes these can be basic partnership tasks, like earning a good salary or keeping a nice house, but normally they are more intimate: cooking a three-course meal, helping your partner clean out the shed or taking their sister to the airport at 3 a.m., for example. People who show their love through caring actions are most likely to say, 'Actions speak louder than words.' The worst thing their partner could do would be not to finish that little job they promised.

If this is your partner:

The stakes have increased since the days when salary-earning and housekeeping truly counted as caring actions, especially as paid work and a smooth-running house can be taken for granted by the majority of people. So look for the extra-special things that your partner might not even have thought about: taking the car to be valeted, installing some new anti-virus software on the home computer or baking a cake. These actions are especially appreciated if they are something you would not normally do. If you are uncertain as to what might constitute a caring action in your partner's eyes, listen to what she or he complains about. At the moment this will feel like being nagged, but look for a twist to turn it into a demonstration of your love. The complaint might be a messy bathroom, in which case don't just tidy up; buy small votive candles and run him or her a hot bath as well.

Affectionate physical contact

Sex immediately springs to mind but often the hugs and spontaneous kisses are more important. These people adore back-rubs and massages and are most likely to say, 'Come here and give us a kiss.' Naturally they can be devastated if their partner pushes them off because they're too busy doing something else.

If this is your partner:

Affectionate physical contact works best when it is taken out of the sexual arena, as the power of an orgasm can overwhelm everything else. Your hand in the small of your partner's back as you guide her through the door, stroking the back of his hand as you watch a movie together or a kiss on the nape of the neck as you pass in the hall; all these are simple non-sexual ways of showing love. Feedback is particularly important for this language, so don't be afraid to ask which contacts were appreciated and which felt uncomfortable or ill-timed.

Appreciative words

If anybody is likely to write romantic poetry it is this group. They want the whole world to know their partner is special by dedicating 'Angels' to 'the love of my life' at the local karaoke bar or placing sloppy adverts in the paper on Valentine's Day. They are most likely to say, 'I love you,' and be upset by their partner brushing them off with, 'You're just saying that . . .'

If this is your partner:

Compliments are very important to these people and they want their partners to be cheerleaders urging them on to even higher achievements. Not only work but also chores about the house and arranging a social event all need praise: 'Thank you for choosing such an interesting play,' or, 'You got a really smooth finish on the paintwork.' As well as offering appreciative words make sure your body language matches. When you tell your partner, 'I love you,' look directly into her or his eyes. These partners also enjoy giving compliments, so accept them graciously. It might be tempting to try to brush them away: 'It was nothing,' or, 'Isn't that what anybody would have done?' Instead go for the simplest and most effective response: 'Thank you.'

Present-giving

Whether it be an expensive piece of jewellery or a chocolate bar bought on the way home, present-givers love to surprise their partner and will go to great lengths to pull off a stunt. They are most likely to say, 'I saw this and thought of you.' The worst thing their partner can do is not appreciate the gift or dismiss it: 'I don't need one of those.'

If this is your partner:

Gifts are an integral part of love and central to our marriage rituals. However, today's culture is obsessed with the value of presents and has forgotten their true message: 'This is something to say that I've been thinking about you.' Cutting an appropriate picture out of a magazine and making your own card can be a hundred times more effective than automatically buying the same old perfume. Don't wait for a special occasion either; lots of little presents will make these partners feel especially loved. What if you are not a natural present-giver? Firstly, get advice – either from people who know your partner's tastes or from the shop assistant. Secondly, look at the type of gifts that she or he gives. This will provide clues as to what makes an acceptable present.

Love Languages in Action

Peter and Elaine had been together for two years. They both knew that something was not right but were unwilling to confront the issues for fear of what they might discover. Finally, after a tense Christmas, Elaine complained that she did not feel loved. It all hinged on Peter's previous marriage – his wife had died five years earlier – and Elaine felt that although she didn't want to compete she still played second fiddle. Peter kept on insisting that he loved her but she complained that, 'Actions speak louder than words; show me.' The more she talked, the more obvious it became that her love language was **caring actions**. So I explained the concept to Peter and he went away thinking. The couple returned the next week wreathed in smiles. 'I looked at my house afresh, through the eyes of someone who might feel excluded, and saw just how many photos of my first wife are up. At least one in every room, some-times more, even in the bedroom,' said Peter. 'I don't need to see her face all the time; it's up here.' He pointed to his head. Peter had taken the photos from beside the bed and reduced the others until one remained in his study and one in the living-room. This **caring action** had really spoken to Elaine, who not only felt loved when she discovered his decision but replied in his love language: **appreciative words**. 'I know it must have been hard for you,' she told him, 'but I really felt that you had understood me.'

Alice and Jasper, who we met earlier, found love languages a breakthrough after several difficult weeks of counselling. During **arguing** – the previous stage in *The Seven Steps . . .* – Alice had repeatedly complained about how little time they spent together. Jasper had countered that his job was very demanding and listed their recent trip to the cinema, a meal out and a summer holiday. When I brought up love languages Jasper quickly spotted that **creating quality time together** was Alice's language. So he turned up at her office, on a day when he was less busy, and took her out for lunch. When bringing work home was unavoidable Jasper took breaks with Alice in front of the TV, whereas previously he would have played computer games in his home office. Alice began to feel truly loved: 'Emptying the washing machine and the other things he'd done were nice, but I really appreciated lunch. You should have seen the look on the other girls' faces when he walked me back to my desk.' Jasper had targeted his energy into Alice's most effective love language.

Kathleen and Philip, the other couple from the beginning of this chapter, also began to speak each other's love language. He started bringing home flowers and she started saying, 'I love you,' without being prompted. In fact it was Kathleen and Philip who introduced me to the concept of love languages. Twenty years ago I had just started therapy with the couple and was making little headway until my supervisor – who seemed to have an intuitive grasp of my clients' problems – suggested I ask about present-giving. My next session with Kathleen and Philip produced the breakthrough; I then started using the idea with other couples and found other ways of expressing love.

While researching this project I was fascinated to discover that someone else had come up with similar conclusions. I found a book called *The Five Love Languages* (Northfield, 1992) by Gary Chapman, who directs marriage seminars in the States. He has slightly different names: **caring actions** becomes 'acts of service'; **appreciative words** become 'words of affirmation', **affectionate**

physical contact becomes 'physical touch'. However, it is basically the same concept.[1]

How to Find Your Relationship's Love Language

Many people will immediately recognise their main love language. If you are unsure, ask yourself to complete these two statements: 'I feel most loved when . . .' and 'I am most likely to complain that my partner never . . .' The second statement is particularly revealing, as what we complain about most is what we long for most. To discover your partner's love language imagine how he or she would complete those statements. It is also useful to look at how your parents showed their love when you were growing up. Some people speak one love language because that is what they heard as children, while others long for what they never had. There is more about finding each other's love language and learning to speak it in the 'Love Cards' exercise at the end of this chapter.

Love Languages in Reverse

If your partner's love language is a fast track to rebuilding **loving attachment**, what happens if you slip up? Robert's love language was **caring actions**. When his partner Elizabeth forgot to pick up the dry-cleaning it became a big deal. He told her, 'This just shows that you don't care.' Elizabeth, whose language was **creating quality time together** thought he had got everything out of proportion. By not understanding Robert's love language she had unintentionally insulted him – just as someone with no knowledge of Japanese culture would be considered impolite if they put a business card

[1] If you would like more information on the subject, I would recommend Chapman's book. It is particularly good at stressing the importance of giving love, while many self-help books concentrate just on receiving.

away without looking at it properly. These simple misunderstandings turn a potentially positive moment between a couple into a negative one.

Dr John Gottman, a professor of psychology at Washington University, set up a special apartment as a laboratory in which to study couples. As his volunteers went through their 'natural' interactions he would observe them and monitor biological changes as the couples discussed areas of conflict. He claims to be able to predict with 94 per cent accuracy who would be happily married, miserable or even divorced within four years. He found that, with happy couples, positive attention outweighs negative attention by a factor of five to one. In other words, for every criticism there should be five compliments; for every time we let our partner down there should be five times that we come through. Sadly, we imagine that one good deed will cancel out one bad, but Gottman shows that our natural instincts are way off the mark. This is why it is vital to target your partner's love language. Firstly, it will help maximise positive interaction and build **loving attachment**. Secondly, it will avoid unintentional negatives. Thirdly, when you do need to 'make it up' with your partner, paying attention to each other's love language can often signpost the most appropriate approach.

What Stops People Communicating Effectively?

It is not only love that is hard to communicate; some clients reach a point where almost everything is misinterpreted. These partners don't mean to cause offence; they even start choosing their words very carefully but somehow still end up with an atmosphere. So what is going wrong and how can **targeting** help here?

Martin and Jackie had a flare-up over Jackie not filling the car up with petrol after she had used it. 'What did I do?' asked Martin. 'I just asked a simple question.' But Jackie had a very different take on the incident. 'He came at me, accusing, all guns blazing,' she explained at their next counselling session. They had sniped at each other and spent an unpleasant evening, each at their end of the sofa, nursing very different interpretations of events. Jackie was convinced that he had been aggressive; Martin was convinced that she had taken offence at nothing at all.

A neutral observer would have been surprised that something so trivial could be so divisive. But the first thing to understand is that neither Martin nor Jackie is neutral. Each of them is viewing the row through their shared history, their past individual experiences – which stretch back to their childhood – and, most crucially, a million and one assumptions. It is these assumptions that undermine good communication.

So when Martin and Jackie brought the incident to counselling I asked them to replay the conversation, but this time I would intervene and help them uncover their hidden assumptions.

Martin started: 'What I said was, "Why didn't you fill up the car after you used it?"'

Jackie was about to jump in but I stopped her. She would get her chance in a minute.

'Why was that important?' I asked.

'Filling it up in the morning takes time and there can often be a queue at the pump. Those ten or fifteen minutes can make all the difference between being on time for work and getting stuck in the rush hour,' explained Martin.

'Did you know this, Jackie?' I asked.

'I know that if he sets off too late he gets caught in traffic,' said Jackie, 'but not about the queues at the pump.'

'I thought you knew how fine the timing can be. Five minutes can make all the difference,' replied Martin.

I had found assumption number one.

'It wouldn't matter so much,' continued Martin, 'if you'd told me when you got back, "Oh, by the way, the car is low on petrol," because I'd have set off earlier the next morning.'

'Have you ever told her that?' I asked.

Martin had to admit that he hadn't. He had sort of assumed that Jackie would know about this alternative approach.

Assumption number two.

Next I asked Jackie to rewind and replay her answer to Martin's question about the empty tank.

'I told him, "There's no need for you to have a go at me,"' she said.

'You sounded quite upset. In what way do you think he was having a go?' I asked.

'He was accusing me of being lazy, not bothering to fill it up,' Jackie replied.

'Did you think Jackie was being lazy?' I asked Martin.

He shook his head. Jackie had just assumed this accusation – assumption number three.

After a short discussion about her childhood Jackie admitted that her father had been very critical and often complained about her not trying hard enough. He would start with a seemingly innocent question about what she'd been up to at school but would soon veer off into a lecture about her applying herself.

Jackie acknowledged that her childhood makes her sensitive to criticism: 'Martin didn't ask about the car in the calm way he did just now in your office.'

'How did he say it?'

'It came out all aggressively.'

In fact 90 per cent of communication happens without words – and this is particularly the case when we are under stress. Martin's tone, hand gestures and delivery had given the words much more punch than he had intended.

Looking at how many assumptions underlie even a simple conversation and how our unconscious body language complicates matters further, it is a miracle that any couple can communicate well, but fortunately love and goodwill normally smooth over any misunderstandings. With this mindset the assumptions are all positive: she was probably rushing back to watch her favourite TV show; he must have had a hard day at work. By contrast, all Jackie and Martin's assumptions had been negative. A partner becoming prickly over seemingly unimportant matters is often an early warning sign of falling out of love. For ILYB couples previously easy-going communication is quickly bogged down by negative assumptions which further exacerbate one partner's desire to leave. So how can you stop hidden assumptions from clouding your communication?

The three-part statement

Assumptions happen because we fail to give our partners enough information. This is why the **three-part statement** is so powerful.

I feel (x) when you (y) because (z).
In Martin's case it would have been:
I feel (annoyed) when you (don't fill up the car) because (I don't have time in the morning and can be late for work).

The beauty of the **three-part statement** is that it is so tightly targeted that it leaves no room for assumptions. Jackie knows exactly what Martin feels because he has told her. She has stopped relying on reading his body language and no longer *assumes* something worse than annoyed – such as angry – because he has told her what he is feeling. The 'when you' in the **three-part statement** keeps things specific. Jackie knows that only a particular behaviour makes Martin feel this way – not her as a person. Ultimately she knows the exact reason for Martin's feelings and can see that there are no hidden moral judgements. Although the **three-part statement** may seem artificial at the beginning, like all these relationship skills it will quickly become second nature. The exercise section has advice on incorporating it into everyday life.

Summary

- There are five main ways of expressing love: **creating quality time together, caring actions, affectionate physical contact, appreciative words** and **present-giving**.
- The power of **limerence** means couples use all five languages simultaneously: they want to spend not just quality time but every moment together; each partner searches for small gestures to show they care; they cannot keep their hands off each other; compliments come naturally; they send cards or pick out spontaneous presents for the fun of it.
- When **limerence** wears off each partner will retreat into one major love language – or possibly two – and expect the other to speak the same one.
- When a partner does not seem to respond, try expressing love in a different way.
- Careful **targeting** prevents misunderstandings, unintended slights and channels energy into the most productive ways of communicating.

Exercises

Love Cards

This exercise is a light-hearted way to help you discover your personal love language(s) and to share the idea with your partner.

1 Get a packet of index cards, or blank postcards, and write the title of one of the five languages on one of the cards. Keep going until you have a complete set: **appreciative words, present-giving, affectionate physical contact, caring actions** and **creating quality time together**. If you have another way of expressing love which

doesn't fit under these categories make up another card. Then create an identical set for your partner. A good tip is to use a different-coloured biro in case they get mixed up.

2 Find a good time. It is best not to introduce this exercise when there is a tense atmosphere, as it requires a certain amount of good faith.

3 Make it sound fun. Everyone dreads the phrase, 'We need to talk.' All too often we interpret that as, 'You need to listen while I complain.' Introduce the cards as a game or a puzzle, 'to help us understand each other better'. You can also explain that it need not take long. I've had couples who completed the love cards in a few minutes; others have taken the whole session to talk through the implications. It's up to you.

4 Give your partner the cards. Ask him or her to spread them out on a table and then put them in order, from the most important way of showing love to the least important. While your partner is doing this you can be ordering your love cards too. It can be off-putting if someone is watching you.

5 Ask for examples. It is tempting to comment on your partner's choices straight away, but first make sure you understand them. For example, if his or her number one is **creating quality time together,** ask which times he or she particularly enjoyed. You could also share one of your favourite quality times and double check that you both mean the same things. Go through each card and ask for more examples. Your partner might have difficulty thinking of an example for the bottom few; it can be hard for something we consider unimportant.

6 Share your examples. Now it is your turn to give examples for your love cards. Keep it positive. Remember it's about what you like doing, not what you don't want. Children respond best to compliments – so will your partner.

7 Compare your responses. Discuss the order in which you have each placed the love languages. What are the differences and what are the similarities? If you have any idea why one is partic-

ularly important to you, share it – for example: 'I came from a family where nobody ever hugged, so . . .' Don't worry if your priorities are very different; the next step will help tackle this.

8 Learn to speak each other's language. Remember, the way we show love is also the way we like to receive it. So try to increase the number of times you speak your partner's favourite love language. This is particularly important if your partner has fallen out of love with you. Ask him or her, 'What one change could I make that you would particularly appreciate?' These tasks should be small and easily verifiable. If your partner's top priority is **creating quality time together**, set a contract for one meal out together each month. Don't leave any loose ends – decide who books the table and the babysitter. For any changes to stick there have to be benefits for both of you, so ask for something small in your language too.

If your relationship has been going through a rough patch, a helpful twist on this exercise is to rearrange the love cards into the order you would like them in the future. One couple I helped started with **present-giving** as their first choice. They explained that this was the only love language that felt safe. When we looked at their ambitions for the future, **present-giving** had dropped down and **affectionate physical contact** had greater importance.

The Love Language Audit

Ask yourself the following questions and pinpoint the last time you used each of the five love languages.

1 When did I last give my partner a compliment?
2 When did I last buy my partner a present without it being a birthday or other special occasion?
3 When did I last take my partner out on a date with just the two of us?

4 When did I last touch my partner in a tender and loving way, without it being a prelude to sex?

5 When did I last do a chore for my partner without having to be asked?

If the answer was in the last few days give yourself a pat on the back; last week is good and last month is also fine. For questions to which your answer was longer than a month, or for those to which you cannot give an accurate response, try to use the relevant language to show your love in a new way.

The Three-part Statement

In times of potential conflict, ambiguous remarks can become so loaded with hidden assumptions – from both the speaker and listener – that clear communication is almost impossible. The **three-part statement** is designed to get as much information as possible out in the open as quickly as possible, and to limit the potential for pointless arguments.

Don't skip any parts of this exercise or improvise, as the recipe works best when followed to the letter.

x) I feel . . .

y) when you . . .

z) because . . .

Very few people can automatically put their thoughts into a three-part formula. It takes practice. Follow these steps:

1 Think back to the last time you wanted to say something and it came out all wrong.

2 Copy down the frame above and fill in each part. For example: 'I feel *humiliated* when you *ignore me* because *I'm trying my best to change.*'

3 Try to come up with four more examples from the past.

4 Now think of something current that you need to communicate. It does not necessarily need to be to your partner – the **three-part statement** works well with sensitive teenagers and work colleagues too.
5 Write down the framework and finish off each part again.
6 Ask yourself, 'Is this statement clear and accurate, and do I need to add anything?' If so, make the necessary changes.
7 Practise the finished statement a couple of times; this will help it flow naturally when you approach the other person.

Step Four

PLAY

'We don't seem to do anything together, just you and me.'
'When I offer a cuddle, you push me away.'
'I'm not talking about sex.'
'Why do I bother?'
'At least we agree on something.'

When a relationship hits the skids fun is the first thing to go. But to be truly close – rather than colleagues running a house or raising children together – you need to reconnect with PLAY.

Chapter Six

How to Boost Real Intimacy

Everybody is in favour of intimacy; it is one of the small number of things of which we all want more. So why does intimacy slip from our grip so easily, with the result that many couples find themselves friends rather than lovers? The usual excuse is that modern lifestyles are stressful and eat into quality time with our partners, but this is only part of the story. Intimacy has been made to equal sex – and nothing else. As we have become obsessed with league tables, performance and delivery, we have tried to make loving intimacy reach targets too. Sex might be reducible to the statistics of 'how often' and 'how long', but intimacy is not so obliging. Plus, in all the sweaty passion of lovemaking, it is easy to imagine that we are genuinely close to our partner. Men are particularly guilty of confusing sex and intimacy and will consider their marriage to be good even if the lovemaking is routine and unfulfilled. Yet even physically satisfying sex can leave both partners feeling isolated, lonely and secretly wondering whether things can ever improve.

Most of my ILYB couples do not complain about their love lives. They normally brush away enquiries with, 'It's fine.' Further questioning reveals polite sex rather than intimate lovemaking. Patrick is a twenty-nine-year-old teacher: 'My pleasure is giving Cathy pleasure.' There is nothing wrong with this, but Patrick had become so considerate that he was not honest about his own needs: 'I occasionally think of trying something slightly different – like making love in the shower – but I don't say anything. What might Cathy think?' Patrick and Cathy were so worried about upsetting each other – and so self-censoring of their needs – that their sex routine had become boring. Worse still, they were unable to talk about these problems, which were pushing them further and further apart.

So what is intimacy and how do we recapture it? Intimacy is made up of three main components: vulnerability, good verbal communication and physical closeness (of which sex is probably only 30 per cent). Get these key ingredients balanced and you will always feel both loved and desired.

Vulnerability is all about being open and risking revealing something about yourself. Not surprisingly it is also the hardest intimate quality to achieve. This is because our fear of getting hurt may be almost as strong as our desire for intimacy. So we hold back and build up our defences as an insurance policy against pain. In the early days of a relationship this 'one foot in, one foot out' approach makes sense. We imagine that things will get easier after marriage but often we become even more scared. Our partners learn so much about our failings as well as our strengths from our new domestic, financial and child-rearing life together that to share too much more can feel like being swallowed up. Also, if you know somebody well, rejection feels more personal and we step up our defences.

Even couples who were good at communicating at the start of their relationship can find their skills evaporating. In the early, heady days of love we never stop talking; we share our opinions on everything from shellfish to Shakespeare. Contrast this with the stress of everyday life, when communication is cut down to the bare essentials – what time you're back, kids needing money for school – as we cross paths in the kitchen. Although this shorthand is very efficient it offers no space for the rich details that taught us so much during courtship. In the gaps we start to make assumptions. We fail to notice that our partner's tastes have changed and our opinions need updating. Worse still, we can swallow our irritations for the sake of avoiding an argument and to ensure the smooth running of the household. The feelings do not disappear but turn to resentment, further distorting good communication.

What about physical closeness? The casual touch on the arm as you make a point; stroking his or her neck as you watch TV; smooching, long cuddles. Sounds wonderful? These little gestures are just as important as sexual intercourse. But why do they disappear from so many relationships after the first flush of passion? Sadly, casual physical closeness is often seen as an overture to lovemaking rather than as a joy in its own right. So if one half is not in the mood – even though they might be enjoying the sensations of the moment – they turn away. After all, they know where it will lead. Very soon these couples get locked in the 'all or nothing' syndrome, where everything beyond a quick peck on the cheek is off limits – unless of course you want full intercourse. These problems are exacerbated for men and women over forty, who find themselves at very different stages with their sexuality. Women whose children are more independent are no longer so exhausted. They feel better, have more time for themselves and feel that their confidence is boosted. Men, on the other hand, are moving in the opposite direction. They are less confident about achieving arousal and will often stay over on their side of the bed unless 100 per cent certain of delivering. Therefore the intricacies of initiating lovemaking often need updating in long-term relationships. What seemed comfortable and safe ten years ago – the hand snaking across the bed – can now make you feel as if you're being taken for granted.

Sexual activity – like love – changes as a couple move through *The Six Stages of a Relationship* (see Chapter Two). While **limerence** is at its height, during **blending**, couples report intense sexual excitement, high frequency and often lengthy lovemaking. One of the great pleasures is slowly exploring every inch of each other's bodies, almost as if each partner is claiming the other as his or her own. 'I almost wanted to climb into him,' explains Jackie, 'and we still joke that when we cuddle I will burrow into his armpit.' This intense sharing diminishes any potential sexual obstacles almost to the point of insignificance and is remembered as a golden period. For most couples this stage lays the foundation for a lifetime of emotional and physical intimacy.

During **nesting** there is a gradual decline in lovemaking. However, the increased knowledge of each other's likes and dislikes can act as compensation and generally there is plenty of non-genital caressing and stimulation. During **self-affirming**, years three and four, sex is most likely to become an issue, especially for couples who have been unable to handle conflict. At this stage different needs for affection begin to emerge but some couples find it easier to turn over and switch off the light than to talk. The unresolved anger does not disappear but instead builds a wall between the couple and shuts down the sexual libido. (If this is you, see the exercise 'How to Be Emotionally Honest' at the end of Chapter Four.) For couples who allow each other to be individuals as well as half of a relationship during the **self-affirming** stage, though, the changes in the relationship create new interest. Each partner learns both to give and to take in lovemaking, thereby avoiding a situation in which one party feels permanently indebted to the other.

Collaborating, stage four, is a time of new activities and many couples also start experimenting with their lovemaking. But this can also be a time when one or both parties feel exhausted – especially if the couple have children. 'I thought Sue never had time for me,' complained Cliff. 'Although I know it's not easy having a four-year-old and an eighteen-month-old, I feel I'm constantly being pushed away.' Over time Cliff had been turned down so often that he no longer felt attractive, despite Sue's reassurances that her refusal was not personal. A good tip for overcoming this problem is, rather than saying no, to make an alternative suggestion. It worked for Cliff and Sue. 'I might not have fancied intercourse, but often I could really have done with a back-rub,' said Sue. 'Afterwards I would return the favour.' Alternatively, Sue learnt to ask for a 'rain check' and offered to make love at the weekend instead.

With **adapting**, after fifteen to twenty years, couples report a decline in the frequency of lovemaking but, conversely, that the quality is better. However, some people have issues about the changes to their body, and their partner's, and about feeling desirable. I would recommend two approaches for this: hiding the offending bits or emphasising them. A sex-therapist friend of mine gets women who feel very conscious of stretch marks or men who are sensitive about post-operative scars to colour them in. She finds that this brings fun and play back into the relationship – always useful – and that afterwards, when the colour has been washed off (maybe together, in the shower), the couples report that the marks were not so noticeable after all. For the opposite approach, the person with bits that he or she feels are undesirable is given the opportunity to cover them up. This partner starts with the fabric of their choice – normally something quite thick – and, over time, replaces it with something thinner. Often the couple move in stages until they end up with just a scarf as they make love; eventually the person with the issue will be ready to go naked again. However, the choice and timings are always up to him or her. This programme was designed to help women after a mastectomy but it works well for anything that makes someone self-conscious.

The final relationship stage is **renewing**. The urgency of orgasmic release is replaced by an increase in cuddling, holding and caressing. Older couples often report the highest level of peace and contentment.

Boredom can become an issue at any stage in a relationship – possibly with the exception of the first year – and is generally an early warning of intimacy problems. And if a lack of intimacy is the problem the answer is play – the fourth step to putting the passion back into your relationship. When we were children play was at the centre of our lives and was a gateway to learning and team-building and an opportunity to let off steam. After we grow up we forget about the simple joys of playing; many people even drop out of sport – the adult-approved form – and become spectators rather than participants. But why is play so important? Firstly, play tackles the three ingredients for intimacy at the same time. Good verbal communication and physical closeness are obvious by-products of play, and in the excitement of the moment there is also vulnerability – nobody stops to think how she or he might look or whether they are being ridiculous. Secondly, play reconnects us to our childlike sense of creativity and that is useful for combating boredom.

The traditional approach to solving sex problems has been to buy a book, but even the best ones – which recognise the importance of good communication and maintaining passion – are largely devoted to new positions for intercourse and improving technique. Not only does this approach put physical contact at the heart of intimacy, but also it assumes easiness with sex, which many couples lack – especially when the bedroom has become an emotional battlefield. It also overlooks the importance of fun and play in lovemaking. The final problem with sex manuals is their one-size-fits-all approach. My experience with ILYB tells me that, roughly speaking, couples fall into three categories:

- *Infrequent intercourse* (perhaps once a month or maybe once every two to three months). Intimacy is a very loaded subject, the source of rows, and has been reduced down to just sex. For these couples I have created the 'Twelve Stops on the Road to Intimacy' exercise, which aims to place intimacy in the context of the whole relationship – in fact, the first four steps are about talking rather than touching.
- *Routine sex life*. Lovemaking happens on a regular basis but has become a task to tick off the list rather than a source of true intimacy and joy. For these couples I have consulted a colleague who specialises in sex therapy and has a reputation for creative and playful solutions. She believes that pleasure is at the heart of intimacy and that many couples have lost sight of this in the hustle and bustle of life or the pressure of bringing up children. For her programme see the 'Pleasure Principle' exercise.

- *Good sex.* Although intercourse is enjoyable, and in some cases extremely enjoyable, the intimacy from lovemaking does not reach the rest of the relationship and one or both partners still feel alone. For these couples I have created the 'Intimacy Repair' exercise.

All three exercises have 'play' at the core, so if you are uncertain which of the exercises will be most beneficial try taking elements from one or more and blending them together. If you get stuck, or start drifting back into old patterns a few weeks later, I would suggest following each of the 'Twelve Stops on the Road to Intimacy' – even if one or two of them seem too basic.

Summary

- Intimacy is crucial to prevent a couple from drifting into a brother/sister relationship.
- Little by little, without either partner intending it, sex can sink to the lowest common denominator: what is easy or what both do not mind.
- Intimacy and sexuality changes as couples move through *The Six Stages of a Relationship*. The challenge is to keep rediscovering what both partners truly enjoy.
- The most common cause of boredom in bed is a lack of intimacy.
- No matter how long a couple have been together, 'play' is the key to unlocking a more fulfilling intimacy.

Exercises

Twelve Stops on the Road to Intimacy

These are designed to be done one per week, but stay at each stop until you feel comfortable. If you wish to move more quickly that's fine. However, just as intimacy normally bleeds slowly out of a relationship it is best reintroduced gradually. Hopefully the earlier stops will become second nature, so they are continued without thinking even while you are focusing on the later ones.

This programme is easier shared with your partner, but do not worry if he or she regards any discussion as an attack; you can instigate the 'Twelve Stops on the Road to Intimacy' on your own. Your changed behaviour will lead by example and create a knock-on effect.

1 *Validate each other.* Compliment or congratulate your partner on a job well done. He or she will probably think you are after something, but just smile and repeat the praise.
2 *Grab opportunities to talk.* Think back to how detailed your stories were when you were courting. Everything is in the detail, for it brings the story to life. Ask your partner to explain something from their life too.
3 *Set aside quality talking time.* Every couple should take stock about what they want from life from time to time. Where are we heading? What are our unfulfilled aspirations? Be vulnerable and really open up about your hopes and fears. The main aim is to set aside enough time for the two of you. We cannot be intimate if our relationship is nothing more than scraps left over from work, family and friends. Guard this time jealously.
4 *Confide a secret.* You might tell friends everything, but are you as candid with your partner? Choose something revealing about yourself to tell her or him. Do not worry if you seem to be doing all the confessing. Like sitting on a see-saw, your actions mean your partner will move too and become more candid over time.

5   *Touch your partner.* Reintroduce casual touching into your rela-
    tionship. Stroke the back of your partner's hand when he is
    driving the car; hold hands while she is watching TV; give him
    a kiss on the back of his neck when he is on the computer.
    Sometimes a touch is worth a thousand words.

6   *Share.* Take one bowl of ice cream and two spoons into a warm
    bath. Couples normally laugh when I suggest this one, but they
    love it. Use only one bowl – after all, this is about sharing. Try
    feeding each other, as this can be very sensual. Feel free to make
    love, but remember this is also about being naked together
    without feeling obliged to have intercourse.

7   *Set the scene.* Take a long hard look at your bedroom. Is it a
    passion-killer? When I've asked couples to describe where they
    make love I've heard about everything, from stacks of bills
    beside the bed to animals sleeping under the duvet. Have a clear-
    out – the bedroom should be a stage for your passion, not a
    dumping ground. Make the room warm enough, the lighting
    kind (candles are a good tip) and lock the door. Finally, add a
    sound system to set the mood and to prevent worries about
    being overheard.

8   *Slow down your lovemaking.* Intimacy needs time. Men often
    head straight for the genitals while women sometimes want to
    get things over as quickly as possible, so as we hurtle down the
    highway intimacy is left on the hard shoulder. Avoid the temp-
    tation to say anything about this during lovemaking. However
    nicely put, such comments will be heard as criticism. Instead,
    slide his or her hands to somewhere else you would like to be
    touched. Add a positive affirmation: 'I love it when you . . .'
    Another way of slowing down is to change position. For example,
    the woman being on top allows her to decide the moment of
    penetration.

9   *Find new erogenous zones.* Where are our erogenous zones?
    Answer: any area where the skin is thin and the nerves are there-
    fore near the surface. The middle of your back; the underside

117

of your wrist; elbows; the nape of your neck; the outer part of your lips – this is why nibbling can be more passionate than plain kissing.

10 *Skip intercourse.* Sexual intimacy is a whole-body experience and intercourse should be an optional extra. Once you can be close without full penetration the stakes are nowhere near so high. Although you might not be in the mood for penetrating or penetration, you are seldom too tired to cuddle or be stroked.

11 *Make initiation a shared responsibility.* The person who always asks or sets the ball rolling for lovemaking risks feeling taken for granted or, worse, being rejected and feeling undesirable. If you seldom take charge now is your opportunity. If it is normally your responsibility, hold back and give your partner space to initiate.

12 *Experiment.* Try bringing something new into your relationship. It might be somewhere new to make love – the back seat of your car, down lover's lane – or something different, like one of you keeping your clothes on while the other is totally naked. They don't need to be big changes, just something to show each other that you've made intimacy a continuing priority.

Pleasure Principle

Many couples who find lovemaking a chore rather than a joy have lost sight of the full range of possibilities for pleasure. In the worst cases life has become a very serious business which almost excludes playfulness. For many others pleasure is concentrated in one or two areas but its effectiveness is blunted by repetition. The best way to explain is to launch into the first stage of the exercise:

1 Think about everything that gives you a warm buzz / real pleasure and write it down. Keep adding to the list – nothing is too trivial. In the movie *Manhattan* Woody Allen's character lists the things that make life worth living as: 'Groucho Marx, Willie Mays [American basketball legend], Second Movement of *Jupiter Symphony*, Louis Armstrong's recording of "Potato Head Blues",

Swedish movies, Frank Sinatra, Marlon Brando, the crabs at Sam Wo's and Tracy's face.' What would be on your list?

2 Look at your list and decide which of the following categories of pleasure, in your opinion, each item falls under. I have listed a few examples to get you going but they are not definitive. For one person a holiday will be an escape, but for another it would be a source of tranquillity; for a third, who might kayak white-water rapids, it would be a source of achievement.

Achievement: Passing an exam; negotiating a discount; finding the perfect pair of shoes; closing a deal at work.
Tranquillity: A beautiful view; watching the water lap at the side of a boat; lying in a warm bed on a cold morning.
Irresponsibility: Putting your feet up for five minutes and reading a magazine; a quick round of golf; making finger puppets at the movies.
Excitement: Driving a fast car; horse-riding on the beach; scoring a goal.
Sensual: Roasted spring lamb with mint sauce and new potatoes; listening to Leonard Cohen; the smell of freshly roasted coffee.
Escapism: Getting silly drunk; meditation; dancing; buying a lottery ticket.
Nurturing: Watching a child sleep; doing some voluntary work; introducing a friend to a really good book.

3 The great thing about lovemaking/intimacy is that this provides one of the few forums that can supply all the above pleasures at the same time. But how balanced is your list? Do all your pleasures cluster together under one or two headings? How many of the pleasures are shared with your partner?

4 Generally couples without enough intimacy in their lives have both lost sight of the *irresponsible*, and although each might individually have *excitement* and *tranquillity* they no longer share these pleasures together. Here are some ideas, under each heading,

which are a pleasure to share together – away from the bedroom. What other ideas can you come up with?

Achievement: Go on a five-mile walk together; landscape the garden.
Tranquillity: Go to the beach and skim stones across the waves together; find somewhere to play Pooh-sticks.
Irresponsibility: Rediscover any forgotten childhood pleasure, like pushing each other on the park swings or running down a hill together singing 'Jack and Jill'.
Excitement: Visit a theme park and go on a white-knuckle ride together; go to the races.
Sensual: Go to a concert together; fill the house with fragrant flowers.
Escapism: Have a weekend away; learn to salsa together.
Nurturing: Plan a special day out for your partner; cook a favourite meal.

What have I got in my hand?

Sharing different pleasures will rebalance your intimacy away from the sexual arena; now it's time to bring the fun into the bedroom. This next game can be as sexy as you wish to make it.

- Each partner finds an ordinary household item that has the possibility of being sensuous: a small paintbrush, a silk scarf, a pot of strawberry yoghurt, skin cream or an ice cube. Do not tell each other what you've found – in fact you might like to tease about the possibilities as anticipation is part of the fun.
- In the bedroom, each partner strips down to underwear and flips a coin to decide who goes first.
- One partner closes her or his eyes while the other gets out their secret item.
- Slowly, gently, the person with the secret item moves it across their partner's exposed skin.
- The partner with closed eyes takes a few minutes to become accustomed to the sensations; meanwhile the other person finds different ways to caress them. Really get into the possibilities and find new

places and new ways to touch (the only off-limits thing is playing in a sadistic way). How could you confuse? How could you give pleasure? Please avoid the obvious erogenous zones at this stage.

- After at least five minutes have passed the person with the secret item asks, 'What have I got in my hand?' The person being touched can either guess or ask questions – 'Is it something found in the kitchen?' – but he or she cannot open their eyes.
- After the touched partner has guessed correctly, or given in, he or she can choose to continue to be touched or ask to switch over and the game starts again.

Intimacy Repair

When sex is good but a physical release more than an emotional connection, try staying awake for five minutes after having an orgasm. I know this is tough for men: drifting off to sleep after making love would be near the top of my list of pleasures. However, pillow talk offers a wonderful opportunity to connect. Some couples use the warmth and security after making love to give a few compliments, but others talk in ways that would be impossible at any other time. I had one client who was locked in a toilet as a child and subsequently suffered from mild claustrophobia. She told her husband that being in the missionary position brought flashbacks of being shut in, especially when he collapsed on to her at the end of their lovemaking. He, of course, had no idea and promptly suggested trying different positions. Subsequently their intimacy went from strength to strength, but without the post-lovemaking closeness this conversation would have been impossible.

Step Five

TAKE RESPONSIBILITY

'If only you wouldn't keep putting me down.'
'What about you?'
'Have you ever thought that if you were a bit nicer I might be too?'
'You don't give me much encouragement.'
'Why is it always my fault?'

It is always easier to take the plank out of someone else's eye than deal with the speck in our own. Nowhere is this truer than in relationships. Although our partner's behaviour will have a huge impact on us we are often quicker to blame than to accept our own part in the unhappiness. This traps us into thinking we should wait for our partner to change rather than to TAKE RESPONSIBILITY.

Chapter Seven

Identity: Does Loving You Stop Me from Being Myself?

Over time partners in a relationship become more and more like each other. It is only natural that one partner's tastes will influence the other and that living together will file away the rough edges of each half's personality. This gradual fitting-together generally makes for a peaceful coexistence. However, some couples take this a stage further and become too alike. Why should this be a problem? Firstly, as discussed earlier, difference provides the spark that keeps love alive. Secondly, too much similarity can become suffocating – indeed many ILYB couples grow as similar as two peas in a pod, and frequently one half complains that they have lost their identity. Worse still, in terms of the health of the relationship, this partner ends up believing that the other is stifling their personality. When this happens there seems to be only one solution: separation. This is terribly unfair, because what is actually happening is far more complicated than it appears. Both parties are playing a part in this merging of identities, and for this reason the next step in putting the passion back is taking personal responsibility.

Stacey arrived at my counselling office in tears. She was twenty-five but had been with her partner from the age of eighteen and was now finding the relationship so claustrophobic that she spent as much time away from home as possible. Out came the familiar incantation: a) I love him but I'm not in love with him, and b) no arguments – even though she had run up a large credit-card debt during her many 'escapes'. Her main complaint was that the relationship stopped her from being herself: 'I don't know who I am. I've lost myself,' and she started crying again. 'That's why I've just got to leave him,' she explained. From Stacey's account I expected to meet a controlling partner. Carl joined us for the next session and could not have been more accommodating: 'Did I say anything about you going out? In fact, I'm not stopping you doing anything.' Stacey did not answer but seemed to retreat into herself. She turned into an entirely different woman from the one I had met before. 'What is it that you want?' Carl asked. There was a long silence. Finally Stacey said, 'I can't be the person that you want me to be.' It was Carl's turn to become quiet. 'Now I've hurt him,' Stacey started crying again. 'I didn't want to do that.' Under all the pain there seemed to be an unspoken question: Does loving you stop me from being myself?

Stacey is not alone in finding that her relationship robbed her of her personal identity. 'The rooms of my house seem so crowded. Pets, children's toys, my husband's files when he works at home,' said Barbara, thirty-four and married for fifteen years. 'Nothing seems to belong to me. Even the kitchen, which is sort of my space, is constantly being invaded by kids raiding the fridge. If I walk down the street at dusk and look into other people's rooms they all seem so cool and spacious. Like lighted stages where the owners are in control, autonomous. I find myself listening to friends who've got divorced and envying their talk of a door of their own.' Lucy, in her late twenties with a daughter of eight and a son of five, would understand these feelings too: 'There are so many demands on my time. I've had to bottle up the needy part of myself while I've attended to the children. I don't have time for books, so I've put them away and the prospectus from the local college too. But try as I might – because I love my children and my husband – the needy part hasn't shrunk. It wants to smash out and destroy everything.'

Both Barbara's and Lucy's partners were keen to help. Barbara's husband promised to keep his work things tidy and talked about creating an extra room in the loft. Lucy's husband agreed to take the children swimming on Saturday afternoons so that Lucy could read in peace. But somehow these well-intentioned plans were sabotaged and nothing really changed. So what was keeping these couples stuck in the same patterns? We needed to look much deeper than the symptoms: no room for Barbara and no reading time for Lucy. Both couples told me that they got on well and enjoyed the same things, but when I asked Lucy for more information she listed eating out, cinema and mutual friends before petering out. All of these were fine, but they did not evoke any passion from Lucy. In fact Lucy and her partner David had not been to the cinema for six months. When I asked about personal passions I was met with a blank face. I had to remind Lucy about reading, and I finally discovered that David used to play golf but had abandoned it when their son was born. Barbara enjoyed interior design but did not feel she could really indulge herself as she needed to take her husband's tastes into consideration. Now, while compromise is fine – and an essential component for building a relationship – there can be too much of it. Both these couples had been so intent on having a happy partnership that they had lost sight of themselves as individuals. It was no wonder I had difficulty uncovering their individual interests: they had been sacrificed – a little here, a little there – to create amorphous couple tastes. So why do some couples become too alike?

The Six Stages of a Relationship Revisited

One of the key ways in which a relationship will change over time concerns each partner's attitude to 'difference'. When a couple first start dating they look for similarities and shared interests. One partner will watch the other compete at a moto-cross rally in the pouring rain; the other attends both the dress rehearsal and the performance of their beloved's amateur operatic society. In the first stage, **blending**, all the differences are subsumed into becoming a couple. During **nesting** the differences start to reappear – perhaps during a discussion over which shade of paint to use – and couples no longer pretend that they adore each other's favourite pastimes. However, similarity remains important as a couple build a home together. During **self-affirming** the couple should begin to look at their differences, because two people will have different tastes, standards, rhythms of getting up and going to bed; the list is endless. Most couples row and end up accommodating their differences. However, some couples – particularly those who will go on to develop ILYB – avoid open confrontation and pretend the differences do not exist. One half will drop a hobby – rationalising that there is no time – while the other half will stop seeing a particular friend whom their partner does not like. Instead of resenting the decision this partner will make up an excuse; for example, 'I don't have much in common with my friend any more.' The other tactic for avoiding **self-affirming** rows is for a couple to stress similarities and concentrate all energies on what the couple *do* have in common. Without tackling difference it is hard to move on to the next stage, **collaborating**, during which each partner develops individual projects and brings back new energy to re-invigorate the relationship. The fifth stage, **adapting**, is also tough if a couple have pressurised each other into sharing similar opinions and approaches to the multitude of challenges that life throws up. The final stage, **renewing**, is a mirror of the first one. Once again the couple become everything to each other and difference is less of an issue.

The following diagram shows what happens to difference from the first date onwards, and how it can undermine a relationship if not properly addressed during **self-affirming**:

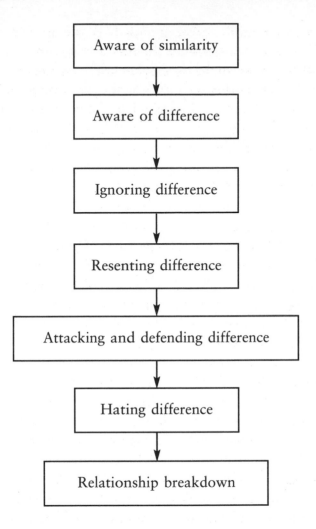

Ignoring difference

This is why being 'best friends' as opposed to partners can put a strain on a relationship. We choose friends who are like us and who share similar interests. We do not have to live with our friends 24/7, however, so we can ignore our differences and concentrate on the similarities. Also we often have different friends at different stages of our lives, as our interests and needs change. The friends who do stay go through cycles of being very close and then seeing us less often. So instead of confronting differences it is easy to let the relationship drift. Partnerships do not have the same flexibility. When a couple describe each other as 'best friends' it always sounds an alarm bell that tells me to check out how they handle difference.

Resenting difference

The first warnings of identity issues and more general relationship problems occur at this stage. A bit like a hairline crack in the sitting-room wall, they do not require immediate attention and may not develop into something serious. On the other hand, the crack could mean subsidence and half the house collapsing. So what are the signs that someone is resenting difference? The following would alert my attention: small plans or decisions have become contentious; one or both partners are keeping an imaginary score card on past disputes; couples tiptoeing round each other. The best way out of this trap is to stop ducking the issues and have an argument. Becoming angry releases pent-up resentment and the real issues can finally be faced. Often these are different, and frequently less scary, than the ones imagined.

Attacking and defending difference

We all want the best for our partner, don't we? We are happy for them to grow and fulfil their potential. Meanwhile our partner will do everything to back our ambitions. This is the public face of many relationships – especially among ILYB couples, who usually have a warm and mutually supportive partnership. Yet underneath everything is much murkier. Returning to the couple we met at the beginning of the chapter, David understood Lucy's desire to return to full-time education. They had met at university but Lucy had dropped out when she became pregnant. He was happy to pay lip-service to her returning, 'one day'. But in reality he was attacking her desire to do something different and be someone other than a wife and mother. He used a classic technique: practical objections. 'I'm really behind Lucy's ambitions, but how are we going to cover looking after the kids? Of course I can help out, but it's more than that,' he explained. 'There's all those hours of essay-writing, and her money from that part-time job isn't just for luxuries.' Every time Lucy solved one problem he was ready with another. But this was more than just a case of a husband trying to hold his wife back. Although David might have been attacking Lucy's attempts to be different, she too was busy defending the status quo. In counselling we had negotiated Saturday afternoons as Lucy's time for some serious reading while David took the children swimming. But week after week Lucy would find something else she needed to do that prevented her from sitting down even to this small amount of study. No wonder they were stuck: both of them were frightened of change. David was frightened that new studies, new friends, new qualifications and new opportunities could mean that Lucy no longer wanted him. Meanwhile Lucy was worried, partly about upsetting David but also about whether she was up to the challenge of being a mature student. Unfortunately, because neither wanted to 'hurt' the other they had suppressed/failed to confess these feelings. Lucy might have been unhappy but David was not getting much out of the relationship either. He had been so busy defending the status quo that he had little idea what he wanted from the future. Because they were unable to deal with difference Lucy and David's relationship was stuck in the stalemate position of 'attacking and defending'; both were prevented from reaching **collaborating** and achieving their ambitions.

The Paradox of Love

We all need to be loved. The more we love someone, the more important his or her love becomes and the more frightened we are of losing it. So we worry that if we do not do what our partner wants he or she will reject us. But how do we deal with different tastes, standards and attitudes? Every relationship faces this problem, partly because no two people are alike but mainly because we are programmed to choose a partner who makes up for the qualities we lack. In the best-case scenario these differences are catalysts for growth rather than estrangement. However, difference can become so threatening that a couple use strategies, often unconsciously, to protect themselves from the pain. These strategies include: attempting to control your partner; pretending to be indifferent to the difference; fitting in with your partner and subsuming your personality into theirs. Nobody sets out to be either controlling or a doormat – they just get frightened. Here comes the central paradox: almost everything we do is to protect us from pain, but most of the pain we feel comes from this protective behaviour.

With ILYB couples, these strategies for protecting from difference slot together into three major combinations:

Control/compliance

One partner is in charge and the other falls in with their wishes. From traditional sitcoms, we would immediately recognise the overbearing wife and the timid husband. In real relationships it is often more complex, with couples swapping control and capitulating over different issues. Take Martin, a thirty-two-year-old lorry driver, and his partner Jackie, a twenty-eight-year-old office manager: Martin was in charge of their social life. He would hold court with their group of friends, decide how long they stayed and where and with whom they spent their leisure time. Jackie would go along with his wishes. However, Jackie controlled almost everything in the home – the budget, where everything was kept, what they ate, when and how they washed up – and Martin would fall in with these dictates. Some couples can rub along with these tight demarcations for years, until something breaks down the walls. In Martin and Jackie's case it was the arrival of a baby. She found herself overwhelmed at home and he found the restrictions on their social life impossible.

Control is about more than just ordering somebody about or physically intimidating them. Sometimes the partner who seems weaker to the outside world is actually very controlling. Some of the techniques for taking charge without seeming to include angry tears, 'poor me' tears, illness, threats of leaving, guilt-inducing body language (sighing, raised eyebrows, shrugging shoulders), blame, accusations and lectures. Although this list makes control/compliance seem exhausting, in most cases such behaviour can provide a superficially peaceful coexistence. However, the compliant partner will feel more relaxed and spontaneous when the controlling partner is not around. Certainly Martin felt he could only truly relax at home when Jackie was not in, while Jackie felt more herself on the rare occasions that she went out with her girlfriends.

Indifference/indifference

These relationships are deceptively calm, with few lows or highs. The two lives run side by side, in parallel, but the couple have given up wanting much from each other. These relationships were common in the first half of the twentieth century, when the emphasis was on survival of the marriage and personal happiness was considered less important. The modern equivalent of indifference – withdrawing both emotionally and physically – is the workaholic relationship. Here one partner might claim to want more 'couple time' but always has an excuse for a few more hours on the home computer. Rather than challenging this behaviour their partner gets on with his or her life. Other distancing behaviour includes watching television, getting drunk, watching sport and burying oneself in hobbies.

With indifference/indifference there tends to be little talk, no intimacy and plenty of boredom. These couples tell me, 'We have little in common but the kids.' Peter and Nancy had been married for twenty years but Nancy complained, 'I don't feel I really know Peter; he seems withdrawn all the time.' While Peter countered, 'What's the point in talking? All we ever discuss is work and other people.' By avoiding conflict they had never really opened up on the issues that would let them explore and understand each other. Although both 'indifference' partners will have strong separate identities, there is no couple identity. Once children become less central to their lives, one half of these couples will often find the loneliness unbearable. Remember that, deep down, nobody is truly indifferent. Someone might pretend, or give the appearance of not caring, but everybody wants to be loved.

Compliance/compliance

These are the relationships in which both partners are so keen to make each other happy that they give up their individuality for a couple identity. Kate and David not only worked for the same company but also sat beside each other in the staff canteen at lunchtime. When I asked if they ever thought of sitting with their individual work colleagues for a change they both admitted being bored with the current arrangement. 'It would be so nice to chat with other people,' said Kate, 'and then I'd have something to tell David in the evening.' David put it slightly differently but came to the same conclusions. So why hadn't he said anything? 'I thought it was what Kate wanted,' David explained and Kate nodded.

Compliance might seem like the best way to run a relationship; after all, the ability to compromise is essential for a happy partnership. But these couples are so frightened of difference, and therefore so defensive, that they ignore any painful feelings. In other relationships the pain would turn to anger and, yes, you've guessed it, a row. If Kate and David had argued one of them would have blurted out, 'Don't crowd in on me at lunchtime!' Compliance/compliance will ultimately cause major identity issues as nobody gets what they really want.

Although rare among ILYB couples, there are two other strategies for dealing with difference: control/control and control/rebellion. With the first, each half of the couple wants to change the other and even small issues create power struggles. With the second, one half is valiantly trying to change the other while the other is valiantly trying to resist. In small doses there is nothing wrong with any of these patterns for dealing with difference. Sometimes it is necessary for one half to make a decision and the other to go along with it (control/compliance), or to row about important issues (control/control). Likewise there are times when neither partner has the energy or inclination to get worked up over something (indifference/indifference), and others when digging the heels in is more effective than a direct challenge (rebellion/control). The problem occurs when a couple become stuck in one particular pattern or, worse still, retreat into more and more extreme versions of these patterns. In the long term this behaviour will drain all connection, understanding and, ultimately, love from a relationship. Until the day when one partner will wake up, look at their mate lying next to them and think, 'He's holding me back,' or, 'She's a stranger.'

Dealing with Identity Issues

Grand gestures, like moving abroad or ending a relationship, often just take the compliant or controlling behaviour to another country or another relationship. Identity is accumulated through a series of small victories: standing up for yourself; doing something different from what other people expect; understanding your fears and your partner's fears. Here are some pointers on the way:

- *Look at your internal dialogue.* Do you spend more time second-guessing your partner's reaction than examining your own feelings? Do you find yourself trying to 'hold the line', frightened that if you give in over one thing it will have a domino effect and change everything?
- *Identify which of the unhelpful patterns you and your partner fall into.* Understanding a behaviour is halfway to changing it. Even if you find yourself falling into the old patterns, keep one eye free to observe yourself. This will make you doubly aware of the pitfalls and less likely to fall into the same traps next time round.
- *Take responsibility.* Don't cast yourself as the victim; look at your contribution to the pattern. As the old saying goes: *You can't change anybody but yourself.*
- *Try to understand, instead of trying to convince/cajole/control each other.* Without understanding it is impossible to build a

proper compromise. (For more on this see 'Break Out of Controlling Behaviour' in the exercise section.)

- *Look at the expectations that underpin your view of the world and yourself.* Where does each expectation come from? How much of your identity has come from your parents? How much from your friends? How much from our wider culture, religion, the media? How much of this belongs to you? (See the 'Unpicking Expectations' exercise at the end of the chapter.)
- *Aim for a compromise.* Is there a middle way that would balance individual and couple identity?

This process described above helped Stacey and Carl find a way through Stacey's identity crisis. Her internal dialogue was full of questions like, 'Is it OK to want to go out this often?' and, 'Will Carl be upset with me for wanting to go?' Carl's internal dialogue had gone along similar lines: 'Should I say something about her going out so much?' and, 'What will she think about me if I ask her to stay in?' From the beginning of their relationship Carl and Stacey had both been so keen to please each other that their relationship had been compliance/compliance. More recently Stacey had run up large credit card bills and Carl had tried to keep spending down: rebellion/control. Next, with **taking responsibility**, Stacey admitted that her shopping habit had been like a reckless teenager's and that Carl had been like a critical parent; this allowed them to have an adult-to-adult discussion, creating a proper budget with money set aside for entertainment. During **understanding** Carl learnt that nights in front of the TV made Stacey feel old before her time; Stacey learnt that Carl thought they should be saving to start a family. We had finally uncovered the unspoken expectations that had been driving them apart. Where had these expectations come from? Carl's parents had had children in their mid-twenties and, as he said, 'It just feels like the right time.' However, Stacey's mother had regretted having children early and had always advised her daughter to 'see something of the world first'. Finally the couple were ready for a compromise. Carl started joining Stacey for some of her nights out and saving for a trip to the USA. Stacey agreed that she would like to have children before she turned thirty.

Meanwhile Lucy and David just needed a frank discussion about both their fears. Lucy was able to reassure David that she was not planning to leave and he was able to be more supportive. Lucy decided to start carving her own individual identity by taking an extra part-time A level course at her local adult education centre. 'I wanted to check that motherhood had not completely destroyed all my brain cells,' she explained, 'but also to check that I really want this before we splash out a lot of money.' David was happy to babysit on her college nights.

Summary

- Too much compromise is as bad as too little.
- Try to find a balance between being one half of a couple and being yourself.
- Do not ignore identity pains; these are normally indicative of a deeper problem in the relationship.
- Secure partners encourage each other to have their own identity because they know this will not undermine the relationship.
- Doing what we want, and need, for ourselves while continuing to care deeply for our partner is not always easy. However, it can be done by understanding each other's differences rather than ignoring or protecting against them.

Exercises

I'm in Charge/You're in Charge

Endlessly compromising and trying to second-guess what your partner might enjoy can become boring after a while. A friend had a novel idea for holidays: he would be totally in charge for one day and his partner for another. 'I really used to look forward to it,' says Jamie. 'It gave me a chance to get to know Sherrell better. I could almost hear the tone of her voice in what she chose.' Even the children would have their allocated day, 'although that sometimes got a little hairy'. The rest of the holiday would be the usual family compromise. The rules are as follows:

1 During your day you choose all the activities. Apart from something that would completely terrify your partner, the choice is entirely up to you; follow your heart's desire.
2 The day starts at breakfast and ends at bedtime – what food, where you eat, where to visit or whether to lie around doing nothing are all up to you.
3 Your partner agrees to enter into the spirit of your day and to try, with good grace, to enjoy your choices as much as possible.
4 On another day you swap over and your partner chooses.
5 Afterwards discuss what you have learnt about yourself and each other. Ask yourselves: What could we incorporate into our normal routines?
6 Before agreeing to this exercise it is worth having a side discussion about any additional personal rules. Here are a few issues to discuss: Does the person in charge have the right to ask for sex? Is there anything that would be totally unacceptable to either one of you?

The exercise can also work at home, with each partner 'in charge' for one day at the weekend or for whole alternate weekends. The same rules as above apply; the only proviso is that the day is devoted to pleasure – a mini-break at home – rather than catching up on chores and DIY.

Break Out of Controlling Behaviour

The object of this exercise is to understand both your partner's behaviour and your own. Take an issue that causes a lot of tension between the two of you – something that you have argued about frequently in the past or need to argue about!

1 The partner who is having an identity crisis or wanting change starts. If this is both of you, flip a coin. He or she talks about how they see the problem, what they want and how they feel. The other person simply listens.
2 The listener can ask for amplification or clarification but nothing else. No defending, no answering back, no comforting or reassuring. Just listening and understanding.
3 If the person who is listening feels tempted to speak, he or she should first ask themselves: Am I trying to convince or defend? If the answer is yes, bite your tongue. If the question aims to clarify or to dig deeper, feel free to speak.
4 When there is a lull in the conversation, check that you have properly understood your partner: 'What you are saying is . . .' or, 'Have I understood properly, that you feel . . .'
5 If an argument starts, stop and look at the protecting patterns: control/compliance, control/control, indifference/indifference and control/rebellion. Have you fallen into one of these traps? Alternatively look for expectations that have turned into dicta (see the 'Unpicking Expectations' exercise below).
6 The object of the exercise is not to find a solution to the difference but to understand.
7 On many occasions the problems disappear without any action plan. This is because understanding the reasons behind our partner's contentious behaviour makes it easier to tolerate. Often our tolerance makes our partner soften their behaviour,

which in turn increases our tolerance and sets up a virtuous circle.

If you are working through this book alone, put yourself in the listening position. Ask your partner why he or she feels so strongly about a point of dispute and follow the exercise from there. If your partner refuses – 'You know only too well' – explain that you want to double check that you understand; this will take them off the defensive. When you've finished hearing and truly understand all their viewpoints, ask, 'Could I explain where I am coming from?' If your partner feels understood he or she will be open to offering the same courtesy to you. So, if your partner refuses to listen, keep trying to understand before seeking to be understood.

Unpicking Expectations

1 Below is a list of potential conflicts. Write down beside each one what it means to you and/or what you believe is the approach of a right-thinking person. For example, beside *debt* you could write: a necessary evil; shame; a personal failure; good money management; a fact of life.
2 Go through the list as quickly as possible, so that you record your first spontaneous thought.
3 Afterwards return and ask where these expectations come from: mother; father; friends; media; priest; wider culture; politicians.
4 How do these expectations feed your arguments? Are any of your expectations out of date? Do you need to change any of them? Which are particularly important to your identity?

Sex; money; Sunday morning; debt; television; role of a man in a relationship; role of a woman in a relationship; flowers; being late; paying bills; play; Christmas; credit; experimenting in bed; health; marriage; how time is spent; Saturday night; friends outside the relationship; affection; entertaining at home; the past; communication; hobbies; bringing up children; tidiness; meal times; housekeeping; dress sense; work; alcohol; disciplining children; promptness; birthdays; interest; presents; behaviour at social functions around other people; sport; the bathroom; cuddles; education.

Want to Change But Can't Change?

Forging a new identity is tough. Below the journey is broken down into six more manageable chunks:

1 *Ask yourself if you really want it.* Sometimes we try to change something – get fit, give up smoking or start evening classes – because we feel we ought to, because someone else is putting pressure on us, because society expects it or because we like the picture of us doing these things. However, deep down we might not really want to change.

2 *What are the benefits of staying where you are?* If you are stuck, there is probably some hidden benefit to not changing. Once you have truly understood the obstacles to change you will be better placed to climb over them.

3 *Break the change down into smaller parts.* Getting from today to the future can seem an impossibly long journey. For example, moving house involves a million and one choices and plenty of opportunities for disaster. But when broken down into smaller chunks – like researching schools in the new area or finding an estate agent – everything seems more manageable. Once those tasks are achieved you can move on to the next ones and pretty soon you will have arrived at your final destination.

4 *Sell the benefits of change to your partner.* If we know our partner will have doubts about a project we tend to be very tentative about asking: 'I don't suppose you'll like it but . . .' This immediately makes it easier to say no. Alternatively we can even provide ammunition for their side: 'I know we're short of time but . . .' Worse still, we fail to convey the importance of a project so that our partner does not understand the consequence of a refusal. So look for all the benefits to you, your family and your

partner. What could make him or her support the change? Finally, find out as much detail as possible and be ready to answer questions. Everybody fears the unknown and the more information you have the less overwhelming that change will be.

5 *How can you make the first step?* It is very easy to put off change until tomorrow, then the day after and then for ever. Choose one small job that will get the ball rolling today.

6 *Keep going.* There are always setbacks, but remember that nothing lasts for ever and these difficult times will pass too. Even the most successful people face dead ends and occasional failure. What makes them different from everybody else is that they are not discouraged.

Frightened of Change?

If your partner is seeking a new identity the changes involved can feel pretty scary. If you want to change but are worried how your partner will react, that can also be a scary place. Either way, here are the three keys to coping with change:

1 *Understanding.* Because you fear change you see it as something bad. Yet change is neither intrinsically good nor bad; it is all down to how you look at it. For example, we might think of rain as bad but in a desert rain would be wonderful. It's all down to our attitude. So the first step is always to look for the positive aspect of something new. If you can't see one immediately try looking a bit further into the future. How might it look in three months' time, a year, two years? Secondly, ask what would happen if you didn't change. What is the downside of staying where you are?

2 *Relax.* Scientists have discovered that when we're under stress – such as during times of change – our brain operates differently. With our very survival under threat we use the less sophisticated parts of our brain inherited from our reptile ancestors. Yet this is the very time when we need to think something through rather

than just act instinctively. So next time you're stressed by change, find a way to relax and calm down. Take deep breaths, go for a long walk, dig the garden or spring-clean the house. Think back to times when you successfully dealt with change – there will be plenty of examples as you're better at coping than you think. Look at what worked last time and decide which skills can be used today.

3 *Name your fears.* When you are relaxed, close your eyes and picture the proposed future. Where will it be? What will it be like? What will your partner be doing? Make the picture as detailed as possible. Now try to analyse what is particularly worrying. Write each of these fears down in a sentence. Go back to the picture and try to imagine other things that could be unsettling you. Write these down too. It is better to have a list of fears on a piece of paper – however long – than a large amorphous terror in your head. Go back to the list and cross off anything which, on reflection, is a molehill rather than a mountain. Finally, discuss your fears with your partner. He or she might be able to offer reassurance or provide more information to take the edge off your anxiety. Even if some fears remain you will have a clearer grasp of the most important issues.

Chapter Eight

Is It the Relationship or Something Else?

Life is complicated but we like to keep our problems as simple as possible. We worry that if we continue to unpack our unhappiness we will be completely overwhelmed. One problem therefore feels much more manageable than a whole stack. However, in our desire to keep things simple we can sometimes end up tackling the wrong cause or blaming our partner for something that is not their fault. So how do we sort out which issues belong in our relationship and which belong elsewhere?

In many cases the unhappiness has simply been deflected from one part of someone's life on to their relationship. Paul was unhappy at work: 'I found the city increasingly stressful, I hated the commuting.' He really wanted to write thriller novels. 'I could escape into a world of my own, time flew. However, I had a family and a lifestyle to maintain, and how could I find time to write?' Paul had started to resent his partner, Debbie, but never really talked to her about it. After he had the ILYB conversation they had a general chat, during which Paul discovered he'd been making assumptions. It turned out that Debbie preferred a happy husband to new cars and exotic holidays. So they restructured their lives and Paul went part-time. However, his novel still did not flow and eventually, in counselling, Paul discovered he was frightened of failing in his new career. It had been easier to blame

Debbie for holding him back than to look inside and take personal responsibility.

In other ILYB cases, issues which seemed to be relationship problems turned out to be one partner's unresolved childhood problems. For example, George, forty-five and working for a large insurance broker, complained, 'I truly feel that nobody understands me. I talk until I'm blue in the face and nobody takes a blind bit of notice. I shut myself away in my study but she keeps knocking on the door.' Relations between George and his wife Tracy, a stay-at-home mum, had gone from bad to worse and George was questioning whether he still loved Tracy. 'I can't understand it,' says Tracy. 'I do listen. In fact I've heard so much about his blessed office that if he was ill I could probably walk in and take over. But still he says I don't . . .' and she made inverted comma signs with her hand, '. . . "really listen".' My gut instinct was that George sounded rather like a stroppy teenager, and indeed he did have a fourteen-year-old son. I knew George's parents had divorced when he was young and, as it turned out, he had also been fourteen when this happened. How did you feel? I asked. 'Nobody listened to what I thought or what I wanted,' George replied. His son reaching the age he had been during the trauma of his parents' divorce had reawakened long-buried emotions. It was a personal, not a relationship, problem. With this knowledge, Tracy stopped taking George's mood so personally. They talked and averted an ILYB crisis.

Alternatively, general feelings of dissatisfaction and unhappiness with a relationship can be a mild form of depression. Unfortunately depression is hard to diagnose, because everybody gets the blues from time to time. Answering yes to five or more of the following questions can indicate a serious depression:

- Are you eating too much or too little?
- Are you finding it hard to sleep or sleeping too much?
- Do you feel tired all the time or generally lacking energy?

- Do you feel inadequate?
- Are you less productive at home or at work?
- Do you have trouble concentrating or making decisions?
- Do you have a tendency to brood over things, feeling sorry for yourself or pessimistic about the future?
- Does the world seem grey?
- Are you easily irritated?
- Do you rarely enjoy or feel interested in pleasurable activities?
- Are you prone to crying?

Anyone recognising two or more symptoms should also speak to their doctor – especially if the symptoms have existed more or less constantly, with no more than a couple of months' relief, for two or more years. Other suggestions for dealing with depression include: consulting a nutritionist to check on diet; cutting down on alcohol consumption; taking more exercise – an aerobic-style workout releases endorphins, the body's natural feel-good hormone.

Sometimes the 'something else' behind ILYB can be someone else. Although couples with ILYB seldom arrive at my counselling office complaining about an affair, I often find their long-term problems have reached a head because one partner is having an 'inappropriate' friendship. These friendships start out innocently enough, as very few people go out 'looking for an affair'. First there are the tingly feelings from just talking together about something mundane, like the first-quarter sales figures. Next come the longer conversations, during which each half opens up first about their real attitudes to work or colleagues, then life in general and sometimes their own relationships. These 'friendly chats' turn into long lunches – supposedly about work but the office is barely mentioned. Before too long comes the first touch – often something innocent like simultaneously reaching for the bill. Both 'friends' feel the charge of electricity. The 'friendship' starts to become more and more important. He's a good listener; she's really able to open up. He tells himself, 'She helps me deal with my stress'; she thinks, 'Why can't I have friends?' The 'friends' share their real feelings and discuss how they should not be getting this close. They start having long clandestine phone calls, sharing sexy texts and intimate emails. Anybody eavesdropping or reading these messages would immediately recognise that this pair are flirting. For the 'friends' this relationship is becoming increasingly significant to their day-to-day happiness. They might even agree to stop calling but their resolve weakens after a few days. This is the point at which the 'friendship' can tip over into a full-blown affair, with either prolonged kissing or intercourse. Or maybe it became an affair – in all but name – a few steps back. That is the problem with 'inappropriate friendships': no individual step along the journey is actually that wicked, but before long the steps have added up to a genuine betrayal.

Inappropriate friendships not only lead to affairs, and all the resulting pain, but also make it impossible to work on the central relationship because all the emotional energy is diverted into the friendship. Oliver and Tina, married for twenty years, had all the classic signs of an ILYB relationship: neither shared their true feelings for fear of rocking the relationship; until recently they had had a superficially happy relationship; both had lost parents in the past two years. However, beneath Oliver and Tina's politeness was a testiness that could barely be concealed. It only took a few neutral questions before Oliver erupted about Tina's friendship with a work colleague. 'Yes, we're friends. What's wrong with that?' she countered. Oliver was determined not to lose his temper. As calmly as possible he produced a telephone bill that showed seven phone calls to one number, totalling three and a half hours, on just one day. Tina was furious but kept a tight control on her feelings. 'He listens to me,' she finally said. 'I'd listen to you,' said Oliver, 'but if I added up all our conversations from the last month, the last three months, I doubt they would add up to three and a half hours.' With the truth finally out in the open we could begin to work on their relationship. Fortunately for this couple, Tina's inappropriate friendship had not tipped into **limerence** – always a risk – and she was still able to focus on her marriage. When does a friendship become inappropriate? Of course it is possible for members of the opposite sex (and same sex among gays and lesbians) to be friends. The acid test is how much the friends are telling their partners and how much is omitted. True friendship is open to public scrutiny; inappropriate friendship is concealed.

So far in this chapter I have discussed the more obvious 'other causes' for ILYB: deflection; recurring issues from the past; depression; emotional infidelity. The next group are harder to pinpoint as they are buried deeper under the relationship.

One of the most useful perspectives comes not from psychology but from the American marketing guru Abraham Maslow, in his book *Motivation and Personality* (HarperCollins, 1954). His 'Hierarchy of Needs' shows that when basic requirements have been satisfied we move on to higher aspirations. For example, once someone has a full belly he or she can worry about somewhere safe to live, and then about a relationship and being loved. He believes that in the 1950s the average consumer was satisfied 80 per cent of the time in their physiological needs, 70 per cent in their safety needs, 50 per cent in belonging and love needs, 40 per cent in self-esteem/prestige/status, but was only satisfied for 10 per cent of the time in their top need, which he called 'self-actualisation': personal fulfilment and realisation of potential.

Look at commercials today: products like soft drinks are no longer aimed at quenching our thirst, a basic physiological need, but instead offer the illusion of satisfying our higher needs, such as identity. Marriage seems to have been climbing the same ladder. Our grandparents placed more emphasis on being a good provider/housekeeper. Twenty years ago, when I first saw couples professionally, they were asking for more love and companionship. Today people with ILYB are asking their partners for the highest need of all: 'Help me become the best that I can be.' Although many social commentators complain that we expect too much from relationships, I think this only becomes a problem when it collides with another twenty-first-century phenomenon: denying ageing.

The average age at divorce in Britain, according to the Office for National Statistics, is now 42.3 for men and 39.8 for women. The mid-life crisis is normally treated as the butt of a joke: 'What's the best way to cover a bald spot?' Answer: 'A Porsche.' We are particularly encouraged to laugh at men who suck in their paunches and try to relive their glory days by buying fast bikes and cars or dating much younger women.

For some reason society has no equivalent stereotype for women, yet I counsel many who are dealing with similar mid-life problems. In fact one third of my clients – both men and women – and probably 90 per cent of all ILYB cases are facing something akin to a mid-life crisis. All of them have woken up one day and thought: Life is too short to . . . Everybody comes up with a different example but everybody is facing the same ticking clock.

I do not use the term 'mid-life crisis' in my counselling, however, as men are quick to disassociate themselves from it even though their wives might agree. Often when I ask both male and female clients when their problems started, as part of my standard assessment, he or she will immediately protest, 'It has nothing to do with turning forty.' The second reason I avoid the term is because the problems can strike at any time. In fact books have been written about the quarter-life crisis: twenty-five-year-olds who feel time is running out. My final objection to 'mid-life crisis' is that it does not have to be a crisis with all the drama that implies.

So what is going on and why does it have such an impact on relationships? Forgive me for stating the obvious: we are not going to live for ever. Although everybody knows this fact, it does not stop us from believing that we are immortal. For some men the wake-up call is the traditional hair in the comb or worrying about declining sexual prowess: at twenty they managed three orgasms in a night and now they are hard pushed to come up with one. For some women it is the awareness that fewer men are noticing them on the street. They begin to compare themselves unfavourably with younger women, envying their slim bodies, their energy and how easy everything seems.

The death of a loved one, often a parent, can also be a wake-up call. There is no more concrete proof that we are not immortal than sitting by a parent's hospital or hospice bedside, witnessing their decline. Even more startling is the death of a contemporary – perhaps in a car accident or, worse still, some illness – as the illusion of mortality belonging to the generation above is stripped away. Everybody eventually faces the truth that their time on earth is finite. At this point some people will ask: What is the meaning of life? or, How can I make sense of my own life? Others will decide that life is too short to be unhappy or in an unhappy relationship and search for remedies. Unfortunately there is a third reaction: denial. These people will take refuge from an unpalatable reality by drinking too much, burying themselves at work, having affairs or cosmetic surgery. People in this third category risk turning a natural reaction and readjustment to ageing into a crisis.

During existential questioning many people reach for self-actualisation, the highest level of Maslow's 'Hierarchy of Needs'. According to Maslow, 'Discontent and restlessness will soon develop, unless the individual is doing what he is fitted for. A musician must make music, an artist must paint and a poet must write if he is to be ultimately with himself. What a man can be, he must be.' At first sight this seems a perfectly feasible goal, except that most professions today are not as clear-cut as being a musician, artist or poet.

What about the people whose work is made up of hundreds of different tasks with no clear-cut core? What about the others who don't particularly like their work and have no desire to be the best ever accounts clerk? Maslow tried to study what self-actualisation might be like but found it extremely difficult to find subjects who met his criteria. In the end he had to settle for just forty-five people: a strange combination of personal friends and acquaintances, twenty students who seemed to be developing in the direction of self-actualisation, plus historical and contemporary figures. Even then he could find only two 'fairly sure' historical figures to study: Thomas Jefferson and Lincoln – but only Lincoln's last years. He found six 'highly probable public and historical figures' and seven 'who probably fall short but who can yet be used for study'.

Maslow detailed his subjects' psychological health but had trouble reconciling their strong individuality with their ability to love and be loved: 'These people cannot in the ordinary sense of the word be said to need each other as do ordinary lovers. They can be extremely close together and yet go apart quite easily. They do not cling to each other or have hooks or anchors of any kind. One has the definite feeling that they enjoy each other tremendously but would take philosophically a long separation or death. Throughout the most intense and ecstatic love affairs these people remain ultimately masters of themselves as well, living by their own standards even though enjoying each other intensely.' In my opinion, these self-actualisers sound rather cold.

Becoming everything that one is capable of becoming seems to run the risk of destroying other people en route. Even a cursory reading of biographies of the famous suggests that, although we might enjoy their music, books, films, etc., we would probably not wish to be married to them. Even Maslow warns that the road to self-actualisation could be a blind alley: 'Higher needs are less perceptible, less unmistakable, more easily confused with other needs by suggestion, imitation, by mistaken belief or habit.' He was writing in the 1950s, before advertising, marketing and public relations became so sophisticated and all-pervasive. Today we have to be very watchful or, instead of truly discovering ourselves, we are sold a holiday on a Greek island, a bottle of beer or a new car.

Unfortunately all this general resentment and bitterness – from growing older and our desire for self-actualisation – gets aimed at

our relationship and in the process turns something perfectly serv-
iceable into something broken. One of the main reasons our relationship bears the brunt is explained by the 'at least we're doing
something' factor. However painful and disruptive separation or
divorce can be, at least these couples feel that they are moving out
of their current situation towards a different script. When it comes
to big questions like, 'What is the meaning of life?' or, 'How can I
ever fall back in love with my partner?' the temptation is to do
something, *anything*. Soap operas reinforce the 'something must be
done' mentality. Good drama needs plenty of action and in soaps
people tend to confront now and think later. Secrets always come
out and characters always choose the most dramatic option. However,
what makes for good soap operas does not always make for happy
relationships. As compelling as it may be to act for the sake of
action, this is not always the best way forward.

Spirituality

Ultimately, underneath the so-called mid-life crisis and striving for
self-actualisation, there is probably a search for spirituality: making
sense of the world beyond the self-centred and materialistic. For
some people this can also include a search for some greater power,
either mystical or religious. However, when listening to my ILYB
clients – especially those who want to leave their relationship – talk
about their life in the future – their expected bliss, fulfilment, contentment and even completeness – I am often reminded of a spiritual
quest.

A good example would be Martin, a thirty-eight-year-old salesman:
'Some mornings while I stand on the platform waiting for the 7.50
I start thinking, what's it all about? Surely there is something more
than daily reports and targets. I want my time to count – rather
than just being hours that are filled until the next day – and I'm
standing watching the same discarded newspaper supplements blow

across the rails. If I started again there would be not only space and time to think but the possibility of meeting someone who would make even the seconds count.' For Martin, love had become the passport out of his mundane existence into a better tomorrow. Although **limerence** might temporarily have the power to transform, it cannot last for ever, and while **loving attachment** makes for a more complete life, on its own it cannot make an empty life meaningful.

So, if not with love alone, how can we make life more purposeful? Why are we here? What is the meaning of life? How do I fill this void at the centre of my life? These are profound questions, and unfortunately all the books and potential answers are either full of platitudes or they leave one thinking, yes, but so what? I believe the problem is that each of us has to find our own answer: something that fits our world view, deals with the issues from our particular upbringing and ultimately confronts our unique doubts, questions and personality. My answer is not going to be your answer, but at risk of adding to the pile of platitudes, I will share my thoughts about creating a fulfilled life in the hope they might kick-start yours:

- *Create rather than just consume.* Instead of watching sport on the TV, go out and play one. Instead of grabbing a convenience meal, take the time to cook something from scratch. Alternatively, take an adult education class in pottery, music or creative writing; the list is endless. Sadly we live in an age that only values something if it earns money. Don't let this common misconception stop you; if a hobby brings you pleasure, do it.
- *The journey is more important than the destination.* Travelling with an open mind and heart is more important than actually arriving. With this attitude, contemporaries' travel quickly becomes less important and the risk of pointless jealousy subsides. If life is a race – something I doubt – at least think of it as a marathon rather than a sprint.

- *Embrace death as a constant travelling companion.* After suffering a major bereavement in my thirties I learnt that death could be a friend rather than the enemy. With every major decision or fork in the journey I am always aware of the time-limit on life, and love, and am guided to make the fullest use of my share. Richard Holloway, former Bishop of Edinburgh, puts this more poetically in his book *Looking in the Distance: The Human Search for Meaning* (Canongate, 2004). He concludes: 'Our brief finitude is but a beautiful spark in the vast darkness of space. So we should live the fleeting day with passion and, when the night comes, depart from it with grace.'

These are only a few first thoughts, as probably we spend our whole lives redefining our personal big questions, testing our answers and, in the light of fresh experience, starting all over again. If you are unsure where to start your search for meaning, try re-balancing your life. Career-orientated people might need to spend more time with the family; someone who has focused on child-rearing and the home might need interests away from their own four walls. As with a mid-life readjustment, it is helpful to look back over the first half of your life, decide what is lacking and what could complete the picture for the second half.

The 'I Love You But' Crisis and the Link to Our Childhood

At first sight it seems tough that our relationships act like a magnet for a whole range of other problems. But twenty years of counselling couples has shown me that a good relationship is very effective in healing deep-seated personal problems. Maybe some hidden, intuitive part of our brain understands this power and is therefore determined to lay a range of disparate personal problems at the relationship's door – even if they do not really belong there.

To explain this idea I need to outline the basic tenet of psycho-analysis: our first relationship, with our mother or primary care-giver, will shape all our subsequent relationships. The 'good parent' will provide a baby with food and comfort when he or she cries; psychoanalysts believe these children will grow up into trusting and open adults who make good relationships. An inadequate care-giver who is wrapped up in his or her own problems might leave a crying baby unattended or be erratic in feeding him or her; psychoanalysts believe these children will be untrusting, find it hard to make rela-tionships, and may even suffer severe mental illness. Most people's experiences will fall somewhere between these two extremes, and indeed psychologists use the term 'good enough' to describe the parenting received by the majority of us.

The most famous piece of research into the influence of upbringing on personality was conducted in the 1950s by the psychoanalyst John Bowlby, a former head of the children's department of the Tavistock Clinic. Among a group of baby rhesus monkeys, some were raised normally by their mothers, some received just food and water, and a third group were also given a surrogate (soft cloth round a wire frame). Not surprisingly, those not given any nurturing turned into delinquent monkeys and those raised with their mothers were well-adjusted. The baby monkeys with the surrogate fared worse than the monkeys with mothers but significantly better than those with only food and water. Bowlby argued that both our sense of security and our anxieties have their roots in our relationship with our primary care-giver. His work has led to a theory called Separation Anxiety. A study by Ainsworth, Blehar, Waters and Wall – *Patterns of Attachment* (Erlbaum, 1978) – found that people fall into three categories: those who had a 'good enough' childhood and find it easy to get close to someone else (secure attachment), who make up 56 per cent of the population; those who had bad experi-ences and find it hard to trust other people (avoidant attachment), who make up 25 per cent of the population; and those whose unful-filled childhood needs mean they can never get enough love. People in this third category find others are reluctant to get as close as they would wish (anxious or ambivalent attachment) and make up 19 per cent of the population.

At first it is very depressing to think that our adult relationships are so strongly shaped by our experiences as babies. After all, we cannot return to being a small infant again and undo the harm – well, not without dressing up and giving the neighbours a lot to talk about. However, a loving adult sexual relationship does provide a second chance to learn about closeness. It is almost as intimate as the bond between mother and child, and indeed many lovers even use baby talk as a sign of affection. So how does this work in practice? Taking my clients' childhood histories, I am frequently amazed by how much abuse some have suffered and yet they still grow up into balanced, normal adults. Time and again, through a good choice of partner and plenty of hard work, these damaged children have forged a relationship that not only reduces past pain but provides the strength not to pass these problems on to their own children. I could give an extreme example but I think a middling one would be more enlightening.

Angela is forty-eight and has been married for twenty-seven years: 'My father left and returned several times when I was growing up, so I don't really know how old I was – probably about eight – when he never came back. Although my parents' fights had been terrible and I hated listening to my father beat my mother, the worst part was that after he left not one word was said about what happened, not one. If my friends asked after my father I was instructed to tell them he was at work. It was terrible keeping that secret, terrible. Even as an adult, when I tried to talk about him my mother just froze me out.' Angela's mother kept a stick by the door with which she would not just chastise her daughter but beat her in cold fury. It comes as no surprise that Angela found it hard to form relationships. 'However, I found a wonderful man and it wasn't easy to trust him, but I did. The proudest day of my life was standing hand-in-hand with my husband, watching our daughter get married. I have the sort of relationship with her where we laugh a lot and talk about anything, the polar opposite of my relationship with my mother. On that day I really thought, the buck stops with me. But I couldn't have done it without my husband's support and sometimes his intervention.'

Implicit in falling in love, and sometimes actually stated, is the pledge: I will look after you. This is the same as the implicit bond between the good (or, as a psychoanalyst would say, 'good enough') mother and her baby. No wonder it feels like such an extraordinary betrayal when someone falls out of love with us. The reaction is beyond rational, but then we are dealing with the part of our personality which was formed when we were babies incapable of logical thought.

An adult sexual relationship might provide the opportunity to go back and work through all the most difficult issues: trust, closeness, separation and, of course, love. However, it is not a magic bullet. I chose the word 'opportunity' very carefully, because a couple need courage, determination and persistence. Sadly, many couples give up too soon, frightened off by the arguments and the pain. Yet what is often mistaken for an impossibly damaged relationship can actually be evidence of two people struggling away with difficult, deep-seated childhood issues, and therefore a sign of hope. We pick partners who are like us or who we feel complement our background in some way. By this I do not mean racial, religious or socio-economic influences – although these play a part – but family quirks. R. D. Laing, one of the fathers of modern psychiatry, wrote this about our families: 'We are acting parts in a play that we have never read and never seen, whose plot we don't know, whose existence we can glimpse, but whose beginnings and end are beyond our present imagination and conception.' Each person's family script will influence not only their personality but their choice of partner. An example of how we 'click' with some people better than others comes from the 'Family Systems' exercise which is often used to train new counsellors. When the course starts the trainees are strangers. They are asked to walk round the room and, with no talking, pair off. Afterwards they compare backgrounds and the surprise is always how well their families match. Perhaps both had trouble showing emotions and becoming angry, or there was a divorce. Whatever the link, it seems we all have an internal play waiting to be cast. We search for other people to act out the issues we were unable to resolve as children. Our partners have to speak the same language, and want to play the same scenes, or there is simply no connection.

Belinda and Thierry have been married for ten years but when they first met they were surprised, despite coming from totally different cultures, at how similar their families had been. 'Dad left Mum when I was eight – and he wasn't a particularly good dad. Thierry lived with his mother and grandmother. So we had both come from fatherless households,' says Belinda. One of their mutual tasks was learning how to be a couple. Thierry explains: 'It was really confusing. We knew about mums – they were fantastic – but had no idea how to be a wife or a husband. What are these creatures supposed to be like? What do they do?' It would have been tougher for Belinda if she'd been drawn to a man brought up in a very traditional family, whose family script would probably say that men are in charge, making him less willing to negotiate than Thierry. Conversely, Thierry would have been baffled by the expectations of a woman brought up in a patriarchal family and the demands she might make of him. Finding someone with whom to work through unconscious past issues can be very healing, but it will also cause tension. This is why ILYB can be positive: one partner is no longer prepared to hide behind being nice and is ready to dive into the complexity of their past to discover a more fulfilling relationship.

Summary

- Unhappiness is like a cancer: it slowly spreads through a life infecting every corner – relationship, work, spirituality and friendships. However, the place where the pain was first felt might not necessarily be the source of the original infection.
- Although few couples seek counselling because of bereavement, when I ask clients to identify when they first had relationship problems one of the most common triggers is the death of a friend or family member.
- With spiritual issues – which our society is particularly uncomfortable in addressing – the pain is likely to be expressed elsewhere, such as in our relationships. If this is the case, splitting up is not cutting out the cancer but merely exorcising the secondary infections. The original unhappiness is left unchecked to ravage further.
- People expect a lot from relationships and that 'love can conquer all'. While love has incredible healing potential, a couple needs to invest energy and determination in their relationship too.
- The main message of this chapter for someone with ILYB is to look at the bigger picture and not to put all the blame on the relationship. If your partner has ILYB, the message is to try not to feel completely demoralised or give up hope too soon.
- Both partners should look afresh at the relationship, to take responsibility for their share of the problems and no more.

Exercises

Self-diagnosis: What Else Could Be Lurking Behind Your ILYB?

The following questionnaire is designed to help someone with ILYB take stock. Some of the twenty-five questions will seem a little strange, but humour me and keep going. Don't over-analyse, just write down your immediate answers. There's no need for an essay, just a few notes and key words, although you may wish to write at length, especially if your thoughts seem trapped going round and round in your head. The choice is up to you. In the answers section you will find an explanation of each question, how to interpret your answers and how to build the bigger picture.

1   How long have you been feeling unhappy?
2   Can you put a precise date on it?
3   How old were you at this time?
4   Think back to when you were eighteen. How would you have envisaged yourself at this age? What would you have expected to have done or achieved?
5   What ages were your children when you first started feeling unhappy?
6   What was happening in your life in general when you first became unhappy? Try to make this answer as detailed as possible.
7   What was happening in your partner's life?
8   What was happening in your best friend's life?
9   What was happening in your children's lives?
10 What was happening at work?
11 When you have had problems at work, how have you dealt with them?
12 What would you consider to be your main problem at work today?
13 What was happening in your parents' lives when you first became unhappy?

14 Look at your parents' lives. How do they cope with adversity? Have they had any mental health issues, like depression, anxiety or excessive worrying?

15 Focus on your unhappiness today. If you had to choose just one thing, what is troubling you most?

16 Have you ever felt like this before?

17 What impact is this problem having on your relationship?

18 When you have had difficulties with your partner in the past, how have you dealt with them?

19 Have you had similar problems with anybody else? How have you dealt with them?

20 What are the three main strengths in your relationship?

21 What would you change about your partner if you could? Try to be as specific as possible.

22 How would you describe your sexual relationship?

23 What would you like to happen right now?

24 How would you like your life to be in the future? Make the answer as detailed as possible. Where would you be living? What would you be doing? What would the house look like? Who else is there?

25 How might you be able to make this happen?

Interpreting your answers:

1 This question is checking whether there is a general background of unhappiness.

2 It helps if you can pin down the start of the current problems. Obviously it doesn't have to be to the day, but within three to six months is very helpful when making connections. For example, reaching the same age as a parent who died can trigger a depressive episode or general unhappiness.

3 Think about your life stage and the issues that people face at this age.

4 We often forget the preconceptions we carry about with us. This

question is designed to help you look at yourself through your younger eyes and reassess.

5 Remember what was happening in your own life at the ages your children were when you first became unhappy. It is amazing how often the events in our sons' or daughters' lives bring back issues from our own childhood. The most classic case would be that your own parent left when you were this age. We think we have dealt with everything but back it comes, to haunt us again.

6 The more detailed the picture the easier it is to find trigger points. So try to add a little more information; maybe find some photographs from that time which will jog your memory.

7 A relationship is such an intimate affair that events in one partner's life will necessarily influence the other.

8 What friends are doing can create a mood that affects our lives too. Often if one couple in a social circle divorce it will have a knock-on effect.

9 We identify so much with our children that their set-backs will always find echoes in our own lives. For example, playground bullying may make us acutely aware of being bullied in the office or remind us of our own childhood unhappiness.

10 We spend so much time at work, or thinking about it, that we often base our identity on it. What light can it shed on your issues?

11 This works in conjunction with question eighteen. Contrast the differences between problem-solving at work and at home. Do they reinforce or fight against each other?

12 Are the problems at work different or similar to the problems at home? If the two sets are diametrically opposite it is tempting to dismiss any connections, but more often they are flip sides of the same issue.

13 We need to look not only at overspill from your parents' lives, but at any echoes from how they made you feel as a child. For example, do they still seem controlling, distant or infuriating?

14 This question aims to pick up any inherited mental health questions. The older we become the more like our parents we become.

15 What field of your life does this come from?

16 What are the patterns?

17 Is your relationship mirroring the problem or is it the source of your problem?

18 This works in conjunction with question eleven. Men often approach work and home problems very differently. If there is a difference, how do you feel about it? Which more accurately reflects the real you?

19 Is there something about your partner that makes you act differently from how you would in other arenas of your life? Is this a good or a bad thing?

20 Sometimes we lose sight of the good things and it is worth remembering them.

21 If you have a general answer – for example, I wish they would be more patient – make it more specific by adding an example: I wish they would be more patient when I'm late. This will give you a concrete goal for change.

22 If someone had a magic pill that would solve any sexual problems between you and your partner, how would you feel? What does this tell you about your relationship?

23 Another question about setting goals.

24 As well as the details of the imagined life, I am always interested in when someone imagines it happening: in one year, five years or ten years' time? Often the deeper someone is in crisis, the harder it is to put a date on the imagined future. If you have very little for this question, try again. Don't censor yourself. This is just a fantasy and in a fantasy you can do anything.

25 Once you have a clear picture of where you are going, the secret to achieving change is to map out a clear path from today to the imagined future. Often the first step is the hardest, so make it something small and easily achievable. What comes after that?

It will probably take several days to let these questions settle. Give yourself some space and then return to your notes. Divide a fresh piece of paper into three columns marked 'personal', 'relationship' and 'neither'. Go through your answers and place each issue in the appropriate column. Is there anything else you wish to add? Usually the answer lies in the column with the most entries, but sometimes just one entry can overwhelm all the others.

Is it the Past or is it Today?

Although the first exercise is designed for someone with ILYB, this exercise is for partners also, as sometimes the partner still 'in love' has issues lurking from their past too.

Spend an evening with old photographs albums and home movies.

1 Look at the pictures of your parents and imagine your partner has never heard any stories about them. What sort of man was your father? What three words would best describe your mother?

2 Concentrate on the way your parents made you feel and then start to make connections between yesterday and today.

3 Look at photographs of you and your partner when you were the age your children are today. What was going on?

4 Get out a recent picture of your children. Are there any reflections from what is happening in your children's lives today on to your own past?

5 Finally, assess whether any of these photos or stories connect with or throw a fresh light on your present problems. Is there anything that you did together in the past that could be revived to help your relationship today?

Step Six

GIVING

'I really appreciated what you did for me yesterday.'
'No problem.'
'It got me thinking and I'd like to do something in return.'
'There were no strings attached.'
'It will be my pleasure.'

Sometimes the smallest gestures, particularly when done with an open and generous heart, can make a big difference. This is especially true when you are up against overwhelming problems – like your partner falling out of love. If, however, it is you who has lost the love, the five preceding steps will have made you take stock and find enough goodwill for your partner to feel GIVING.

Chapter Nine

The Theory of Tipping Points

When a relationship is in crisis most couples think they need to make a big effort to get big results. Often they vow to try harder and be different: more thoughtful, more open, more helpful round the house – add your own shortcomings to the list. For the first few days both partners display model behaviour, but of course it cannot last. The result is more bitterness and even depression.

A fresh perspective on how to effect change in a seemingly imposs- ible situation can be found in a recent business book, *The Tipping Point* (Little, Brown, 2000), in which Malcolm Gladwell writes, 'We have an instinctive disdain for simple solutions. There is something in all of us that feels true answers have to be comprehensive and that there is virtue in dogged and indiscriminate application of effort.' He goes on to praise the 'Band-Aid Solution' (tightly focused and targeted interventions): 'Critics use it as a term of disparagement. But in their history Band-Aids have probably allowed millions to keep on working or playing when they would otherwise have had to stop.'

So when relationships are not satisfactory the answer is not to try harder but to think smarter. To this end it is important to under- stand the laws of change. Gladwell examines how ideas catch on and describes the moment when something crosses over from specialist to mainstream as the 'Tipping Point'. For example, in the second half of 1996 an email address went from being a nerd accessory to something that nearly everybody possessed. As with a line of dominoes, a small push will ultimately have a big impact. Gladwell claims that 'one imaginative person applying a well-placed lever can change the world'. I thought the 'Tipping Point' theory might also help explain how relationships can slip almost overnight from 'OK' to 'unhappy'.

In my first interviews with clients I have always asked them when their difficulties started, mainly to find they centre around the classic life changes that put relationships at risk: having a child, bereavement, moving house, redundancy, new job, etc. Although these important events make us take stock they were seldom given as the real cause of a couple's problems. The 'Negative Tipping Point' – where the relationship went from satisfactory to unhappy – seemed to come sometime later, although few couples could pinpoint exactly when this happened. Yet if I asked for reasons why previous marriages or live-in relationships had failed, the majority offered these definite life changes as answers. Could it be that we retrospectively attach big issues to a relationship breakdown because it makes sense of the big changes in our lives? After all, who would admit to seeking a divorce because of damp towels left on the bed or failing to take out the rubbish?

The 'Tipping Point' theory, however, would suggest that a build-up of what my clients call 'stupid things' is the real cause of marital breakdown. Remember, the key idea is that little things can make a big difference. In his book Malcolm Gladwell gives the example of cleaning graffiti from subway trains in New York. More people travelled on the network, and with more passengers around there were fewer muggings and crime went down dramatically. A virtuous circle had been set up. My clients, on the other hand, seemed to be trapped in a downward spiral where 'forgetting to empty the dishwasher' could seed a divorce. So instead of concentrating on major issues I decided to focus on the little things.

Julia and Graham were in their thirties and their most common argument was about cleaning their young children's shoes. She nagged and he could not understand the fuss. Under this seemingly trivial dispute we found two further layers. Firstly, Julia's father had always cleaned her shoes and therefore she believed that good fathers did the same. However, Graham had been brought up to be self-reliant and clean his own shoes. Secondly, the shoes represented their attitudes to bringing up their children. She wanted to nurture them while he wanted to make them self-sufficient. Once we had this insight the shoes ceased to be an issue and the relationship dramatically improved. Instead of being defensive Julia and Graham began explaining, and this knowledge meant better communication which in turn further increased their understanding. We had begun to build a virtuous circle.

Gladwell identified the two key elements for reaching a positive 'Tipping Point': the law of the few and the stickiness factor. The first undermines an old myth about relationships, that both halves of the couple have to want to change. As with my eighty/twenty rule about arguments, economists talk about an eighty/twenty principle in the market, workplace and wider society. They believe that in any situation roughly 80 per cent of the 'work' will be done by 20 per cent of the participants. Thus 80 per cent of crime is committed by 20 per cent of criminals and 80 per cent of road accidents are caused by 20 per cent of motorists.

In other words, a few people have a disproportionate effect on what happens. The same principle applies in relationships. We like to think of them as equal partnerships but often one half works harder at maintaining the relationship than the other. Many couples arrive in counselling because the partner who used to be responsible for providing 80 per cent of the relationship glue has given up. Paula, a thirty-seven-year-old recruitment consultant, was typical: 'Why should I make all the effort? I kept all the conversation going at mealtimes; I even kept in contact with his mum. But Jake made no effort to fulfil my needs. I felt alone in the relationship so I just withdrew.' They were stuck, angry and waiting for the other to make the first move. I sympathised with both of them, for in their different ways they each felt under-appreciated. After several weeks I threw my hands up and asked, 'Do you want to be right or happy?'

Next week they returned with smiles: Paula had been less critical of Jake and he, in turn, had been more willing to help round the house. They had achieved a positive 'Tipping Point', but it had required Paula (the law of the few) to take the initiative. Paula was so pleased that it ceased to matter that she had made 80 per cent of the initial effort, because both were now contributing more or less equally.

So why are some messages heard while others fall on deaf ears? The second law, the stickiness factor, is the answer. Malcolm Gladwell talks about a health trial to make students have tetanus inoculations. Yale University tried various educational booklets – some were just informative while others had gory pictures – but the take-up rate remained stubbornly low. However, one small change made 28 per cent of students have the jab: including a map showing the health centre and the times when shots were available. Tinkering with a message can often make it stick. If someone is not listening to us we find more and more dramatic ways to get their attention – shouting, tantrums, threats, walking out – when a small change can often be far more effective.

In the case of Paula and Jake, Paula learnt that by using humour she could ask for something without coming across as critical. Since discovering *The Tipping Point* I have spent more time getting clients to find different ways to communicate rather than repeating the same message or behaviour louder and louder.

When I look back with clients at the end of counselling they are often astounded by how much has been changed by so little. Robin and Tamara, two teachers in their forties, are typical. 'Instead of stomping off I learnt to stand up for myself verbally,' says Robin. Tamara learnt almost the opposite: 'I thought I listened, but if he said something I didn't want to hear I interrupted and effectively shut him up.' These small but effective changes allowed them to deal more successfully with their major life issues – in this case Tamara's mother's increasingly poor health – without even needing to discuss them in their weekly counselling session. They had dramatically improved their communication skills by one small, key intervention.

Tipping the relationship back into the positive is easier than couples first think, but on every occasion either one partner or both must decide to be generous and giving, thereby kick-starting the healing process.

What Stops Couples from Finding Their Positive 'Tipping Point'?

Our attitudes to relationships are underpinned by a set of assumptions so fundamental that we take them completely for granted and rarely check if they are really true. Here are four that could be stopping you tipping from negative into positive.

Nothing I say or do has any impact

When I see a client on their own, because their partner has declined an invitation to join in, they often despair about being able to influence their other half. They feel completely powerless. Melanie, twenty-nine, was convinced of her partner's ability to spoil her day: 'He'll criticise my driving – "You could have got a tank through that space" – or he's not phoned when he's going to be late and I'm left in the dark. It's no accident; he knows how to get me riled.' With a little encouragement Melanie admitted she knew which of his buttons to press too. 'With each meal Michael puts a small heap of salt on the side of his plate and then keeps dipping his food in it,' she explained. 'If I say anything about how damaging this is to his health he gets really irritated – which I doubt is good for his blood pressure either.' If she was aware of the negative buttons to push, surely it followed that she knew the positive buttons to get his co-operation too? 'He loves to be complimented,' she admitted, agreeing to try this strategy. It took a while for Michael to respond – perhaps he was angry or suspected an ulterior motive – but instead of giving up I encouraged Melanie to keep praising him. The results were impressive and soon her and Michael's relationship began to improve.

Although both parties have to be on board to improve a relationship it only takes one person to start the journey. Pushing positive rather than negative buttons will ultimately create enough goodwill to recruit the second partner into joining the mission. Indeed Michael started phoning Melanie, not just to tell her if he was going to be late home but for a general chat.

Turnaround Tip: To get into the mood for pushing positive buttons think back to your courting days and what your partner enjoyed. Is there something you could repeat today?

Me, me, me

This block makes people concentrate on how something impacts on them but they then forget to make a leap of imagination and consider the effect on their partner. For example, Melanie found it hard to accept compliments from Michael. When he said her new hairstyle suited her she would shrug it off with a joke: 'At least it looks slimming.' Eventually Michael stopped giving compliments and Melanie started complaining that he never paid her any attention. So why did Melanie find compliments hard to accept? 'I feel all self-conscious, like I'm the big "I am . . ."' But did she imagine how Michael felt? Finally she stopped thinking and said quietly, 'When I make a joke of it he probably feels belittled.'

Turnaround Tip: Next time something upsets you acknowledge the impact – preferably out loud – and then ask your partner how the problem makes her or him feel.

Keep on going to the end of the road

This block is caused by having one fixed idea about what will save a relationship and pushing continuously in that direction, no matter what. When Gavin and Mary started counselling I saw each of them on their own for one session. Unable to cope with conflict, they had simply stopped talking to each other – fearing conversation would only cause more rows – but they ended up with even more misunderstandings. The situation was dire and Gavin despaired for the future: 'I've done everything to build a bridge: I saved up money to buy something special for Mary's fiftieth birthday and I threw a party with all her work colleagues invited, friends and family, but she barely acknowledged me. When I had an inheritance and put all the money into our joint account – to pay off the overdraft – she thanked me, but it didn't make any difference. I don't know what else to do.' When they started joint counselling Gavin was determined that they should sort out their finances so he brought all the bills and statements along to the session. Although they were back in the red again Mary sidestepped the money issue and the session went round in circles. Gavin did not want to provoke an argument so he said nothing and instead kept throwing me dark looks. 'You see, I've tried everything,' he seemed to be saying. For many couples this is the point at which one or both parties give up and believe divorce is the only answer. Except Gavin had not tried everything: he had just kept on going to the end of the road.

Malcolm Gladwell's *The Tipping Point* is full of stories about individuals who made a big change to their community or turned a small business into a multi-million dollar company, starting what he calls a 'social epidemic'. He writes, 'The world – much as we want it to – does not accord to our intuition. Those who are successful at creating social epidemics do not just do what they think is right.' He goes on to describe how these successful innovators try other avenues – even ones that everybody else would consider counter-intuitive, or even stupid. Gavin's intuition had told him that money was the root of their problems. Indeed they were seriously in debt and he had tried everything to solve their financial problems. But he had not tried everything to save his marriage. Within a couple of sessions it became clear that Mary wanted Gavin to talk to her, not about money but using the normal exchange of views and news that make up the day-to-day chat of a happy relationship. Once Gavin started conversing – rather than keeping on to the end of the 'money' road – their relationship tipped into the positive.

Turnaround Tip: If you feel you've tried everything, write a list of this 'everything'. Next go through the list and cross off all the items that have sent you down the same old road. Finally, think counter-intuitively. What haven't you tried yet?

Old dogs can't learn new tricks

This block assumes not only that our partner cannot change but that it is morally wrong to ask. However, Gladwell writes, 'What must underlie successful epidemics, in the end, is a bedrock belief that change is possible, that people can radically transform their behaviour or beliefs in the face of the right kind of impetus.' He goes on to add, 'We like to think of ourselves as autonomous and inner-directed, that who we are and how we act is something permanently set by our genes and our temperament. We are actually powerfully influenced by our surroundings, our immediate context, and the personalities of those around us.'

Week after week in counselling I meet people who are worried that their partner will not change and others who complain, 'She wants me to be something I'm not,' or, 'He knew I was like that when he married me.' Yet week after week I see that minor accommodations – rather than fundamental shifts in character – will satisfy the other half's needs and lead to a more fulfilling relationship.

Returning to the couple with the money issues, Mary's fear was that Gavin wanted to change the core of her personality. She believed, 'I work hard and I deserve to treat myself.' (Indeed Mary's job did involve a long commute and work she found rather tedious.) Mary was convinced that Gavin wanted to turn her from a spender into a saver. In reality Gavin was worried about how much money went on eating out. 'Restaurants are a waste of money,' he complained. Mary fought back: 'I deserve to be pampered and looked after.'

Ultimately a compromise was found: Gavin would buy the best cuts of meat and all the trimmings for a wonderful meal but would cook it himself. 'I even put on my best suit and pretended to be the maître d',' he joked. 'You should have seen the look on Mary's face when I showed her to our dining-room table which I had laid with our best tablecloth, cutlery and flowers from the garden.' Mary felt indulged and Gavin was pleased about the money saved. Had they changed? Yes. They stopped going to fancy restaurants (except for birthdays and other special occasions). Were they happier? Most certainly. Had they fundamentally changed each other's personalities? No. Except this no longer mattered because they had made minor adjustments that had reaped large rewards.

Turnaround Tip: Write down everything that you would like to change about your partner. Next go back and take the items concerning temperament or personality – which are hard to change – and turn them into specific patterns of behaviour, as these are easier to change. For example, instead of 'be more thoughtful' put 'take me out on Valentine's Day'.

Find Your Own 'Tipping Point'

Often a major change can come from a small internal shift in one or other partner. Here are four small suggestions that will help achieve the sixth step to putting the passion back into your relationship: **giving**.

- Be aware of your own internal, self-imposed obstacles. Each partner often waits for the other to commit to improving the relationship. Often they have little tests in their mind – 'If he loves me he should take more notice of me,' or, 'If she loves me she should show more affection' – except neither partner tells the other so the tests remain secret. Instead be generous, throw away the tests and make the commitment to change.

- When you wake up think: 'What is the one thing that I could do today, no matter how small, that could improve my relationship?'
- Next time you and your partner fall out try agreeing with them – not for a quiet life, but with love and respect. By this I mean really trying to understand why they hold what seems like a very contrary position. Give him or her the benefit of the doubt, after all this is someone you respect and if they hold a position dearly it must have some validity.
- ILYB is caused because couples choose a quiet life/the easy option. Therefore adopt a new personal motto: 'I'll never make it easy for myself again.' Whenever you are faced with two choices always go for the most challenging. The more you put into your relationship the more you will get out of it.

If you are looking for some bolder 'Tipping Point' ideas or your relationship is in crisis and needs something more intensive, look in the exercise section below. In fact I would go further: these are two of the most useful exercises in the whole book, so read them anyway!

What if We Have Separated? Is it Too Late to Try Tipping Points?

After a break-up the temptation is either to withdraw into neutral mode or to become angry and push negative buttons. However, with ILYB most people are ambivalent about ending their relationship and therefore secretly looking for reasons to stay rather than leave. Obviously it will take much positive button-pushing to turn the relationship round, but stick with it and monitor yourself for negative button-pushes. For every negative slip, I would recommend at least three positives to counteract the effect.

Summary

- Small changes can start a positive cycle and ultimately have a big impact on the relationship. Instead of trying harder, try thinking smarter.
- When deeply held assumptions are not challenged a relationship risks not only continuing down the same old road but also remaining oblivious to any alternative.
- It is never too late to change.
- Never underestimate the impact of a single generous – and open-hearted – gesture.

Exercises

Positive Reinforcement

Tipping Points are about finding new ways of looking at things. With a fresh perspective small changes can lever large ones. Here is a personal example from dog training, which might sound strange but stay with me:

Puppies are extremely exhausting. They have to be watched constantly or they start chewing the legs of the dining-room table that belonged to your great-great-grandmother. Although a puppy wants to please it does not understand English and has no idea what is good or bad behaviour. I spent so much time telling my puppy 'no' that he probably thought it was part of his name. When I took Flash off to puppy socialisation/dog-training the instructor asked us: 'What do you do when your puppy is lying down quietly?' I stuck my hand up: 'Breathe a sigh of relief.' Another class member added: 'Get on with the housework.' Neither of these was the correct answer. 'It's what most people say,' explained the instructor, 'but that's the last thing you should do. How does a puppy know what is good behaviour if you completely ignore him when he does it? What happens when he's been naughty?' We all smiled because we didn't have to answer the question: the puppy got our full attention. 'You're all reinforcing the bad behaviour with negative attention and not rewarding the good,' the instructor explained.

From then onwards, if Flash was napping in the sun I would tickle his tummy and praise him. When he got overexcited and started rushing round the house I ignored him. At first I had to think consciously about rewarding good behaviour. But after a few days Flash began to calm down and I soon realised the extra effort was more than worth it – I was actually saving time by not chasing him round the house.

Here are some tips for using positive reinforcement to 'train' your partner:

1 Think back over the past twenty-four hours. How many times did you criticise your partner's behaviour or nasty habits? How often did you praise them? Which came out on top, positives or negatives?

2 Stop giving negative attention. Instead of complaining when, for example, he watches too much football or she has too many nights out with the girls, wait for the behaviour that you wish to encourage. If your goal is more time together, reinforce this positive on your next joint outing by telling him or her, 'I'm really enjoying sharing this with you.'

3 Positive reinforcement is built around gratitude and compliments. Don't overlook this as nobody can have too many of either.

4 Don't take anything for granted. Jeff had moved into Martina's house but was having trouble feeling at home. Eventually Martina agreed to remodel the place completely so Jeff had a stake too. When all the work was finished Jeff told her, 'I know it has been hard for you, especially as it meant borrowing a lot of money and you don't feel comfortable doing that. So I just wanted to

let you know that I really appreciate it.' Of course Martina knew all that, but having it acknowledged and said out loud was really important. Think of something you appreciate about your partner but which normally fits into the category of 'goes without saying'; this time give the thanks out loud. Make the compliment as detailed as possible. Which sounds more heartfelt: 'Thank you for all you do,' or, 'Thanks for taking my car in to be serviced today, it really made things easier for me'?

Flop/Flip Technique

When under stress we have a limited number of ways of responding. For example, we might shout, fly off the handle or go silent. If this does not work we up the ante, screaming, not speaking for days or even trashing the house. Soon we are trapped in the same loop, our behaviour becoming more and more extreme. Does this sound familiar? Here is a simple trick to break out:

1 Next time you're about to launch into your usual response, stop and think: What could I do differently?
2 It doesn't matter what. Honest. Anything is better than the usual response; we know where that leads and that it does not work.
3 Try the alternative response and watch your partner's reaction. It will probably make them think too and may also prevent him or her from slipping into a standard response.
4 Think of the opposite to your normal behaviour and try that as an alternative. Instead of going quiet, start talking. Instead of throwing ornaments, straighten them. It is amazing how often an opposite behaviour is the key to better communication.
5 Remember: stop using the flop response and instead flip it over!

Step Seven

LEARNING

'Things seem to be going much better.'
'I agree.'
'Sometimes I worry that it's too good to last.'
'That's in the past.'
'What if we slip back into our old ways?'

Successful organisations have learnt that staying where they are is not good enough; they have to improve continually. It is the same for relationships and the best way to avoid stagnation is to make a commitment to keep on LEARNING.

Chapter Ten

The Six Special Skills of Successful Couples

Towards the end of their counselling many couples reach a moment of bliss where all their hard work begins to pay off. **Loving attachment** blossoms and a glimpse of reawakened **limerence** helps them believe that, once again, the two of them can climb mountains and defeat all comers. This magic is fleeting, however. Before too long they remember how easy it is to fall from the heights of **limerence**, the pressures of everyday life, the demands of our twenty-four-hour work culture and the paucity of support for couples. The bliss turns to fear. So how can we protect our relationships?

It is not only relationships that are under pressure: a run of bad judgements can put the future of well-respected high-street stores at risk and public institutions can easily find themselves accused of being 'out of touch'. Providing the same level of service is no longer enough: competitors get an edge; customers expect more and more. This is why many businesses champion an idea – first developed by companies like Toyota – called the 'Continuous Improvement Culture'. Many schools have also adopted it. This idea suggests that unless something is getting better it is actually in decline. Therefore management and headteachers are not satisfied with being good – and certainly not good enough – but instead strive to be better. Although our relationships should be protected from these market forces we can adapt some of the better ideas.

Learning provides the edge that keeps a relationship fresh, ensures nothing is taken for granted and provides avenues for making **loving attachment** deeper. But how do we learn what makes relationships happy and fulfilled? This is hard for ILYB couples, especially as many of them report that their friends regard them as the partnership least likely to have problems. In addition, the professionals offer only scattered clues as most psychologists have concentrated on studying failing relationships. I therefore decided to search scientific journals and my own casebook to discover what makes for a happy relationship. I found that successful couples tend, often unwittingly, to have cultivated six good habits, which can provide goals to help all relationships improve continuously. I have started with the easiest habit to adopt, but they work together. Like *The Seven Steps* . . . , incorporating one habit into your relationship will make the next easier.

Six Good Habits for a Happy Relationship

Investing: setting aside time together

When things go badly a couple will spend more time apart, which breeds yet more misunderstanding. Once work, commuting time, sleep and watching TV have been deducted from a normal week the average British couple spend little time in each other's company. According to the Office of National Statistics approximately three and a half hours per week (or just twenty-four minutes a day) is all that is left for shared social life, sport, hobbies and interests. Even a small amount of extra time together can pay dividends: Professor John Gottman of the University of Washington – who studied several hundred married couples interacting and kept in touch with them for several years afterwards – proposes an investment of five hours a week to make a profound difference.

Nick and Anna tried **investing** as part of a wider attempt to make their relationship work. Their social life revolved around their circle of friends, so they reserved one evening a week for each other and, despite friends' tempting offers, this appointment came first. When their night coincided with a Shakespeare production in the local park, for which their closest friends had already booked them tickets, they came up with a second way of **investing**. During that particular week they set aside fifteen minutes each evening to chat over the events of the day. Through this kind of small talk Nick and Anna were able to keep up to date with each other and important issues emerged naturally. 'This was much better than Nick announcing, "We need to talk",' said Anna. 'That would send me into a panic and make me all defensive.' By prioritising their time together successful couples demonstrate on a daily basis that they treasure their relationship above everything else.

Laughing together: using shared jokes and running gags

For many successful couples laughter is a tool to knock the edges off a hard day. 'Laughter really does help,' says Elizabeth, a fifty-four-year-old laboratory technician who has been married to Derek, a marketing executive, for twenty-one years. 'We laugh at ourselves, our families, the bizarre habits of neighbours and old movies on the TV. Sometimes it's the only thing that gets us through.' 'We have certain sayings,' explains Derek, 'that would probably mean nothing to anybody else, but I'll tease her that she'll never play for Leicester Ladies' Lacrosse again and she'll tell me that the knackers yard would be too good for me.' Germany's Max Planck Institute of Human Development has noted that happily married couples are good at stepping out of an argument for a moment so that they can make little repairs for their wrongdoings. A common way of diffusing the moment is to make a joke – this is particularly effective when someone pokes fun at themselves.

Marrying actions to our words

Social psychologists argue that only 10 per cent of communication is verbal, but somehow we expect our partners to trust our words rather than our behaviour. In the rush of day-to-day living it is easy to buy off a partner with 'of course I love you' rather than take the time to show it or act thoughtfully. This is why many couples arrive at counselling with one partner complaining about being taken for granted. Their partner is often mystified. 'But you know I don't,' is the most common defence. Frequently the complaining partner snaps back: 'How?' The conversation grinds to a halt. By comparison, successful couples demonstrate love and appreciation and perform small acts of caring – the cement that holds a relationship together – rather than just paying lip-service.

Many of my clients balk at this idea of consciously deciding to demonstrate their love, complaining that it would feel artificial. Some feel that saying 'thank you' all the time is stupid. Others go further: 'Why should I thank my husband for doing the washing-up? It's not as if they're just my dishes.' These clients worry that being too free with compliments will devalue them. With small acts of caring – for example, he irons a blouse for her or she collects him from the station – they fear that taking over a task, even on just one occasion, is tantamount to having responsibility for ever. But does it have to be like this? Successful couples show that really powerful praise, thank yous or small acts of caring come from out of the blue. The occasional 'have I ever told you that you've got beautiful eyes?' or 'I really appreciated the way that you rallied round while my mother was ill' will be remembered for a long time. The power of small acts of caring lies in the fact that they are one-offs. In cases of ILYB it is more effective to *show* your partner your deep affection than just to *tell* them about it.

The art of compromise

Instead of having winners and losers, or unbalanced power, successful couples find a middle way. An example would be sharing out household duties according to who has more time. When chores are rigidly divided there are often niggling resentments. Compromise is very different from compliance (just giving in) in that partners will put their viewpoint strongly and maybe even fight for it. Rather than digging in and never giving ground, though, successful couples will look for a meeting point. This is corroborated by the findings of Professor Gottman. The best predictor for which of the couples studied in his laboratory would stay married was how well they argued and resolved their differences. This turned out to be more important than the type of issue faced and even its severity.

David and Simone, two teachers who had been together five years, learnt to compromise, but only when they were heading for a break-up. Although the couple had few fights, both partners had entrenched positions. David was keen on hang-gliding but Simone felt that it took him away too often and did not leave enough time for them as a couple. Generally David went once a month and Simone policed this tradition – in case hang-gliding ate into more weekends. When David's hang-gliding club proposed a long weekend away Simone put her foot down and they had a series of nasty fights. 'David doesn't get much holiday and we like to use what there is for a decent break,' Simone explained. But eventually she decided to be generous: 'I decided to stop going on at him about hang-gliding because it was casting such a big shadow over our lives. He knew how I felt and it was pointless going on about it.' Ultimately Simone had a nice surprise: 'David didn't really go hang-gliding that much more, just the occasional special opportunity, and it stopped being an issue.' David added, 'With the atmosphere much better at home I've been getting away from the office earlier and spending more time with Simone. It's funny but I found that I had been defending "me" time and really there was no need.' Both Simone and David discovered they had been fighting over an arbitrary line in the sand. Their new compromise worked better, each of them felt more relaxed and their relationship flourished.

Taking risks

When we first fall in love **limerence** provides a magic cloak of omnipotence that blinds us to the risks of starting a new relationship. However, once **limerence** wears off each partner will start defending themselves and putting up barriers. Successful couples continue to take both small risks (like upsetting their partner) and bigger ones (like one partner retraining and meeting a lot of new people) while, by contrast, ILYB couples prefer to play safe. If they decide to take a risk it is nearly always a sign that the relationship is on the mend. Rita fell out of love with Joe after nineteen years and three children together. Since his wife had confessed her true feelings Joe was even less likely to rock the boat. 'My policy is to stress the positive,' he told me at our first counselling session. However, as we worked through the seven steps he became bolder. 'We were out shopping and she took my hand, after months with no physical contact, and I wanted to know why,' Joe explained. 'Normally I would have kept my mouth shut, in case I heard something I didn't want to hear or maybe she would take her hand away.' This time Joe took a risk and told Rita how much he enjoyed the contact. 'I told him it just felt right to hold his hand,' said Rita, 'and later we had a long conversation over coffee. I hadn't meant the hand-holding as some grand gesture but the more we talked, the more important this impulse seemed.'

Another example of taking risks is Amy, a twenty-six-year-old singing teacher, who was offered a contract to work in France. Her initial response was to turn it down. 'It involved four months in Paris and, although I liked the picture of me sitting at a pavement café in Saint-Germain-des-Prés,' she explained, 'it would mean being apart from Allan.' The idea of being stuck at home while his partner had an adventure did not appeal much to Allan either. 'If I was honest,' he admitted, 'I could picture her being swept off her feet by a sophisticated Parisian.' However, Allan decided it was best to give Amy his blessing and she took the job. The Eurostar train link allowed them to spend 50 per cent of their weekends together, and Allan took some holiday in Paris and learnt French too. 'I could really get into the way of life over there,' he said, 'buying fresh croissants and *pains au chocolat* for breakfast. The quality of the ingredients for cooking was an eye-opener.' Ultimately Paris became an adventure to share together and Amy's contract an opportunity to grow together rather than a threat. Both falling in love and maintaining love involve taking a risk, without which there is little learning or growth.

Giving each other some independence

Successful couples allow each other freedom to grow, even if this means doing things without each other. At the other end of the scale are couples who lean on each other to the extent that one, or both, fear they would collapse without an all-encompassing togetherness. Most couples sit somewhere in between these two positions, but during challenging times most of us are likely to become more controlling or clingy.

The importance of some degree of independence has been underlined in the study of lesbian couples. Women have a reputation for being keen on intimacy and being good at it. In theory, therefore, lesbian relationships should be extremely stable. In 1983 American sociologists Philip Blumstein and Pepper Schwartz interviewed 4,314 heterosexual couples (either married and cohabiting), 1,875 gay couples and 1,723 lesbian couples. They returned eighteen months later and found the couples least likely to break up were the married heterosexuals (14 per cent had split), followed by cohabiting heterosexuals (29 per cent) and then gay couples (36 per cent). Most likely to break up were the lesbian couples, at a startling 48 per cent.

So what makes an all-female couple the least likely to stay together? This was the task that Susan Johnson of the University of Wisconsin set herself in her book, *Long-Term Lesbian Couples* (Naiad Press, 1990). She gave questionnaires to 108 lesbian couples, across twenty-one US states, who had been together for ten years or more, then she followed up many responses with interviews. At the beginning she thought the high break-up rate could be caused by the pressures on lesbian couples, and the lack of support, from mainstream society – even though gay couples face the same problems. Her second theory was that lesbian couples were too quick to consider themselves couples, hence the old joke: What does a lesbian bring on a second date?

Answer: A removal van. However, having completed the research she concluded that successful lesbian couples were prepared to allow each other to be different. 'You may think you are living as part of the same relationship but you're not,' Johnson wrote about her own relationship. 'My partner says ours is the easiest relationship she has been in; I say no, for me it is the hardest. For a long time we argued about who was right. It took us several years to realise we're not in the same relationship. She is living with me – one experience – and I am living with her – a very different experience.'

Why should gay men's relationships last longer than those of lesbian women? A possible answer – and one that reinforces the issue of giving each other independence – is the gay attitude to fidelity. McWhirter and Mattison, who tracked the development of gay couples, found that after five years none of the partners were sexually exclusive. 'There are rules about what is acceptable, which include no flirting with other people when we're together and a ban on bringing other men home,' says Scott, who has been with his partner for seven years. 'We also have a pact to tell each other about any outside adventures. Our heterosexual friends find our arrangement extraordinary, but in my opinion it is better and more honest than the sneaky affairs conducted by many straight people I know.' Gay men are, therefore, less likely to expect their partner to fulfil each and every one of their needs.

All couples like the idea of their partner being the same: having the same experiences; interpreting reality in the same way; coming to the same conclusions. Yet this is not only impossible but also probably undesirable. Sameness is fine but equally important is an awareness of differences, so that each partner can create a clear space for themselves as an individual within a relationship. This is why independence – both in the physical sense of being apart from time to time and in the intellectual sense of being allowed to have different thoughts and come to different conclusions – is so important.

The lesbian couples interviewed by Johnson brilliantly sum up one of my most important themes for ILYB and offer hope for all long-term couples. One woman said, 'There is no such thing as a relationship without conflict. You have to have some kind of acceptance of that; it just ain't gonna happen. Another person is not the answer. There ain't nothin' out there that is perfect.' Nearly all the couples in Johnson's book had been through some crisis that could have split them up. May, in an eighteen-year-long relationship, was typical: 'I think sometimes – this sounds silly but I think it's true – people don't hang in long enough to know that you live past it [the crisis]. It does not have to be this big gaping wound; it can heal. People aren't patient enough.'

I started this chapter by explaining that successful long-term couples had unwittingly developed six positive habits. Here is a bonus. May's quote underlines that just by getting to this point in your relationship you have already developed one skill that underpins everything: PATIENCE. This is a vital foundation for *The Seven Steps*: the work ahead is hard but ultimately very rewarding.

Summary

- While unhappy relationships fail for a multitude of reasons, happy ones all succeed for the same ones: these couples have cultivated six special skills.
- *Investing* will encourage a couple to *laugh together*. *Marrying actions and words* will create goodwill for the *art of compromise*, which in turn makes *taking risks* easier and *giving each other some independence* becomes a possibility.
- **Learning** completes *The Seven Steps to Putting the Passion Back into Your Relationship*. A commitment to continual learning will both renew a relationship and keep it on track.

Exercises

Building New Habits

Many couples start out with good intentions but after a couple of weeks everything starts to slide. The advantage of habits over good intentions is that they build in three key factors for lasting change: *simple events*, which *happen regularly* and can be *easily measured*.

Take the first habit as an example: spending more time together. The temptation is to organise a grand gesture, like a cruise or an expensive night out. However, these fail to become habits because, by their very nature, they cannot happen regularly and therefore the benefits quickly fade. By contrast, eating together in the evening can become a habit. It is definitely *simple,* can *happen regularly* – possibly most weekday evenings – and is *easily measured*. At the end of a month a couple can look back and check how often they ate together. If this idea appeals, here are some practical tips to reap the benefits of this habit:

1 Don't have the television on or allow other distractions that stop the two of you talking.
2 If one of you gets in much earlier, have a sandwich or something to keep you going.
3 Alternatively, set up a meal together at the weekend – like a long breakfast on Sunday morning – and treat it as a fixed part of your routine.

• What new habits would you like to introduce to your relationship? How can you break them down into something *small, repeatable* and *measurable*?
• Think round a new habit, like I have done with eating together, and try to spot any stumbling blocks in advance.

Laughing Together

If you and your partner have few opportunities to laugh together

– indeed many couples' shared social activities are very serious, adult activities, like eating out – here are some ideas:

1   Visit a comedy club.
2   See a funny film at the cinema or a farce at the theatre.
3   Try something difficult together, like ice-skating.
4   Do something ridiculous together for charity, like running a three-legged race.
5   Tickle each other.
6   Show each other your baby pictures.
7   Go to the beach and build a sandcastle.
8   Visit a children's petting zoo or a farm.
9   Share something that you haven't done since you were a kid.
10 Paint a picture together.

If your relationship has reached crisis point

Chapter Eleven

Having the 'I Love You But' Conversation/ Hearing the 'I Love You But' Confession

Up to this point I have tried to address both someone who has fallen out of love and their partner at the same time. However, this is where a couple with ILYB issues can end up in two very different camps: one partner needs to talk and get feelings off their chest; the other is in shock. So I have divided the chapter in half, starting with making the confession and then moving on to how best to react.

Having the ILYB Conversation

'At Sunday lunchtime I'll be sitting round the table with my family; my body is there but I wish I were somewhere else,' explains Grant, a forty-five-year-old building society manager. 'My wife is laughing and the kids are talking ten to the dozen. The whole thing should be perfect. I love my kids to bits and Jill and I rub along fine, but I feel so alone. Sometimes she'll catch me thinking; she calls it my 'faraway face': "What's up?" "Nothing darling." How can I tell her that inside I'm dying?'

Many people with ILYB hold back. They instinctively know that there are few things more devastating than learning that someone has fallen out of love with you. Yet having these feelings trapped inside is also extremely painful.

So what can be done? The first instinct of most ILYB sufferers is to hope something will change: 'I'll feel different after the summer holiday/Christmas/moving house . . .' Add your own example to the list. But this kind of bargaining seldom provides more than temporary relief. In some of the cases I have counselled as many as ten years have elapsed between first doubts and the final confession. Normally the gap is between three and five years.

How do you know it is time to talk? A sure sign is the growing tension between negative feelings inside and superficially pleasant behaviour on the outside. Once someone reaches this stage they start snapping and their partner feels as if he or she is walking on eggshells. Grant wished he had come clean before his marriage got bogged down in pettiness: 'I hated myself because I'd pick, pick, pick all the time: how much noise she made in the bathroom in the morning; the way she'd sing in the shower; the way she'd turn her handbag out to look for a mint. A thousand and one things that had never bothered me before all made me seethe. I was like a bear with a sore head and I knew that if I didn't say something soon we wouldn't even be friends any more.' ILYB is difficult enough without loading the situation with unnecessary animosity.

For some people a strong attraction to someone at work or a friendship that is in danger of crossing the line is the catalyst for an ILYB confession. Daniel, a forty-eight-year-old compliance manager, found himself drawn to a female colleague. 'The weekends seemed grey and endless at home,' he explained. 'When my heart started racing on Monday morning, as I chose clothes that I hoped she would like, I knew I had to do something.' Daniel had been suffering with ILYB for three years but had said nothing for fear of hurting his wife. 'I knew that an affair was almost inevitable. If not then, certainly a few years down the line. What would hurt my wife more: telling her how I felt or cheating on her?' Even when 'nothing has happened' it is better to make a full confession and explain how serious the problem has become.

Once you have decided to confess there is no right or wrong way to go about it. Some people prefer to set up a rendezvous. This has the advantage of committing a couple to talking but it could worry the partner who is ignorant of the true nature of the conversation. Another option is to secretly stage-manage the confession: make sure the children are out and that there are no likely distractions, then spring the discussion on the other half. This cuts out the chance of the partner worrying in advance – and conjuring up some life-threatening illness – but risks him or her interrupting, pleading work pressures or asking for a rain check. The third alternative is to wait for an appropriate opening, such as when the other half asks what is wrong. The topic comes up naturally but this option can easily become an excuse for putting off the confession – indefinitely. For this reason I would recommend setting a time limit on waiting for an opening.

A few words of general caution: don't bring up ILYB in anger, after a couple of drinks or during an argument; avoid Christmas, birthdays and anniversaries (otherwise these dates will always bring back memories of the confession); although neutral places – like restaurants – can provide good forums in which to talk, avoid old favourites as this can taint a partner's previously happy memories. Whatever the choice, set aside plenty of time to talk: your partner will want to go over everything again and again. In most cases the confession will be the start of a series of conversations.

The most important element in the ensuing discussions is to be 100 per cent honest. Some people with ILYB try to spare their partner's feelings by releasing the bad news bit by bit. This strategy will not only destroy trust but also magnify the pain. Frank, a fifty-eight-year-old service manager, did not put all his cards on the table straight away. He had met Christina relatively late and, without the distraction of children, they had been able to dedicate plenty of time to their shared interests: classical music concerts, theatre and walking.

Frank knew Christina would be shattered even by the thought of divorce so he led her to hope that their marriage could be saved. She started cutting out helpful articles but he would not read them. Eventually she confronted Frank and he told her the truth. 'I'm not a little girl who'd been promised a pony,' said Christina. 'It was so demeaning and for the first time in our marriage I found I couldn't believe what he told me.'

Other people with ILYB are often economical about what, in their opinion, has gone wrong with the relationship. 'I thought it was kinder not to tell him just how miserable I felt. Why grind his face in it?' explains Sheila, a forty-four-year-old care worker. 'Would it really have helped if he knew that I didn't think he pulled his weight, leaving me to earn most of the money; that I thought he was selfish in bed and how he sometimes bored me?' None of these things are easy to hear, but keeping them back robs a partner of the opportunity to change. As discussed before, avoid damning a partner's character when communicating criticism and concentrate on the particular unwanted behaviour and how it makes you feel. For example, Sheila could say, 'I need more foreplay,' rather than, 'You're a lazy lover.' Even when badly phrased, the truth is always preferable to kindly intended lies.

In other cases the person with ILYB tries to be straightforward but their partner chooses to minimise the confession, either by dismissing it outright or putting the most optimistic spin possible on it. In these circumstances I recommend finding an alternative way of delivering a message – for example, write a letter or send an email. (For more advice on the clearest and the kindest way of communicating difficult feelings see the **three-part statement** in Chapter Five.)

What if there is someone else involved? An affair makes an ILYB confession a hundred times more complicated. Has the affair undermined the primary relationship? Did problems in the primary relationship cause the affair? It is a real chicken-and-egg situation: very difficult to unravel even years afterwards and impossible under stress. However much ILYB is a contributing factor, the 'innocent' partner will be primarily concerned with the betrayal. Therefore it is best to confess to the affair first and leave the ILYB until the initial shock has worn off. When the other partner is ready he or she will want to know what caused the affair and this is the moment to talk about ILYB.

What happens after the initial confession? You will probably feel a short burst of relief: at last your secret is out in the open and the pretence has finally stopped. However, once your partner's shock wears off, be prepared for him or her to turn angry, sad or even to take on all the blame. The next few days will be full of drama and on many occasions your preconceptions about each other will be challenged. This will be tough but ultimately it can be an opportunity to grow together. Sheila expected her partner, Robert, almost to roll over and play dead: 'It was such a shock because all his resentments came tumbling out: how I'd used my bigger salary to dictate what we could and couldn't afford; how demanding I'd become; how I wouldn't listen. He was a lot tougher than I thought and, although what he said made me angry, you know something? I started to admire him again.'

Sometimes the ILYB confession can be a prelude to reconciliation, especially where one partner feels that previous attempts to rescue the relationship have been ignored. Jennifer had been unhappy with Bob, a construction worker, for many years and felt that she was bringing up their two sons alone. 'Every time I tried to talk he just shut off. It was like an invisible barrier dropped down in front of his eyes,' she explained. 'I thought I could carry on for the sake of the boys but one morning I just snapped.' Unlike in most ILYB relationships, Jennifer had to put up with a lot of abusive language and on some occasions Bob would punch the wall. 'I had to explain that I cared deeply for Bob but I didn't love him any more,' she said. 'I think he would have found it easier if I'd told him I hated him.' However, the news galvanised Bob into action. Within a week he had arranged individual counselling. 'I don't like the person I've become either,' he told me. Jennifer didn't know what to do. Could she really trust Bob to change? The first month was the most difficult, but once the truth was out in the open Jennifer and Bob found they could talk honestly and began to negotiate.

Planning a trial separation?

Generally I am not in favour of these, especially in the first few weeks after the confession when there is a lot to discuss. However, some people find it easier to think away from the pressures of family life, and in the words of many of my clients: 'Maybe if I'm away I'll find that I miss him/her.' Certainly the space allows each partner to unravel which issues belong to them personally and which to the relationship.

- Your partner will probably be against the idea, fearing that it is the first step towards permanent separation. Even if you have no clear idea of how long you need to be apart, try to give an estimate. A tightly defined separation – with clear goals – will seem less threatening than something open-ended. One of my clients went away for a long weekend while another chose six months. Most couples settle on somewhere between one and three months.
- What about the children? Obviously a lot depends on their age and for how long the parent is going away. On the one hand, if reconciliation is possible, it seems tough to worry them unnecessarily. But on the other, studies into the long-term impact of divorce show that children suffer most when marital break-up comes out of the blue. Generally children pick up on the atmosphere in the house and the worry of not knowing is worse than having all the facts.
- It is best to tell the children about a trial separation together. This act of physical togetherness underlines that you will continue to co-operate as parents whatever the future brings. Children often process emotional issues through very practical concerns; for example, 'Will Daddy be here for my birthday?' Before talking

to the children, think through the separation and how it will impact on them. In this way you will already have an agreed plan. Most children need time to digest the information, so expect this to be the first of several conversations.

- When should the temporary separation start? Look at your diary and negotiate how to deal with joint social occasions over the next month. Should you cancel them? Should you still attend together, even though you are temporarily separated? Should just one partner attend? Or should you wait until a certain event has passed before starting your temporary separation?

- Start to discuss the day-to-day practicalities. Where will you live? What contact should there be during the temporary separation? It is important to plan some time together to talk and take stock during your break – maybe even a date? In this way, there is the potential to court each other again.

Hearing the ILYB Confession

'It was like strolling along a quiet street on a sunny summer afternoon: a nice neighbourhood with well-tended lawns, kids playing and men washing cars. When out of nowhere a car came hurtling round the corner, mounted the pavement and knocked me down. As it flipped me in the air and my face hit the tarmac, I noticed my husband was driving the car. Why was he doing this to me?' This is how Margaret, who had been married for seventeen years, described the impact of hearing her husband confess, 'I love you but I'm not in love with you.' Just like in a car crash, she felt shocked, disorientated, confused and very frightened. She kept thinking, 'There must be some mistake,' and, 'What do I do now?' But, unlike in a road-traffic accident, there was no ambulance on the way and nobody to offer a cup of sugary tea.

Although the situation may seem bleak there is one enormous positive: all the relationship problems are now out in the open. The work of finding a way back to **loving attachment** can begin. But first you need to cope with the fallout from the ILYB confession. After a crash the first step is to walk round the car and assess the damage. The same goes for hearing that your partner does not love you. Firstly, is he or she telling the truth? When a couple have been dating/seeing each other for only a few months one partner can try to break off the relationship by using ILYB. These partners hope it will soften the blow, partly because they do not want to hurt their date and partly to ease their own guilt. To be brutal, it is doubtful if these people know the true meaning of love and all their previous declarations should be taken with a heap of salt.

The second set of circumstances in which ILYB can be a handy cover-up is when one partner is having an affair. These people think bad news is better broken in stages. 'I thought that he wouldn't get so angry if I held back on the affair for a couple of days,' explained Jill, a thirty-eight-year-old fitness instructor, 'because my lover was not the cause of our problems, just a symptom.' Often with celebrity break-ups the couple will deny that anybody else is involved but a few days later one half will be caught out by a photographer with a long lens. The partner is left doubly betrayed, firstly by the cheating and then by the lying. In other cases there is no affair but the partner is indulging in an 'inappropriate friendship' – either over the Internet or with flesh-and-blood colleagues at work. Here are a few questions to uncover an inappropriate friendship:

- Are you talking on a personal level with someone else?
- Are you calling or emailing someone just to chat?
- Have you been out for lunch or a quick drink after work with someone?
- Is anyone becoming more than a friend?
- Have you touched anyone in an intimate way?

Having satisfied yourself about the facts behind ILYB, the next job is to find some first aid. Speak to a member of your family or a long-term friend who will listen and sympathise rather than take charge. Some partners who have been told ILYB feel disloyal confiding in others. However, the road back to a healthy relationship can be long and arduous, so good support is vital.

Often, in an attempt to gain control of an out-of-control situation, the dumped-on will magnify their weaknesses and promise to change overnight. When Tony told Maria ILYB he also confessed that he was unhappy with their sex life. She jumped on this scrap of information, read a million books and promised a better future. Maria was truly in overdrive, overwhelming Tony with love and hoping to win him back. For fear of embarrassing Tony in front of their friends, Maria kept her problems to herself. Although thoughtful, this decision proved to be counter-productive. Her friends would have stopping her from taking all the blame and humiliating herself. Remember the first of my *Three Laws of Relationship Disputes* (see Chapter Three): All arguments are 'six of one and half a dozen of the other'. Tony needed to take the blame for not speaking up sooner and also accept some responsibility for their inadequate sex life.

After assessing the damage and getting support, the third part of recovering from hearing ILYB is to get angry. After a brief burst of fury many people who have been dumped on get weepy, or too nice and too forgiving, and many try to minimise the news. Although shock and denial are natural responses to a catastrophe – and that's no understatement for something that puts relationships, families and homes at risk – these reactions stop a couple from really addressing the problem. In contrast, anger will bring issues, concerns and desires to the surface. It also shows your partner that you care, take the problems seriously and really wish to work on your relationship. Without anger the gut instinct is to reassure – 'It'll be all right' or 'I'll try harder' – just the sort of 'nice' but passionless response that drained all the love out of the relationship in the first place. If you are having trouble accessing your anger, either speak to a supportive friend/family member or look at the 'Unable to Get Angry?' exercise at the end of this chapter.

Next on the agenda: begin thinking about the changes that *you* would like. This surprises many clients who would rather keep the spotlight on their partners. Maria was particularly reluctant to talk about her issues: 'If I tell him my problems he'll think the situation is hopeless. No, I've got to concentrate on the positive.' But this can easily be seen as dismissing the crisis or – even worse – not really listening. After some prompting Maria began to think about her needs too. 'Tony keeps himself to himself; I don't know what he's thinking of half the time,' she explained. 'When he doesn't share his feelings with me I don't really feel like sharing my body with him.' Finally both Maria and Tony had something concrete to aim for that could improve their **loving attachment**. Their relationship began to turn around. Tony would chat about his day on his return from work, while Maria would try one of the tips from her magazine – for example, keeping good eye contact during their lovemaking (rather than closing her eyes or turning her head away). The following week Maria and Tony came back with smiles on their faces. He had talked and she had looked, and both felt more intimate with one another than they had for years.

The plan worked for Tony and Maria because it had fulfilled three basic requirements:

- *The needs had been expressed as a positive.* When you tell your partner, for example, 'You don't talk to me', it doesn't matter how nicely you put it – he or she will hear this as a criticism. The natural response to criticism is either to get defensive or to attack. However, a positive request – such as, 'I'd really like to understand more about your job' – invites a positive response.
- *They had asked for something concrete.* Some requests, even though they are positive, fail because the other partner has no real idea where to start. For example: 'I'd like us to spend more

time together' is fine, but how long, how often and what will the couple do? Contrast this with, 'I'd like us to walk the dog together on Saturday morning.'

- *It had been small and easy to do.* Instead of offering something ambitious, like a new position for intercourse or sexy lingerie, Maria had agreed to something she knew would be achievable: keep her eyes open during lovemaking. Instead of intimate chats about love and where the relationship was going, Tony had agreed to talk about something more neutral: his work.

For more about setting positive goals, see 'Accentuate the Positive' in the exercise section.

What if my partner asks for a trial separation?

- Obviously it is easier to work on the relationship if the two of you are under the same roof, so be certain that your partner is determined to leave rather than just floating the idea.
- Unfortunately it is impossible to keep someone at home who is determined to leave, and resisting the inevitable will soon become counter-productive. Instead of the focus being on your partner's ILYB it switches to your 'unreasonable behaviour'.
- I know it is tough, but agreeing to a trial separation puts you in a stronger bargaining position than if your partner just walks out in exasperation. So give the break your blessing, but first ask for a month together to absorb the news and work through some of *The Seven Steps* . . . 'When Frank first told me about the temporary separation I was heartbroken, and I must admit I did everything to stop him, including using emotional blackmail,' Christina confessed. 'Ultimately I couldn't change his mind. OK, he stayed, but he was miserable and certainly it wasn't going to make him better disposed towards me. If I loved him – which I do with all my heart – I had to let him try.' This act of generosity helped Frank and Christina find a compromise: a temporary separation but one during which they saw a lot of each other.
- Look at the practicalities: Where will your partner go? What

choices would be acceptable? What would be unacceptable? How often will you meet up? My advice would be to ask for at least one 'date' a week – by this I mean a couple of hours doing something pleasurable, just the two of you. If you have children, build in opportunities to meet as a family. How often should there be telephone contact and under what circumstances? Don't wait until the month together is up to start discussing the practicalities – particularly somewhere else to live – as this will help your partner realise your 'blessing' is genuine.

- Spell out all the 'rules' of engagement so there is no room for misunderstanding. I have counselled cases where one partner believed that he was free to see other people while his partner thought they were still working on the relationship. If both parties have a clear understanding of the temporary separation this kind of bitterness can be avoided.

- How long should the trial separation be? There are no hard or fast rules but it will make the time apart easier if you know the duration. Your partner will probably be unable to give any idea how long he or she needs. If your partner is particularly hard to pin down I would advise you to suggest a possible duration – for example, three months. Most people will reply either 'not that long' or 'I'll need more than that'. Keep going until you have found a possible duration to discuss. Your partner might still be resistant to a fixed period and indeed it is hard to predict how either of you will feel. So view the end of a trial separation as an appointment for an in-depth discussion rather than a definitive decision on whether to try again or split up. ILYB needs time and it is always better to renegotiate a longer break than to force the issue too quickly.

What if my partner has already left?

- All is not lost. The ideas in this book can still be used on the occasions when you have contact – in particular see Chapter Nine, *The Theory of Tipping Points*.

- Keep the lines of communication open. My advice is to try the opposite of what you did before, as this will bring some fresh air to the situation. If you've always talked at home, go out to a coffee shop. If you've talked in restaurants have a take-away. In fact, do anything that will change the old dynamic.

- It is important not to go into overdrive and push your partner further away. Read the advice in the next chapter (*Coping Day to Day*) before attempting any of the relationship rescue strategies.

Summary

Confessing ILYB
- The longer you leave it, the harder it will be for your partner.
- Make sure you are as honest as possible. Any attempts to dissemble will just hurt your partner further.
- Expect the unexpected, but be ready to talk – probably more than in all your conversations in the past five years added together.
- If you need a trial separation or some 'space' to think, give your partner a clear and detailed picture of what you need.

After hearing an ILYB confession
- Everybody reacts differently to bad news; there is no right or wrong way.
- Instead of focusing on your partner's dissatisfaction and becoming trapped by their mood swings, start thinking about what she or he needs to do to win you back too. This change of attitude will stop you sliding into depression and provide some direction for your life.
- Although extremely hurtful, an ILYB confession can be the beginning of a more emotionally open and fulfilling relationship.

Exercises

Planning to Confess?

Think back to past bad news that you had to give or hear. Maybe you told an employee that he or she was being made redundant, or perhaps you were on the receiving end of such news? Perhaps when you were young your parents split up, or you can remember them telling you about a grandparent's death? If you are gay or lesbian, what about coming out to your parents? Write down all the things that made it easier to break unexpected news or to hear it; next think of everything that made the experience more painful. This will give you a list of dos and don'ts, and although these are not accurate predictors for your confession this process can help you prepare.

Accentuate the Positive

Generally it is easier to say what we *don't* want than to ask for what we *do* want. That's why, when trying to make things better with our partners, we end up either complaining or simply describing the problem.

1 Look at these typical complaints and see if you can turn them into a positive, then find a request for a small but concrete goal. *(Some possible answers can be found in the* Appendix *at the back of the book.)*

- Why do I always have to clear up?
- Will you stop mauling me?
- You never initiate sex.
- You're always hanging out with your friends.
- I hate it when you avoid me.
- You are way too critical.
- Why can't you lighten up?
- Why didn't you phone me?

- You do nothing with the kids.
- Isn't it about time you fixed the hall light?

2. Thinking of your complaints about your partner, write down the top three and turn them into positive requests: what you want rather than what you don't want. If you can't find a concrete goal, ask yourself: How will I know when this goal has been achieved?

Examples
Complaint: *You sulk to get your own way.*
Positive Request: *Please tell me outright when you disagree.*
How will I know when this has been achieved? *When we can happily go shopping together.*
Concrete goal: *Let's choose the new taps for the kitchen together.*

Complaint: *I'm always the driving force.*
Positive Request: *Don't leave all the decisions to me.*
How will I know when this has been achieved? *When my partner arranges a night out.*
Concrete goal: *Actively planning a holiday together.*

Unable to Get Angry?

If you find yourself being 'too nice' to someone who has told you ILYB, here is a list of my top seven anger prompts. Write the ones that apply to you on a card and keep them handy at all times. Next time you feel weepy or depressed, this card will provide a shot of anger to keep you going.

1 He/she told me that he/she doesn't love me any more.
2 She/he has kept these feelings to her/himself for ages.
3 He/she has put our relationship at risk.
4 What is the impact on our children/friends/families?
5 I feel I am putting more effort into saving this relationship than her/him.

6 What gave him/her the right to reject me?
7 He/she might want to see other people. How will I cope with
   that?

Can you think of three more personal anger prompts? Even if it is
something that seems petty: 'After I spent my mother's inheritance
on buying him a new car,' or, 'After all the girls' nights I picked
her up at three in the morning.' Don't try to rationalise the feelings. Write them down on your card.

Chapter Twelve

Coping Day to Day

After the initial shock of ILYB wears off, a couple will often be overwhelmed by a million questions: 'What's going to happen?' 'What if . . . ?' 'How will we cope?' Of course there are seldom any simple answers; discussions about the future go round in circles and the pain never seems to lessen. So what can be done? The first part of this book provides a long-term strategy for rescuing a relationship, but what happens in the meantime? This chapter contains less directly relevant material for you if you are the one who has fallen out of love, but it will provide insights into your partner's state of mind. The next chapter focuses on guilt, however, the issue that affects most people with ILYB in the first weeks and months after the confession. Whichever side of the ILYB split you are on, be gentle with each other. This is a tough time for both the partner asking the questions and the other half who has no adequate answers.

The biggest fear of someone who has been told ILYB is that the relationship might be over; indeed the fear is so big that it pushes aside nearly every other question and lurks, barely disguised, behind the others. This problem is multiplied a hundred times if the partner has asked for a temporary separation. Gary, a primary school teacher, found himself cut adrift from his normal routine when his partner of five years, Nicola, went to stay with her mother: 'I worried she would turn Nicola against me. I worried what friends would think;

I worried whether I'd be able to afford the flat on my own; I worried that I would never taste her baked polenta with goats' cheese salad again.' To make matters worse, Gary's brain was simultaneously churning over past memories of golden moments together, the pain of getting through that day and the void where the future used to be. At work Gary was good at coping with emergencies, but this time he felt completely de-skilled. In fact he was facing the two biggest challenges for someone living through a temporary separation: worry and over-analysing. Although these normally come as a pair – and feed off each other – they are subtly different. While worry is about what will happen in the future, over-analysing is normally about what happened in the immediate past. So what can be done to stop these twin enemies from overwhelming you?

Beginning with worry, the first secret is to cut the future down into manageable chunks. Instead of stewing – often needlessly – about a distant tomorrow, try concentrating on getting through the next few weeks. This approach helped Gary: instead of being immobilised by the prospect of spending months and months of empty weekends without Nicola, I asked him to focus on that coming weekend. When would be the dangerous moments? He had football on Saturday morning, so no problems there. What about Saturday night? He decided to arrange a drink with an old schoolfriend. Sunday lunch was another problem, so he would invite himself round to his parents. Sunday evening he would be preparing for his next week at work, so he was happy to be home alone. Once he had broken the weekend down everything seemed more manageable, until he let his focus drift again. 'What about our summer holidays?' he groaned. Normally I would sympathise, but in a crisis it is vital to concentrate on today. 'That's not your responsibility at the moment,' I told him. 'Your job is to make it through the next week.'

The second tip is to gather the facts, as this will prevent you from worrying in a vacuum. Visit a Citizens Advice Bureau or a solicitor – most are happy to give an initial consultation at a reduced fee

– to find out where you stand financially and legally. Next, find a friend who will provide a sounding board and help sort the reasonable from the unreasonable fears. Ideally this friend should be someone who will just listen and not offer to wade into the crisis, as this will only complicate matters.

Thirdly, accept that everybody worries. It is a sensible and natural response. The goal should be to worry less about matters beyond your control – like, 'Will he phone?' or, 'Will she want to see me this weekend?' – and concentrate more on things that you can directly change – like your own behaviour. During Gary and Nicola's trial separation Nicola threw a Sunday afternoon barbecue to celebrate her birthday. She invited Gary, her parents and various shared friends. Unfortunately Nicola's father insisted on grilling the meat his way. 'Nicola lost her temper and stormed back into the house. My instinct was to ignore the incident – even though they were really shouting,' Gary explained, 'but then I realised that's what I'd always done and what I'd always done had brought me to the point where I almost had to beg for an invite to her birthday party! I needed to change, but how?' He decided to do something different and followed her inside. 'I listened to all her complaints about her dad, and she had a little weep. I kept thinking: *What would I have done before?* Probably offer to have a word with him. So again, I told myself: *Try something different.* So I just heard her out and, do you know, that seemed to be enough.' The birthday party became a turning point for Gary and Nicola. While Gary's trick of finding a different approach from what he'd done in the past didn't always come up trumps, it worked often enough to get them out of their relationship rut. Perhaps more importantly, he stopped worrying about what Nicola would do next and focused instead on how he could be different.

After worry, the second most common problem is over-analysing. While it is hard to find any benefits in worrying, the ability to analyse a problem properly is normally an asset. However, the stress of an unwanted separation – or the threat of one – can tip useful introspection over into negative thoughts, and instead of fresh insights it can offer only a distorted lens on the world. The person trying to save the relationship starts playing relationship detective: endlessly going over a telephone conversation for clues; dissecting how well a meeting with their beloved went; putting all the facts together to try to build a bigger picture. Over-analysing teases a million angles out of an issue until someone can no longer think straight and becomes chronically indecisive or, alternatively, panicked into bad choices.

So how can you tell where healthy introspection ends and over-analysis begins? The first will normally range over the whole of the relationship while the second focuses on events over the past few months – often to the exclusion of everything else. While healthy introspection will throw up new strategies for healing a relationship, over-analysing goes round in circles, ending up nowhere. Zoë did a lot of hard thinking after Murray told her that he didn't love her any more, and many of her conclusions helped to improve the relation-ship. However, after he asked for some space to get his head straight, Zoë went into overdrive: 'Everything became a clue to whether he was going to come back to me or not. How long did it take to return my text? Did he want to come round for Sunday lunch? Reports from a mutual friend over his state of mind seemed to take on a huge importance. If he seemed to be missing me I'd be up in the clouds. If he was tired and wanted to go home early I'd be depressed for days.' When Murray called during her down days she'd be snappy and often attack, despite being pleased to hear from him. In our coun-selling session Zoë learnt to stop looking for a deeper meaning behind Murray's behaviour, to relax and enjoy her time with him. So what is the secret?

Phase one: *Realise that over-analysing is not constructive.* People keep doing it because they feel they are getting great insight and stripping away the rose-coloured glasses. But more often than not someone who over-analyses ends up feeling bad about themselves or their partner. The next time you catch yourself over-analysing, put up a mental 'stop' sign and distract yourself with something pleasant like exercise or a hobby; play with the children or pick up a magazine. Eight minutes of distraction has been found to be enough to lift your mood and avoid depressing thoughts.

Phase two: *Reschedule your thoughts.* Tell yourself that you are not avoiding the problems but putting them off to a better time. When the rescheduled time comes you will probably find everything feels less overwhelming or the problems might have simply disappeared. This rescheduling is especially important in the evening, as it is best to avoid distressing thoughts before going to bed.

Phase three: *Commit your thoughts to paper.* Do not censor yourself – rather like taking dictation, write down everything. Then look back over your notes and underline just the concrete events, not your interpretations. Keep on going back to these facts. Discuss them with a practical friend who will look for solutions rather than be sympathetic and fan the flames of over-analysis.

Phase four: *Look for simplicity.* In most cases the most straightforward interpretation of events is always the best. For example, Murray probably did not return Zoë's text message because he was in a meeting, not because of any sinister reason.

In my experience, people who over-analyse fall into three main patterns: the angry, who end up blaming other people (like Zoë); the self-critical, who blame themselves; and the swamped, who become overwhelmed and are prone to becoming depressed. There is a questionnaire in this chapter's exercise section ('Are You Prone to Over-analysing?') to diagnose whether or not you suffer from over-analysing and, if so, into which category you fall. Each category has special tips and advice.

Coping During a Temporary Separation

My clients often ask about the likely outcome of a temporary separation. It is difficult to know how to respond, firstly because there are no statistics and secondly because each case is different. For some people a temporary separation can be very constructive. When Simon, in his fifties and a solicitor, left his wife Margery for 'time to think', she became very brave. 'We'd meet up from time to time – so I could give him the mail and things like that. Once I asked him if I'd see him at the weekend and he told me, "It depends how we get on today." I was furious; I stood up in the restaurant and told him that I didn't want to be judged. He got all flustered and then apologised. He didn't realise I felt that way. When I thought back, he was probably right because I normally tell Simon what he wants to hear.' Her back might have been against the wall, fighting for the relationship, but she decided her best option was honesty. Margery had got in touch with her anger and discovered that it stopped Simon walking all over her.

Conversely, Erin, a thirty-one-year-old housewife whose husband of seven years left 'to get his head straight', felt a complete failure: 'I had put my family at the centre of my life. Everybody thought we were a great little family but on the inside I felt worthless.' The sense of rejection can be even worse if the current loss gets mixed up with a past one. Erin's mother had died when she was a teenager and many of the old feelings of abandonment came back when her husband left – even though it was just for a while. While Erin was stressed it was pointless trying to deal with the past pain; the priority had to be making it through the immediate crisis. It was important to ease the worst jags of pain without letting her regress back into little-girl mode. (For more advice see 'Beat the Blues' in the exercise section.) However well or badly your temporary separation is going, do not be tempted to take any long-term decisions in the first three months. You will be in shock and this is not the best time for considered judgement. But be assured: it will get easier.

What If My Partner Is Slipping Away?

The first option is to try to communicate in a different way.

- If you normally talk face to face, write a letter.
- Alternatively, fewer words can be more powerful than many – especially if you are someone who would normally write an eight-page letter. Buying a greeting card, sending a text or scrawling a message in lipstick on the mirror could make your partner take notice.
- If you don't often talk intimately on the phone or seldom email each other, these are other options.
- In other words, anything that will surprise your partner or stop them from thinking 'same old same old' and switching off.

If the above fails, step back and stop chasing.

- If your partner is trying to grapple with why s/he has fallen out of love, it is not helpful to be constantly asked: How are you feeling today?
- Forever telling your partner that you still love them is counter-productive. S/he will probably say, 'I know', which does not provide the reassurance that you are looking for *and* reinforces in your partner's mind her/his lack of feelings.
- I have avoided gender stereotypes – of women who like to talk through a problem and men who like to retire to their potting shed to think through their problems – because I have met plenty of men who want to engage and women who want to retreat. However, it is worth remembering that clichés contain a large dash of truth. Have you been asking your partner to respond in a way that makes you feel comfortable but them uncomfortable?
- If your partner is a talker, invite him or her to unburden themselves. If you have done this before and failed, try again as s/he might not have taken your first approach seriously or perhaps your offer was too tentative to be believable.

219

- If your partner is a thinker, give them even more space. Through your eyes it might feel as if you have already done this, but from your partner's perspective it might still have seemed as though you were pursuing or placing demands on them.
- Pamper yourself. Get a new haircut or a day of beauty treatment – anything that will shift the focus away from your partner and on to you.
- Do something that you enjoy rather than something you hope will bring back your partner.
- Try to enjoy life. I know this sounds hard, especially after your life has fallen apart, but who is your partner more likely to want to spend time with? a) Someone who is weeping all the time and staying at home, or b) someone who is upbeat and out doing interesting things?

What Should I Do If My Partner Shows Signs of Recommitting to the Relationship?

- If you have found the strength to step back and refocus your life, you will probably have piqued your partner's interest and he or she might start asking questions.
- Don't get too excited or enthusiastic. These first days of reconnecting are rather like the early days of courting, when it is better to be warm and encouraging than to throw yourself at someone.
- Accept some of the invitations to spend time together, but not all of them, and certainly do not cancel prior engagements.
- Keep the dates light and fun. Just like your original courtship, don't get too heavy too soon.
- Wait for your partner to bring up difficult subjects – like your relationship or the future – and don't say, 'I love you,' first as this invites a response that your partner might not be ready to give.
- If at any time your partner starts to back-pedal, check whether

you have begun pursuing again and rededicate yourself to focusing on your own life.

- Stay cool until you are 100 per cent certain that your partner is equally keen.

Summary

- While this chapter has mainly been addressed to someone who has been told ILYB, the next one is mainly for their partners.
- If you are prone to worrying, break the issues down into smaller chunks and concentrate on those within your control.
- Over-analysing can be as destructive as taking a relationship for granted. It falls into three types: angry, self-critical and swamped.
- If your partner seems to be slipping away it is time to try another strategy.
- Embrace the advantages of living in the moment. After all, we can only actually change anything in the present.

Exercises

Stop Worrying

The secret is to live in watertight compartments and not to stew needlessly about a distant tomorrow.

1 Make a list of all your worries, then cross off those that are not immediately relevant for the next month. If you are feeling very positive, try to bring your window of worry down to just the next week.
2 Looking at the worries that are left, write beside them three practical things you could do to solve them.
3 If the answer is nothing, make a deal with yourself and refuse to think about the worry for half an hour. Get some fresh air – a walk can lift your spirits and help you think things through.
4 Ask yourself: Honestly, what is the worst that could happen? Prepare yourself mentally to accept the likely worst case and then expend your energy on calmly improving on it.
5 Avoid caffeine and sugar and cut back on smoking and alcohol: all these are stimulants and will make your mind race even more.
6 If you can't sleep at night, picture your worries on the piece of paper. Tell yourself: 'There's nothing I can do now,' then imagine screwing up the paper and throwing it out of a pretend hole in your head. Do it several times until you feel more calm.

Are You Prone to Over-analysing?

Although this quiz is meant as a bit of fun it has a serious side too. It will help you discover your analysing style and offer some specially targeted advice.

1 You have a blazing row with your partner and find yourself repeating all those insults you promised you'd never use. Do you think:
   a)   About all the other ways you have let your partner down.

   b)   I should make a grovelling apology – even if deep down you feel you were in the right.

   c)   It's my partner's fault for provoking me.

   d)   Arguments happen in even the best-regulated families.

2 You make an extra special effort to seduce your partner in the bedroom, but he or she rolls over and starts snoring. Do you think:

   a)   If they are not interested in me they must be getting it somewhere else. I knew that new member of their department was trouble.

   b)   Considering how much weight I've put on it's a miracle anyone ever fancies me.

   c)   My partner didn't thank me for preparing supper either; he/she always takes me for granted. Why did I ever fall for such a selfish man or woman?

   d)   My partner has probably been working too hard.

3 During a telephone conversation with your partner there are a lot of awkward silences. Afterwards you find yourself dwelling on it. Do you think:

   a)   Why can't the two of us get on, and why do I keep rubbing everybody up the wrong way? Do I actually get on with anybody?

   b)   Maybe if I could be more tolerant we could still be friends.

   c)   Why do I have to do all the work?

   d)   I'm not going to let it spoil my day.

4 During your temporary separation one of your best friends has a dinner party to celebrate their birthday but invites neither you nor your partner. What is your reaction?

   a)   Could everybody have been talking about me behind my back and decided deliberately to exclude me?

   b)   You phone the member of the group that you're closest to and find out if you've done anything to upset the hostess?

c) I wouldn't have wanted to go anyway.
d) My friend probably couldn't fit everybody round the table, or maybe it was embarrassing to invite just me.

5 Your partner tells you that his or her mother was remarkably quiet when told the news about your problems. Trying to keep things light you joke, 'Are you sure she hadn't been swapped with someone else's mother?' Your partner laughs. But later, do you think:

a) He/she will be upset that I've run down his/her mother and think I'm not supportive enough. Worse still, I will never be told anything again.
b) I'm always putting my foot in it and must engage brain before mouth.
c) She deserved everything and more – the way she criticises everybody she had it coming to her.
d) If my partner is upset about my comments he or she will say something about it.

6 Which is closest to your personal motto?

a) There are more questions than answers.
b) Must try harder.
c) Why is everybody always picking on me?
d) What you don't know can't harm you.

7 Your partner leaves a note asking to meet up that evening. What do you think?

a) How will I tell the family we're splitting up and how will I ever find anybody who fancies me again?
b) You go over every recent conversation again in your mind and work out what you have done to upset your partner.
c) It's all her or his fault. How can she or he expect loyalty when they treat me like this?
d) I'll find out what it's about soon enough.

Mainly a = Swamped Analysis

In your head your thoughts have logical connections, so you can easily jump from a potentially barbed comment about your partner to your appearance, and maybe on to how one of your parents seemed to ignore you – even if, in reality, the thoughts have nothing to do with each other. The result is that you are flooded and do not know where to turn.

Tip: Next time you feel overwhelmed, stop and unpack all the different thoughts. Behind nearly every one will be someone else's voice telling you what to do: 'You should make the most of yourself'; 'You shouldn't let someone down'; 'You should always be nice'. Until you are overwhelmed with a tyranny of 'should'. With each 'should', stop and ask: Who says? Is their advice still appropriate today or in this situation?

Mainly b = Self-critical Analysis

It is easy for you to talk yourself down and, despite being perfectly capable, you have a low opinion of yourself. Even when there is a positive spin on something you will always take the opposite interpretation. You are probably a worrier too.

Tip: Firstly, you cannot change the past, so there is no point running yourself down. Secondly, learn to forgive yourself. With forgiveness you do not get bogged down with guilt and can move on to solving the problem. Finally, when thinking back over something, ask yourself if you are giving too much weight to negative thoughts. Be aware that there are positive and neutral possibilities too.

Mainly c = Angry Analysis

Although not quick to lose your temper, you often stew over things and end up feeling bitter. Sometimes this can be a cold anger – often very deadly. On other occasions you simply explode. Because you do not like yourself in this mood you try to avoid the problem with a quick-fix solution, which often leads to long-term complications and is fertile ground for future dissatisfaction.

Tip: You have high expectations of yourself and everybody around you. However, life would be easier if you could sometimes accept things the way they are and move on. For example, when your practical mother is not more openly loving, embrace her good qualities rather than getting angry about the rest. Next time somebody upsets you, do not think, 'How could they do this to me?' Instead learn to forgive and focus only on the real slights and what to do about them.

Mainly d = Well-balanced Analysis

You do not spend hours thinking something over unless it is a genuine crisis. When you make a decision, you stick to it. These are qualities to applaud. But are you sometimes too busy 'doing' to consider how other people might be feeling?

Tip: In times of trouble your level head is an asset. However, next time you find yourself playing back a difficult conversation, look for what is happening under the surface. What might have been left unspoken? By becoming aware of these extra dimensions you will probably make even better choices.

Beat the Blues

The blues kick in whenever we feel overwhelmed by helplessness. This is why even something very minor, but empowering, can help us break out.

1 Set up small triumphs and easy successes. For example, tackle a nasty chore that you have delayed for ages – like sorting out the cupboard under the sink. Afterwards these jobs will provide a real sense of achievement.
2 Find small boosts to your self-image. Make sure that you get dressed at the weekend, rather than slobbing round in your dressing-gown, or splash out on some new clothes.

3 Help other people. Offering to fix the guttering for an elderly neighbour or volunteering for the girl guides' camp will divert your attention from your own problems, and their praise and thanks will make you feel better about yourself.

4 Compare yourself to someone worse off. Cancer patients often reassure themselves by comparing themselves to someone sicker. Next time you find yourself wishing your life was like that of a lucky friend, try being thankful it is not like that of someone much less fortunate than you.

5 Take up yoga, swimming or some form of exercise, as the natural endorphins lift spirits, help relaxation and take your mind off worries.

6 If you are religious, try praying; if not, look for a meditation class. These are often run by local Buddhist centres. They will not look to convert but rather to teach you to empty your mind. It is a hard goal, but even getting a few moments' peace from an over-active brain can be very uplifting.

Chapter Thirteen

Guilt

'If only I didn't feel this guilty,' moaned Gary, who had been with his wife since they were both teenagers but, at thirty, had fallen out of love with her. Sara still loved Gary and desperately wanted the relationship to work – especially as they had two children together. However, after several weeks' working on the relation-ship the counselling reached stalemate and Gary asked Sara for time apart. During 'space' or a 'trial separation' I stop counselling the couple but offer one or two individual sessions to support each partner through the first difficult weeks. It was during one of these appointments that Gary let out his moan of guilty despair. It is a refrain with which I am only too familiar. From Gary's point of view the 'space' had been going well – too well: 'It is so nice just to please myself. I've had a chance to get stuck into some books I want to read and I'm bang up to date at work. I close that door and cocoon.' During the previous week the whole family had been on an outing. 'We went to the rare farm animals centre and the boys were running around, scratching the pigs' backs, and they even helped feed an orphaned baby lamb,' he explained, 'but leaving after tea was not so easy.' I listened to the details of the day out – only too aware that he had not mentioned his wife once. 'How did Sara seem?' I finally asked. Gary moaned again: 'If only I didn't feel so guilty.'

At this point on the ILYB journey a couple can be almost over-whelmed by guilt: the person who has fallen out of love feels guilty for all the pain he or she is putting the family through; their partner feels guilty for not spotting the problems earlier, or for their part in the crisis. No wonder it sometimes feels as if there is guilt for breakfast, lunch and supper – with a couple of guilt snack attacks in between just to make sure the nasty taste never leaves the mouth. So what exactly is guilt? Why can it be so debilitating and what is the best way to break out?

Guilt is a perfectly natural human emotion and generally a very useful one. We feel guilty when we have done something that violates our personal value system and, assuming that we buy into them, society's values too. Therefore guilt has its positive side: it binds people together and means that most citizens self-police, with the courts intervening only in exceptional circumstances. However, when guilt turns toxic another closely related emotion is often mixed in: shame. While guilt is about an action – for example, parking on double yellow lines – shame is about one's personal unworthiness. In other words, it is about being a bad person rather than a good person doing something bad. Gary felt guilt for breaking his marriage vows, and shame because he wondered what sort of man would leave a woman that loved him. In most relationship break-ups, where the couple hate each other, each party has built up a head of righteous indignation: 'I'm leaving because of his unreasonable behaviour,' or, 'She was a bitch.' Each party might feel guilty about what they did, but neither party feels they are a bad person: 'He made me do it,' or, 'After what she did, what choice had I got?' Couples with ILYB have no such easy excuses and therefore are particularly prone to shame.

Such feelings can often be traced back to childhood: 'If you're a good boy and finish that, you can have dessert,' or, 'Good girls go to the party; bad girls stay at home.' Some parents unconsciously add an extra message: 'If you don't behave I will take my love away too.' This idea that 'good things happen to good people and bad things happen to bad people' is further reinforced by religion, schools and popular TV drama, in which virtuous characters are rewarded and the immoral suffer. With this in mind, it is no surprise that everybody likes to view themselves in the best possible light. Even though we learn as adults that being a good employee does not stop employers from relocating our job to the other side of the world, or being a good father does not stop an uninsured drunk driver from smashing into the back of our car, we still like to believe that these childhood rules apply. Of course we cannot control these random life events, but deep down we cling to the idea that being 'good' will protect us. A relationship crisis challenges this belief and makes us doubly keen not to be seen as a bad person.

Gary did not have the luxury of blaming Sara for his plight and he needed to distance himself from his feeling of being in the wrong. For Gary, and for many people suffering from ILYB, guilt was serving a second purpose. Towards the end of his first solo session he said, 'I know I'm being selfish, but if it's any consolation I feel really guilty about it.' Even Gary did not believe Sara would draw much comfort from his suffering, so we looked more deeply. Finally, Gary admitted, 'I can't be a bad person because a bad person would not feel guilty about asking for a temporary separation.' In effect, the guilt was allowing Gary still to view himself as good. Guilt also protected him from looking at other difficult feelings: anger, pain, grief, regrets; if only I'd done this; if only I hadn't done that. Instead of engaging with these monsters, Gary would try to tame his guilt by phoning his kids or he would distract himself by going for a beer with his work colleagues. These coping mechanisms were fine, up to a point, but they did nothing to address the underlying causes. And while most emotions burn themselves out, toxic guilt can last for ever. Gary might have hated the guilt but he felt even more uncomfortable about the feelings hidden behind it. Plus there was a final advantage to feeling guilty: it stopped him from deciding between returning home and getting divorced.

Breaking Out of the Guilt Trap

The following exercise will be painful and time-consuming. You can write down your feelings or alternatively recruit a supportive friend. The ideal listener would be someone who knows both you and your partner and can be neutral. Avoid cheerleaders who are 100 per cent behind you or anyone likely to feel uncomfortable with your pain and who may want to ease the burden before it has been properly examined. A friend is particularly useful for point two but, if you can be honest with yourself, writing down your feelings will provide the necessary distance.

1 Examine your regrets
Start with everything over the past month and then move backwards over the past year, the past five years, back to before meeting your partner, adolescence. What are the important turning points? What are the 'if only's? Who have you hurt? Are the regrets just about today's relationship crisis or part of a larger pattern?

2 Challenge the toxic thoughts
Taking the most important regrets, ask yourself the following questions: Have I overestimated my responsibility? Have I underestimated someone else's responsibility? Is there any false blame? Have I denied my responsibility? Have I made the past seem very black and white, without contradictions, paradoxes and ambiguities? Did I assume superhero skills – like second sight or a super-smooth tongue – to persuade someone to change?

If your partner told you ILYB, skip the next part and go on to part five. If you are no longer in love with your partner, move directly on to part three.

3 Grieve
Life always involves making choices. If you went to university, you will never know what would have happened if you had started your

career earlier. If you chose not to accept a proposal from a suitor, you will never know what life would have been like with that alternative partner. With these regrets, allow yourself to visualise how life might have been, with all its advantages. Later add the potential disadvantages of the path not taken and the important assets gained from the path you did take.

For current regrets, allow yourself to feel the pain. Choose the catharsis of tears over short-term pleasant distractions or small gestures to compensate. Don't overfill your diary and leave time to be quiet and still.

4 Take stock

When someone starts unpacking guilt it is impossible to predict what will come up. If you have discovered regrets over missed opportunities from the past, look for ways to incorporate those goals from where you stand today.

Are you using guilt as a justification for inaction? If you are not ready to make a decision that is all well and good – many people rush blindly into the future – but be honest with yourself.

Could you have another try at your relationship? Particularly if you are reading this when your ILYB has already reached crisis point, give yourself enough space and time to digest the ideas and try out the exercises.

5 Make amends

Accept your share of the responsibility and apologise. You should neither grovel and beg for forgiveness nor worry about your partner's share of the responsibility. Just a simple, direct apology with no explanations or mitigating circumstances. You could try this out first in a letter, which you may or may not share later with your partner.

Do not expect forgiveness – this might come later. The goal is simply to apologise. Your approach might be received warmly and be the springboard for a useful discussion, but you should also be prepared for an angry response and, under these circumstances, be ready to leave rather than get embroiled in bitter fighting.

Think about making appropriate reparation, a gesture towards repairing the damage. It might be a present, doing something that your partner would really appreciate or, if splitting up, a generous settlement.

When Gary started to **examine** his guilt he found more than he expected. When he first woke up with a sinking feeling – not just unhappy but downright depressed – he had been sure it was due to his unexciting relationship. However, while examining the roads not taken, he started talking about the rock band he had played in with some friends: 'We weren't just popular at school but really had a following in the local pubs. I'm not saying that we were going to be the next Beatles but we had a real chance. Except the music business seemed like a real gamble and Sara and I were getting serious, so I got a proper job instead. I still wonder what my life would have been like if we'd stuck at it.'

His next task was to **challenge the toxic thoughts**, and indeed he had begun to look at his life in very black-and-white terms: success and failure. It soon became clear he felt angry with his parents, school and Sara for not supporting him more. However, once he actually voiced those long-hidden emotions he began almost immediately to take his share of the responsibility for not pursuing his dream. In part three of *Breaking Out of the Guilt Trap* he started to **grieve** for his lost career: 'I could have been playing stadiums all across America, with thousands of screaming fans, but I could have also ended up in drug rehabilitation or penniless on the streets.'

Finally, in **taking stock**, Gary learnt one of the most important things about regrets: it is seldom too late. A successful rock career was unlikely at thirty, but one of the advantages of being older is learning to be more flexible. There was nothing stopping Gary from playing in local clubs as an amateur and reconnecting with his music again. Once Gary had acknowledged his anger at Sara for keeping him in his hometown – and she came to watch one of his impromptu gigs – his attitude to his marriage began to change. He no longer saw his wife holding him back and he became open to re-examining his marriage and rediscovering the passion.

Nicola had effectively fallen out of love with her husband five years before she announced that their marriage was over. Richard knew things had been tough five years ago: 'She'd been on my case: a lot of nagging; I didn't pay enough attention; we didn't do enough together – but what did she expect? Life's not all wine and roses. Except one day she just stopped having a go. I thought: She's off my back – great. She's realised it can't always be like the movies.' But five years previously Nicola had stopped trying to fix the marriage, or, as she put it, 'I'd exhausted every possibility. There was no emotional connection and I just knew I'd be happier without Richard.' However, she decided to wait until their youngest child reached primary school age before leaving the marriage. She had stayed married for the past five years but in her heart and mind she had already left. Meanwhile Richard was living in a fool's paradise.

When Nicola finally told Richard that she did not love him any more he was devastated. He finally understood the depth of her unhappiness but Nicola was already halfway out the door. He tried everything: a week's holiday in Venice, flowers, being more helpful round the house, a giant teddy bear, dragging her reluctantly into counselling. Nicola was feeling terrible: 'I'm such a hard bitch. I tell him something that's wrong and he immediately tries to fix it, but it's not enough. Then he looks at me and I am just overcome with guilt. Guilt with a capital G.'

Nicola's guilt had become like a high defensive wall that none of Richard's gestures to save the marriage could get over. So in counselling we started working on *Breaking Out of the Guilt Trap*. We **examined** Nicola's regrets and she talked about the marriage she had wanted. Richard wanted to interrupt and promise that the future could be that rosy but I stopped him. At this stage he

needed to hear Nicola out. Next I **challenged her toxic thoughts.**
Who had been responsible for all that unhappiness five years ago?
'He didn't lift a finger, I was left to do everything round the house,'
she explained. This time I allowed Richard to present his side of
the story: the extra hours to bring in more money since Nicola
had stopped full-time work and how he had helped with the children. In other words, it was not as black and white as everything
had become in Nicola's mind. 'Why didn't you tell me how you
felt?' Richard asked. Nicola had tried but it had come out as
nagging, which just pushed Richard further away. Who was to
blame?

In this case it boiled down to the first law of relationship disputes:
six of one and half a dozen of the other. When relationship problems get really embedded, however, toxic thoughts can distort everything into right and wrong, with none of the grey bits in between.
During **grieving,** the third part of *Breaking Out of the Guilt Trap*,
Nicola wept for all the unhappiness during the five years she had
lived on autopilot, and Richard's eyes were moist as he listened.
When **taking stock,** Nicola admitted she did not dare let Richard
have a second chance in case everything went back to how it had
been before. 'How can I trust him?' she asked. Trust is difficult to
gain overnight. It takes time. So Nicola agreed to put the divorce
proceedings on hold. There was in fact no timetable, no ticking
clock, except for the one in her head. 'Ultimately, I owe it to the
kids to give him some more time. Perhaps then I can lower my
defences just a little,' she said. When it came to the final step,
making amends, we discovered that they had both already achieved
that: Richard had truly listened to all Nicola's issues (without trying
to persuade her to stay), while Nicola had given Richard a second
chance. Eventually they decided to stay together and found the relationship that Nicola had dreamt about. Unfortunately it needed
Nicola to tell Richard that she no longer loved him, and the very
real threat of divorce, before he truly heard her.

*

In the two case studies above the couples decided to stay together. However, some clients find that they have been feeling needlessly guilty. Michelle had been married to David for eight years and had felt watched at every step. Right from the beginning of their relationship David had been very solicitous for her welfare. Michelle was a keen amateur ballroom dancer and David was always ready to pick her up after practice, no matter how late. At the beginning David's attitude helped the relationship: 'He was always willing to go out of his way and this made me feel special; he certainly didn't have eyes for anybody else,' she explained.

However, David's caring soon turned into jealousy. 'My regular dancing partner is gay but that didn't stop David from making nasty comments about how happy we looked on the floor together. I tried explaining that it was all for show, for the judges, but he thought there was no smoke without fire.' Eventually Michelle got fed up with the snide comments and decided to swap partners. Although she never found someone as good at dancing, she loved David and decided it was worth the sacrifice: 'I thought he'd be more confident about my feelings after we got married. Like changing dance partners, it worked for a while but he'd always want to know where I'd been. I found him checking my text messages and finally he wanted me to give up dancing altogether.' Day by day she felt her love draining away until she told David, 'I love you but I'm not in love with you.'

Michelle felt guilty when she arrived in counselling and David was quick to point out everything he had done for her: 'Remember your marriage vows? I meant every word when we stood at the altar. Didn't you?' However, as we went through *Breaking Out of the Guilt Trap* Michelle became more and more angry. 'You're still trying to manipulate me,' she exploded. 'You can't use guilt to control me now.'

Instead of suppressing or ignoring your guilty feelings, try analysing them. On the one hand, the guilt could mean that you are doing something that violates your personal code of values and your conscience is telling you to stop; on the other hand, you could be taking more than your share of the responsibility for a relationship crisis.

Summary

- Guilt is an inescapable human emotion.
- When shame gets mixed in with guilt it can often turn toxic.
- Letting go of guilt involves examining regret, challenging toxic thoughts, grieving, taking stock and making amends.
- Guilt normally has a message for us. It is better to listen to it than rush headlong into an unknowable future.

Exercises

The Guilt Journal

Buy a ring-bound exercise book, rather than using odd pieces of paper, as you will need to refer back. This exercise also involves a lot of writing, and buying a nice notebook will show a commitment to persevere.

1 Confess. Instead of the thoughts going round in your head, write down everything in your guilt journal. Some of the guilty feelings will be about past events and some of them will be fresh today – it does not matter if the two types of guilt are mixed up. Put the date at the top of each entry, however, so that you can look back and discover which guilty thought preoccupied you and when. Don't worry about style, spelling or grammar – just let everything go in a stream of consciousness.

2 Analyse. You will find more objectivity if there is a gap of two or three days between writing and analysing. Take a marker pen and go back over what you have written; start looking for black-and-white thinking. Words like 'always' and 'never' are good clues. Next try to find thoughts that suggest superhero skills and second sight, and mark these up too. Sentences with words like 'should' or 'ought' are often indicators of this kind of thinking. Finally, look for sentences that blame and underline those too. Maybe one colour for yourself and one for your partner. How do the different colours balance up?

3 Identify the main themes. Although guilt can throw up a thousand and one variations, usually there is only a handful of main themes. Give your theme, or each of your themes, a name. For example, guilt about not supporting your partner enough while their father was dying could be 'hospice'.

4 Questionnaire. For each theme, jot down some thoughts under the following question headings:
   • What could you have done differently?

- Thinking of that time, what resources would you have needed?
- What prevented you from doing it?
- What do you feel angry about?
- Who are you angry with?
- What could you learn for the future?

5 Reflect. Put your journal away for a week and return to it with fresh eyes. Read through everything and allow yourself first to grieve for past mistakes and then to take stock about what comes next.

6 Reopen the journal and answer just one more question: How can I make amends? Write down as many practical solutions as possible, even if some of them seem ridiculous at the time. After you have exhausted all the possibilities – both sane and insane – go back and select the most appropriate.

Note: Some clients find that they feel guilty about something in the past but the person concerned is no longer alive. How do you make amends with someone who is dead? In these cases I suggest writing an imaginary letter to the person concerned.

After the crisis

Chapter Fourteen

How to Bond Again

I love the moment in counselling when it becomes clear that the couple have found their way back to each other. It is rather like the clouds parting on a rainy bank holiday. Nobody wants to acknowledge that the sun is shining – because we do not want to tempt fate – but there is still undeniable hope that the day might be saved. About two weeks later one or both halves will admit, 'I do have feelings.' There is a shy smile and a slight tilting of the head, but the eyes shine. Falling in love again – achieving **loving attachment** – should be easy from here, but it rarely is. Many couples expect something dramatic rather than tentative. In the movies, the hero suddenly realises that he loves her after all and starts a madcap rush to the airport, where his beloved is about to fly off to become a nun in the Congo. Or the heroine is standing at the altar, watching her husband-to-be pick his nose, and suddenly she knows her 'other love interest' would never do anything so horrible – or, if he did, it would actually be rather cute. Of course, at the same moment 'other love interest' is fighting his way through a crowd of guests to stop her from making the biggest mistake of her life. Love always wins out. Real life, however, isn't like the movies. Crucially, it is much more rewarding.

The first shoots of love are green and tender, but many clients want to take them straight out into the big wild world. Some talk about ending counselling: 'Thank goodness, we're out of the woods,' sighed Nina – one half of a lesbian couple who survived ILYB – 'I feel I can breathe again.' However, my advice is never to relax too soon. This couple had been extremely close and ILYB had been particularly painful. In order to persuade her partner Sophia that there was everything to play for, Nina had had to swallow a lot of her own needs. The next week Nina and Sophia had long faces. 'We've had a terrible time,' complained Sophia, 'always picking at each other. The slightest thing would set us off: forgetting to phone when I said I would, or not bringing my plate through to the kitchen. What's happened to us?' After months of being positive, Nina's natural resentment about being put through ILYB was finally coming to the surface.

At the other extreme were Brenda and Mike, who had been living apart for two years and were so frightened of destroying their returning love that they tiptoed round each other. Mike agreed to attend Brenda's family celebration, even though he was worried that they might be hostile to him. This had taken a whole counselling session to set up, so I was keen to discover how everything had gone. 'Fine,' replied Brenda. 'Not as bad as I thought,' said Mike. Their answers sounded too defensive, so I dug deeper and discovered that Mike had escaped from the table between courses and played with the dogs. I asked Brenda how she felt about this. 'Everything has been going so well, I didn't like to say anything,' admitted Brenda. 'But it was rude.'

Go back to the idea that rediscovered love is like a tender plant: before a seedling is ready to thrive in the garden it needs to be hardened off. Horticulturists know that young plants need to be acclimatised gradually: first the heat is turned off and then the covers are raised for a few hours in the daytime; finally the new plants stay out day and night. With rediscovered love, though, some couples throw off the protective covering too soon – like Nina and Sophia – while others are too frightened to say anything, leaving the glass on for ever – like Brenda and Mike – and risking the love turning mouldy. So how do you acclimatise gradually?

Levelling

I have called this chapter *How to Bond Again* because there are two things that still need to happen. The first of these is **levelling,** an open and honest sharing of feelings – for example, 'OK, I will level with you; I've been unhappy too.' In fact, the recommitment to love is not an ending but the point at which really productive work can start. When George, a salesman in his late forties, returned home to his wife Cherie, a legal assistant also in her late forties, they stayed up late, talking, for three nights in a row. 'I really needed to prove to Cherie that I was serious. Previously I would have cut the conversation short, worried about being tired for work the next morning,' said George. 'I think she really appreciated that.' 'When George first opened up,' said Cherie, 'I was relieved but it was like a dam breaking. I found myself talking about my dissatisfactions – in particular how George did not take enough time to woo me before trying to have sex.'

Levelling is very productive but these conversations can easily stall. This is because **levelling** has four accompanying behaviours: blaming, placating, intellectualising and diverting. If you find yourself straying from **levelling**, do not be alarmed as in moderation these behaviours are part of the hardening-off process. Like the good gardener, the trick is to keep an eye open and spot potential frosty moments.

Blaming

Definition: To blame your partner for something that has gone wrong rather than looking at your own contribution. An example of this from Cherie: 'You don't give me enough foreplay,' and from George: 'You don't pay me enough attention.'

Tackling it: Although both George and Cherie were telling the truth, as each of them perceived it, this cast them both in the role of victim. What would happen if Cherie took some responsibility and rephrased her feelings as, 'I don't ask for enough foreplay,' and if George said, 'I don't explain to Cherie what I need from her'? They would both become in charge of their own destiny again. Cherie could show George how she likes to be caressed and George could ask Cherie to switch off the TV when he returns home.

Placating

Definition: To appease your partner with sweet words or by offering something to keep them quiet in the short term, rather than addressing the root problems. George would often say, 'I won't leave you.' Meanwhile Cherie would immediately give in – 'You're right, I've been far too wrapped up in my own stuff' – even if she did not necessarily agree with all George's complaints.

Tackling it: There is nothing wrong with soothing your partner's pain. However, in the long term, constant placating leads to resentment. If George tells Cherie only what she wants to hear, but without really meaning it, he will find it harder and harder to share his true feelings. So what can be done? Placating works well if it is just the first part of a discussion rather than a standalone interaction. Obviously George needs to reassure Cherie he is not about to leave immediately. However, he must go on to explain that without fundamental changes he cannot stay for ever.

Intellectualising

Definition: To place an excessive emphasis on rational thoughts, often with a complete disregard for feelings. An example from Cherie: 'Historically men have always treated women as sexual objects and ignored their needs.' While George would say, 'It makes financial sense to rent a room up in town during the week rather than spend so much on train fares.'

Tackling it: Being rational about a problem can be useful. It helps a couple to step back, get a fresh perspective and make the issues seem less personal, but a lasting solution has to make sense to the heart as well as the head. Intellectualising can also get a couple trapped in pointless arguments – about nineteenth-century sexual etiquette, for example – rather than addressing the real issues. So balance the rational thoughts with feelings, and the generalisations with the personal impact.

Diverting

Definition: To deflect someone's attention in the hope that they will forget the original complaint. The three main techniques are denying, distracting or ignoring. For example, George would change the subject from his bedroom prowess by saying, 'Think yourself lucky that I'm not like my boss – he's got two women on the go.' Cherie would try complete denial – 'I'm always interested in what you have to say' – when often she would rather watch her soap opera.

Tackling it: Sometimes diverting is an understandable response, especially late at night when one partner feels worn down. There is a more honest approach, though: to trade. When George asked, 'Can we talk about this tomorrow?' Cherie would have been more likely to agree if a specific time and place had been suggested: 'Tomorrow, after supper, we'll sit in the kitchen while the kids are watching *The Simpsons*.' Obviously, it is important to honour this commitment. Diverting is only a short-term solution and, used indiscriminately, it will set up all the conditions for slipping back into ILYB over time.

With a little practice, **levelling** became second nature for George and Cherie. George told Cherie, 'I feel disappointed when you watch TV because I want to share my day with you.' And she told him, 'I feel frustrated when you rush sex because I want our lovemaking to be special.' (If you would like more information on **levelling** look at the exercise section in Chapter Five: the **three-part statement** will help you to be open and honest without unduly antagonising your partner.)

Learning

If **levelling** is the first part of truly bonding, the second part will be familiar if you have worked through *The Seven Steps* . . . **Learning**, the last step, is also important for bonding again. In the last few weeks of counselling my ILYB clients are relieved that love has returned but are still wary.

Anna and Nick, the salesman and the teacher, decided to stay together. Although the initial honeymoon period was wonderful, both Anna and Nick were worried that they would fall back into their old ways. So I helped them look at why their relationship had developed problems. 'I was always wrapped up with our sons,' Anna replied, 'and Nick had his work.' 'When we could have had time together, we surrounded ourselves with friends,' Nick added. 'It was like we were frightened of what would happen if it was just the two of us.' What were you frightened of? I asked. 'Arguing,' they said in unison and laughed. 'I didn't want to have terrible rows like my parents,' said Anna. 'My parents never argued, so I suppose I didn't know how to,' said Nick. They had their diagnosis: their love had disappeared because they were never together enough to be intimate and their fear of arguments had trapped them either side of this divide. Next I asked how they had changed. 'We're not afraid to speak our minds,' they answered, again in unison. So what could they do if they found themselves heading into trouble again? Nick and Anna didn't answer; they just looked at each other and I knew the counselling was over. By learning what had caused their problems – and remembering the new skills that had pulled them out – they were confident that they could avoid the same traps in the future.

For many couples this is enough knowledge, but others like to look deeper and learn what attracted them to each other in the first place. As discussed earlier, it is something beneath the superficial characteristics – 'looks', 'sense of humour' or 'easy to get along with' – given by most couples to explain their mutual attraction.

Everybody's childhood leaves them with relationship dilemmas inherited from watching their parents' marriage. It might be 'not showing feelings', 'coping with unfaithfulness', 'temper tantrums' or 'attitudes to loss' – the list is endless. We are drawn to people who have complementary problems and are wrestling with similar issues. For example, Julia, a thirty-five-year-old secretary, had listened to her mother complain about her father – a travelling salesman – never being around. So Julia, in turn, had no picture of how a husband and wife negotiated daily life together. She swore not to make the same mistakes as her mother but unwittingly found herself married to a workaholic who played little part in family life.

Repeating the same mistakes as our parents might seem depressing, but in fact we have a chance to re–enact the dilemmas and find a more comfortable compromise. When Julia understood that her anger about her husband's hours in the home office was exacerbated by memories of her parents' fights, she was able to get her reaction back into proportion. She also admitted that she would have hated her husband to be hanging around all the time, stopping her getting on with her projects. With this understanding Julia and her husband were able to negotiate a routine in which Saturdays were family time but he was allowed to work on Sundays.

Forming relationships – and having children together – will always rub at the old fault lines from the past and make us question the present. While previous generations expected problems, we are more impatient and less willing to tolerate anything less than perfection. Yet if we all hung in longer and believed more we would address the underlying issues and reap the rewards of a doubly intimate and doubly satisfying relationship. If all this sounds like hard work, perhaps a hit of **limerence** will help. (See the exercise section at the end of this chapter.)

What If the Honeymoon Has Stalled?

Four to six weeks after a couple have decided to try again the confidence often begins to slip away and one partner can become quite depressed. In this circumstance it is important to check that all anger has been vented. The pain from a deep wound cannot be healed all at once, but every time it is re-examined a little more of the hurt and anger will be eased.

Both Nina and Sophia, the lesbian couple introduced earlier in the chapter, still had questions to ask each other. Nina wanted to know if Sophia had been falling out of love when they booked a weekend in Venice, as the holiday had particularly good memories for her. Sophia wanted to know what Nina had said to some of their friends – who were like a surrogate family – about their troubles. Although at times raking over the past made Sophia and Nina feel trapped, overall they found the process liberating. 'When I kept something back,' explained Nina, 'which I often did not to hurt Sophia, and I suppose myself too, I would get more and more down. Yet if I did ask, I'd stop feeling so vulnerable.' Finally, after about two months of talking, there were no more questions to ask. 'My trust in us as a couple had returned,' said Nina. If there is still some unresolved anger in your relationship, look at 'Five Useful Subjects to Argue About' in the exercise section.

Ritual can be a potent tool for moving on – hence all religions and cultures holding some form of service to mark a death. Some couples use ritual to lay old pain to rest while others choose to celebrate a new, stronger love. A good ending ritual is to find a couple of objects that represent the bad times and have a small ceremonial burning. Another idea is a holiday away together. (See 'Rituals' in the exercise section.)

The final step to re-energising a relationship is to plan for the future. Sit down and discuss the next five years and listen to each other's thoughts with an open mind. Of course there could be differences, but a couple that have faced and survived ILYB will have learnt all the necessary skills to deal with this. If you are stuck for ideas for the future read 'Finding Your Dream', the **collaborating** exercise in Chapter Two.

What If I Want to Fall in Love Again But It Is Just Not Happening?

Lots of emotions – like trust, sexual desire and, of course, love – are not rational. No amount of arguing or rationalisation will open up the heart. Towards the end of counselling some people with ILYB no longer want to leave, but they are not sure that their relationship can be what they need or whether they can truly open themselves up to love again.

Rod had fallen out of love with his wife, Gemma, after fifteen years of marriage: 'I could see how we'd let things slide, so we decided to make changes and certainly everything feels less claustrophobic. But what if I still don't love Gemma the way that I should?' Gemma had fears about the future too: 'I know it is stupid to ask for a guarantee – life doesn't come with one – but that doesn't stop me wanting one.' So while Rod worried about loving again, Gemma worried about trusting again. What next? This is a hard one, because the solution is a paradox. On the one hand, a couple needs to have worked hard to remove the obstacles to love: anger, hurt, cynicism and impossible expectations. Yet on the other hand, a couple needs to step back and let go. Just as Buddha found enlightenment only when he stopped seeking it and let it come to him, couples with ILYB reach a point where they need to stop pursuing love, trust and reawakened desire. These are slippery emotions and, like enlightenment, they are more elusive when placed centre stage.

In counselling we reviewed Rod and Gemma's previous obstacles to love (not arguing, unspoken resentments and Rod's unnecessarily long work hours) and remembered how much had been achieved. I also asked Rod and Gemma to list any other possible obstacles and we came up with just one minor issue (Rod thought Gemma resented him playing golf, but she was only concerned if it happened every weekend). Finally Gemma turned to Rod and said, 'We'll just have to believe we can do it.' Two weeks later, love and trust were no longer issues. Although neither Rod nor Gemma could put their finger on the reason, after they had stopped worrying the emotions had returned. For couples who are unable to believe, I ask them to behave 'as if' they trust, love or expect to feel sexual desire again. 'What would you do?' 'How would you act?' This 'letting go' phase normally lasts between two to six weeks and at some point the couple effortlessly cross from acting to being. With couples who remain stuck, I encourage them to re-examine their relationship and seek out any remaining obstacles.

A Better Understanding of Love

When couples who have been through ILYB look back at their journey, remembering the knowledge acquired and the new skills learnt, they find a lasting belief in themselves. So what is this knowledge?

- Love is effort. In a good relationship both partners regularly and routinely attend to each other's needs – no matter how they feel. This extra mile is often what is most appreciated.
- Love is about both giving *and* receiving. In a good relationship both partners make sure they find the joy in both halves of the equation.
- Love is courage. In a good relationship both partners share their vulnerabilities as well as their strengths and do not close themselves off, shut down or take the easy option.
- Love is rewarding. In a good relationship both partners support each other and help each other grow.
- Love is most appreciated when a couple thought it was lost for ever but have subsequently found a way back to each other again.

What about the skills learnt?

- To be honest with yourself.
- To be honest with your partner.
- To be upfront about differences, rather than ignoring or hiding them away.
- To negotiate better.
- To find a genuine compromise, rather than one partner just backing down.

Summary

- Provided that ILYB is addressed early enough – and the couple have both been honest about their feelings – there is no reason why they should not decide to give their relationship another try.
- Do not expect reconciliation too soon; in the beginning, a commitment to a better relationship is enough.
- To bond a couple need first to **level** with each other and secondly to **learn** what went wrong; this will give them confidence that the problems will not reoccur.
- When we first fall in love we make fundamentally good choices. The secret of happiness is to understand the attraction and solve relationship dilemmas set by our childhood.

Exercises

Audit Your Reactions

This exercise requires nerves of steel, not because it is difficult but because it is very revealing. Next time your discussions seem to be hitting the buffers, switch on a tape recorder. After fifteen minutes, rewind the tape and look out for:

1 Blaming. These sentences normally start: 'You make me . . .'
2 Placating. Especially excessive use of 'Sorry', 'You're right' and 'It won't happen again.'
3 Intellectualising. Long, rambling sentences which do not seem to go anywhere are a sure sign.
4 Diverting. Are both of you truly listening or are you blocking, contradicting and belittling?
5 How often do you interrupt each other?
6 After auditing the conversation, return to the topics discussed and try to cover the same ground again without falling into the same traps.

Five Useful Subjects to Argue About

The best way to bond is to have a good argument. It gets all the issues out in the open, providing a release of pent-up feelings and a sense that the relationship can get better.

Little things

Small irritations such as stacking the dishwasher badly may not seem like serious crimes, but they can cause huge resentment if not dealt with. Also, if you find conflict especially difficult, these smaller issues can provide a dry run before tackling something really contentious.

Tip: Bring up your niggle at the time – rather than a couple of hours later when it's too late for your partner to do anything about it. Don't hide behind a joke, because your partner will wonder if you really mean it. Also avoid slowly building up to the request with statements like, 'You're not going to like this,' or, 'There's something I need to bring up.' This will put your partner on the defensive. Just ask directly.

Amount of time spent together

With so many demands on our time it is easy to put our partner at the bottom of the list. But if **loving attachment** is not nurtured it withers, so ring-fence time together.

Tip: Don't fall into the trap of concentrating, for example, on the amount of time your partner spends outside the house or on hobbies – this only invites a justification of his or her behaviour or a dispute about the facts. Instead discuss how this makes you feel. For example, I feel neglected/taken for granted/not important. As you are the expert on your feelings, this is harder to contradict.

Different tastes

Differences make things more interesting, highlighting your role as partners rather than best friends or twins. Choose something in the news or a movie you have both seen and discuss it together. Standing up for your views is healthy and you will probably learn something new about each other. These arguments can even take on a playful tone and give the opportunity for mock fighting – very useful if you find confrontation difficult.

Tip: Always have an opinion. If you opt out – 'It's OK, you choose what we do this weekend' – your partner will feel 100 per cent responsible for the success of an outing, which can become very wearing.

Money

Arguments about money are harder to negotiate but provide an express route to important, but often hidden, issues. Money can stand for power, self-respect, freedom, responsibility, security and even love. So when you discuss money, be aware that you're not just talking about pounds and pence and try to delve deeper.

Tip: Get your partner to talk about what money meant when they were growing up. Next, share the lessons you have learnt from your childhood. This will help you see your differences through fresh eyes and find room for compromise.

Sex

This is another tough area but one that can pay real dividends if tackled. Whether the arguments start with, 'You don't fancy me any more,' or, 'Why do you always push me away?' it will bring into the open deeper issues that many couples are too embarrassed to discuss.

Tip: Be extra considerate. Instead of blaming – 'You make me feel . . .' – own the problem – 'I feel . . .' This will stop the argument becoming unnecessarily confrontational.

Rituals

Mankind has always used rituals to mark the seasons. Similarly, we need to mark the end of one phase of our lives and the beginning of another. This exercise will allow you to give the past problems of ILYB a 'decent burial' and look forward to a new closeness.

Check that all the conflict is out in the open

Spend an evening going back over the past months. How does each of you make sense of what happened? What has each of you learnt about the other person? What have you learnt about yourself? If this ends in a row you are probably not ready to close the book on ILYB. If this is the case, look at 'Audit Your Reactions' above and keep talking. If the talk is productive and supportive you are ready for a ritual.

Design a ritual
Find something that seems to sum up ILYB for you. Some clients write an account of what happened, others tear pages out of their diary or gather up the paper used for exercises and decide to burn those. Another strategy is to find something that encapsulates your arguments – like an old golfing sweater or a beer-mat from a night-club – and have a ceremonial trip to the council dump. Alternatively the act can be completely symbolic, like holding a helium-filled balloon on top of a hill, imagining that it holds all the pain and letting it go. Other cleansing ideas could be making paper boats and sailing them over a weir or casting petals into the wind. The only limit is your imagination.

Honour the ritual
If you are writing a letter, or an account of your pain, make sure you do it properly and don't just scribble on the back of an en-velope. Find a location that speaks to you. I had a client who burnt some old pictures on the beach – because she had happy childhood memories there – and watched the tide come in and wash away the ashes. Take time to talk, think and be together. Some clients have chosen poetry and others have even brought music. This all helps to make it a solemn occasion and adds signif-icance. If, for practical reasons, the location is rather ordinary – like the council dump – find somewhere nice to go for a walk or a drink afterwards.

Celebrate the new
Just as marriage needs witnesses, so does a reborn relationship. I always think a feast is a good way of marking an important date, and you could invite people who have been supportive over the difficult times, but discuss together what would be best for your relationship.

Limerence Exercise: Remembering the Magic of the First Meeting

For five years I did a series of magazine profiles of celebrities and their partners. I would always start by asking for the story of how the couple first met. Within seconds the atmosphere in the room would change – any nerves or apprehension would disappear – and I would feel real warmth as people remembered. The secret is in the detail I asked for: Where were you? What were you wearing? What did you eat? What did your partner look like? What did she say? What did he do? Normally people have boiled their 'how we met' story down into one or two sentences which do not provide enough material to trigger proper memories. Over and over again the celebrities – normally on tight time schedules – would stretch the time allocated for my interview. I was taking them back to the height of **limerence** and everybody enjoyed lingering on their passionate memories a while longer.

Either write a short story about your memories of how you met your partner or bring the topic up in general conversation – perhaps over a meal. It normally takes three or four questions to get someone in the mood. To give you an idea, here is the first part of my interview with Twiggy and her husband Leigh Lawson (an actor best known for his role as Alec D'Uberville in Polanski's film *Tess*.) See how many facts I extracted:

Twiggy started: 'In 1985 I went out for dinner at the Caprice in London with three friends. At another table I spotted Jonathan Pryce – who I'd been working with – so I went over to say hello. Immediately this handsome man stood up. It was Leigh, who reminded me that we'd met ten years earlier at a John Denver concert. Even back then I'd thought him really dishy, but we'd both been married so nothing romantic had crossed my mind. This time the chemistry must have been obvious, because I remember telling my friends to stop trying to pair me off. But I must have been curious because I bought a magazine with a big interview with Leigh. I learnt he had been alone for two years and after the trauma of the break-up was not interested in seeing anyone seriously for the next ten years! Three days later Robert Powell and his wife Babs, who used to be in Pan's People, invited me to a restaurant in Chelsea. By a string of amazing coincidences Leigh was invited too. We chatted and laughed but on paper he was trouble. Who in their right mind would trust a gorgeous actor? I was no longer an eighteen-year-old about to jump in head first. So I let him slip away again. Fate had other ideas.'

At this point Leigh takes up the story: 'I thought Twiggy was absolutely gorgeous – but as one of the most beautiful women in the world I knew everybody would be after her phone number. Despite fate throwing the two of us into the same restaurant as each other twice in one week I said goodnight and let her walk away. Perhaps I lacked confidence; perhaps my heart had just got out of intensive care; perhaps she wasn't giving the green light. Although these days Twigs claims she was disappointed that I didn't ask for her number – but she's got to say that! Anyway, five days later I went to the newsagent's for my morning paper and this big blue Jag – with an exquisite blonde inside – pulled up by the kerb. It was Twiggy. She wound down the window and said, 'Do you want a cup of tea?' Even I knew this was the green light!'

Every story of how two people met and fell in love is interesting, so give yourself permission to enjoy your own. With luck there will be things to tease each other about (notice how Leigh does it over asking for the telephone number and Twiggy over the magazine interview), which can be turned into affectionate everyday banter between the two of you.

Chapter Fifteen

If the Worst Comes to the Worst: Making Sense of Endings

In an ideal world this book would have finished at the end of the previous chapter. ILYB relationships can be saved, the passion reignited and both partners – not just the one who fell out of love – can find a deeper and more fulfilling intimacy. But I am a realist. Some people are determined to end their relationship and, no matter how committed their partner might be, ultimately it takes two to make a couple. For other readers it may already be too late and their relationship has already ended. So, after accepting the inevitable, what next?

As the shock of the break-up starts to wear off and the pain really kicks in, most people try to distract themselves: some will have a makeover or take out a gym membership, others will bury themselves in work. In the first difficult weeks there is no right or wrong approach, just something to make it through. However, after this first flush of energy most recently separated people discover that they need to understand the past before moving forward. Slowly but surely, often over a bottle of wine, they will rake over what happened with their friends or family. It might be painful but ultimately it is the right thing to do. In a paper presented to the British Psychological Society Conference, Dr Carla Willig of London's City University identified three main stories commonly used by ex-lovers to describe what went wrong. 'There's such a strong need to have an explanation,' she claims, 'and those people who haven't got one find the break-up more difficult to accept. Of the people I studied there was just one man with no story. He was still struggling through his pain many years later.'

I wrote earlier about Michelle, the twenty-seven-year-old TV researcher whose husband Claude disappeared for two months and reappeared on the other side of the world. Nearly two years later she was still having trouble making sense of her divorce: 'I don't have any answers; that's what makes it so hard. We only spoke a couple of times on the phone, but that's it. I just don't have a proper explanation. What possessed him just to disappear?' It is tempting to think an ex holds the answer – that is certainly the motivation behind many late-night, slightly drunken calls, but these conversations never go anywhere. Each half of a separating couple has to build up his or her own account of what happened and why. In fact, on many occasions these stories will be radically different. Slowly I helped Michelle to piece together what had happened. Claude did not like conflict and never argued. 'He just seemed happy to go along with what I suggested,' she explained. What if Claude did not agree? 'He'd just keep it to himself. I suppose the pressure of bottling it up was just too much,' she answered. It seemed that Claude had taken conflict avoidance to its extreme and just disappeared. Michelle had begun to put her story together.

What types of stories has Dr Willig found? The first story, 'To the Bitter End', is built around the idea of doomed lovers. From the first kiss, every twist in the tale is painful. Every jealous event, bad holiday and discovered secret is used to illustrate how the relationship had problems all along. The reality of the relationship might, in fact, have been very different. But these former lovers use a cut-and-burn technique to obliterate all the tender memories and then move on. This is not normally the choice of ILYB couples, as 'bitter-enders' part hating rather than caring about each other. Sadly, though, I do meet some people who think the whole relationship has been invalidated by the split. Roberta had been married for fifteen years and had a twelve-year-old daughter, but when her husband threatened divorce she said, 'I'm so angry with him. I feel that he has stolen my best years and I can never get them back. Everything is ruined.' The French philosopher Henri Bergson would label this thinking 'the illusions of retrospective determinism'. Bergson argues that we often view historical events as inevitable and, consequently, our present social problems too. With this false logic even the good times at the beginning of the relationship hold the seeds for the ending and are somehow tainted. It is like looking back at a holiday while stranded at the airport waiting for the flight home and feeling the whole trip was a disaster. But no matter how much discomfort the hold up brings, it cannot undo the pleasure experienced at the beginning of the holiday, eating calamari while overlooking the old fishing port.

The second story, 'A Way Out', builds on a similar principle. From the beginning something has not been quite right: the lovers had incompatible habits or different interests. He might have been tidy, for example, while she left her knickers on the bathroom floor; she might have been a computer expert while he was an artist. While the 'bitter-enders' let these small but painful events build up until one finally breaks the camel's back, the 'way-outers' find a dramatic exit. In Dr Willig's study it was nearly always an affair, with another lover providing an excuse for the ending. And indeed, some ILYB couples do find themselves enmeshed in affairs.

The third story, 'Changed Circumstances', has an entirely different narrative. This relationship starts well. After a honeymoon period the couple settle down into a happy life together. But the course of true love does not run smoothly and, as in all stories, there are obstacles to overcome. One partner is promoted and their job takes them away; the children leave home, or the couple simply grow apart – all these new circumstances can undermine what was once a happy relationship. This is the most likely story for ILYB couples as it acknowledges the love and affection, which survive the break-up.

Dr Willig's research also explains why men are more likely than women to be emotionally damaged by relationship break-up. Previously experts simply blamed men's tendency to keep problems bottled up, but it goes deeper than this. By not talking, men are failing to construct an ending for their relationship. By contrast, women, while offloading on to friends, are forever rehearsing and finally settling on a version for their break-up. Whether these explanations are right or wrong is immaterial. 'Any account is better than none,' claims Dr Willig.

Michelle's story does not really fit into any of the three stories identified by Dr Willig, however, which is why I add a fourth narrative. I call it the 'Unwanted Opportunity', and it works for both the person who is left against their wishes and the partner who leaves. 'We had a good and fulfilling relationship which worked for a while,' this story says. 'We both made mistakes and went in different directions. Being single is not what I wanted but I am determined to see the opportunities rather than dwell on what I've lost.' 'Unwanted Opportunity' people use the painful experiences to hone their relationship skills, so when they meet someone in the future they will make the most of it. Many people move on to this fourth narrative after first having used one of the other stories, so arriving here is proof that you have made progress.

When constructing the story of how a relationship ended, some people become fixated on the last painful section and feel overwhelmed. To get a better perspective, take a piece of paper and create a graph: on the horizontal axis write 'time' and on the vertical axis write 'pleasure'. The first meeting with your partner is the zero point on the time axis. From there, plot your whole relationship on the graph, including all the peaks and troughs. Label all the good times so that you do not forget them. Next, examine the bad times. Were they inevitable? What is the balance between positive and negative?

Roberta used this idea to look back over her fifteen-year marriage. She had a high for the birth of her daughter and after that everything was more or less a flat line. Beyond the last three and a half years, Roberta's graph showed that her relationship had been better than she had painted it. 'Obviously I have regrets, but actually it was not all bad,' she concluded.

Looking back over a relationship, many people feel they are a complete failure and find only one person to blame: themselves. Weighed down by a million regrets, and a thousand things they should have done better, they become depressed and start to despair. At this point I would recommend coming from a fresh angle. Machiavelli, the founder of political thinking with his pamphlet *The Prince*, advised the ruling Medici family on how to keep power and influence events in their favour. He is famously ruthless, but still he wrote, 'I believe that it is probably true that fortune is the arbiter of half the things that we do, leaving the other half or so to be controlled by ourselves.' Yet most of us act as if the proportion of things we control is much larger and end up castigating ourselves.

Michelle, whose husband disappeared, took on all the blame. 'I keep thinking that I drove him away; I should have asked what he wanted,' she said. However, through counselling she found a more balanced picture: 'He could have said something if he was unhappy. When I spoke to his mother, she told me that he disappeared without explanation as a teenager too.' Michelle had found that responsibility for the break-up of her relationship was more fifty/fifty.

If taking all the responsibility for a break-up is a mistake, so is going to the opposite extreme and blaming someone else. It might initially be comforting to feel, 'It was not my fault,' and that either circumstances or the other person's wickedness were to blame, but playing victim in the long term makes it harder to find someone new. Instead of saying, 'They took advantage of me,' rephrase this as, 'I should have stood up for myself more.' The first explanation leaves you vulnerable to repeat performances; the second explanation leads to an assertiveness course. In all good films and books the central character learns something about themselves from their trials and tribulations. It is what makes satisfying drama; it also makes for a more satisfying life.

Although it is hurtful when one partner blames the other for the end of a relationship, or alternatively takes on all the blame, it should not be taken to heart. One of the few advantages of splitting up is that the ex's take on events no longer matters. Each half of the couple is heading for a different future and even if one ex-partner has a different story it will not hamper the other's progress.

Closure

Sometimes clients arrive at my office seeking something called 'closure'. After the first time this happened I consulted my dictionaries of psychological and psychoanalytical terms but found nothing. I was surprised. Where had this term come from? It is neither a medical nor a religious concept – the other main sources for psychological-sounding words that enter the general vocabulary. Closure, the idea that we can somehow deal with a past painful relationship, package it up and move on, is such a seductive idea that we have invented our own word and now want to believe in it. But is it possible?

When someone is determined to reach closure I am sympathetic but always probe deeper. Some clients hope to skip some of the pain by rationalising and packing it away. Although this process can help it is not a magic bullet. Other clients have used closure as the cover for some pretty nasty behaviour. Hannah had been having an affair with a married man for three years: 'I had no choice but to go round and tell his wife. She had a right to know and how else was I going to achieve closure?' This is dramatic but never final. The confrontation just launches another round of recriminations. Indeed, Hannah's boyfriend turned up on her doorstep and started shouting at her. 'It was not at all healing,' she admitted.

The best way forward is to repackage the pain into something positive. I helped Hannah look back at her painful parting as the moment she started painting; another client remembered how his former lover had introduced him to meditation. Even bad relationships teach us something. If this does not work for you, take a long hard look at the benefits of staying where you are. This seems mad, because who would want to keep hurting? But sometimes it feels safer to cling on to a failed relationship than to face our fears: 'I'll never find anyone else to love me,' or, 'I can't cope with the loneliness.' Be as honest with yourself as possible and keep digging deeper. Once everything is out in the open the underlying assumptions can be properly challenged, anxieties chopped down to size and a way forward found.

Finally, be patient with yourself. A relationship break-up is as traumatic as a bereavement, so never underestimate what you have been through. Congratulate yourself on your progress so far and be assured that the pain will lessen over time. Although we can never achieve complete closure, we can integrate the past into a better future.

Summary

- Having a story that makes sense of the break-up is the first step to healing.
- It is important to learn from the past before truly leaving it behind.
- Do not place too much blame on your ex-partner or take too much yourself.
- The end of a relationship is like a bereavement.

Exercises

Put Your Break-up Under the Spotlight

This simple test will help you decide how to tell your story.

1 Which statement best describes your arguments?
   a)   S/he never listened.
   b)   We tried to resolve our problems but slipped back into old ways.
   c)   We didn't argue very much.
   d)   Somehow we could never get through to each other.

2 Which statement best describes your sex life?
   a)   Fireworks more times than not.
   b)   We got bored in bed.
   c)   Satisfactory but not earth-moving.
   d)   We had our good times and bad times.

3 Which statement best describes your break-up?
   a)   I'm better off without him/her.
   b)   The affair was a catalyst, not the cause.

c)   We became like brother and sister.
d)   Maybe we could become friends sometime in the future.

4 Which statement best describes how you're left feeling?
a)   I don't know how I put up with him/her for so long.
b)   It could have dragged on for much longer.
c)   It was just one of those things.
d)   As long as I learn something.

5 Which statement best describes your feelings about meeting someone else?
a)   Forget it – not with my track record.
b)   I'm frightened to let anybody get close.
c)   I'll have to wait and see.
d)   I'm generally optimistic.

Mostly a = Bitter End

At least the sex was probably good; many people put up with poor relationships because of the magic of making up after a fight. Try and see the relationship in less black-and-white terms, though; life is drawn from a far richer palette. The main advantage of such a final ending is that you are spared the charade of pretending to stay friends.

Mostly b = Way Out

Beware of a tendency to rewrite history to make your previous relationship seem worse than it was and thereby reduce your guilt. The aftermath of an affair often produces increased levels of jealousy caused by a heightened awareness of how easily relationships can break up. There is also a possibility that you might want to return to the original relationship after time and distance have made you reassess what you've lost.

Mostly c = Changed Circumstances

Remember: a relationship needs the right environment to flourish;

just loving each other is not always enough. These good relationships can also peter out because each person swallows their differences to preserve the happy picture and nothing gets solved. The positives are that you are unlikely to blame yourself or your lover, so there is always the possibility of salvaging a proper friendship.

Mostly d = Unwanted Opportunity
You are making good progress, but do not be surprised if there are times when you feel depressed or angry: recovery is never a straight line and most people will fall back from time to time. If you find yourself stuck in one of these holes it may be worth considering counselling to find a fresh perspective.

Even Split Exercise

1 Take a piece of paper and draw a line down the middle. On one side write 'my responsibility' and on the other 'his/her responsibility'.
2 Starting with your partner's side – as this is normally the easiest – list all his or her contributing factors towards the break-up. Leave space on the page directly opposite so that you can go back later and see if you have a matching contribution.
3 Move down the page and list your contributing factors on your side of the paper.
4 Look back and see if there is again a matching contribution to be written in the opposite column. For example, beside 'he always pushed for more sex' someone might write 'I used sex as a weapon to get my own back on him'.

If you find it very hard to think of anything for either column, ask a friend to help and make suggestions.

Chapter Sixteen

How to Fly High Again

Recovering from a relationship breakdown – especially one not of your choosing – is hard. In my experience, people who swim rather than sink have pulled off a difficult trick. They spend enough time on understanding the relationship (the past), but concentrate on changing things for the better (the future); yet when times are tough they focus down to the next few days (the present). Although the ability to alternate through these three time-frames is useful at any time, it becomes crucial during a personal set-back, such as a divorce. People who are stuck in the past frame risk depression, while those who set off with their eyes fixed only on the future are most likely to crash and burn. People with problems caused by sticking to the present are rarer – most of us find it hard to live in the moment – but occasionally I see clients who are living in the present hedonistic (focused only on feeling good today and becoming trapped in pointless pleasure-seeking) or present fatalistic (just swept along by events).

So how can you be flexible enough to find the right time-frame at the right moment? The secret is to understand the advantages of all three. In the last chapter I looked at the lessons from the past, and Chapter Twelve (*Coping Day to Day*) covers the present, which leaves the third time-frame, the future, for this chapter.

*

The future offers the promise of a brighter tomorrow: no more tears, no more pain and perhaps even a new partner. Not surprisingly, most people want those goals now and indeed many clients ask, 'Why does everything have to be so hard?' I do not answer, partly because I am not a philosopher but mainly because counselling is about helping people find their own answers. If I could fly in an emergency on-call philosopher, he or she would probably answer, 'Because nobody has ever learnt anything important from happiness or success; problems make us grow.' Maybe it is just as well these flying philosophers do not exist, because they would not be very popular. A woman I interviewed for a women's magazine best sums up the typical response.

Nuala Bingham developed a complex viral illness when she was just twenty-nine and her husband, Harry, had to give up a high-flying city career to nurse her round the clock. Three years later, when I met them, her energy levels were still so low that she considered it a good day if she could dress herself. She turned out to be one of the wisest people I had ever met and after the interview she offered help with a problem I had been struggling with. 'For the sake of full honesty, whatever depths and curious rewards this illness has brought,' Nuala explained, 'we would NEVER choose it. Day-to-day life is harder and more wearing than I would wish on my worst enemies. For myself I would choose to be shallow and well rather than tortured and deep.' I offer another extract from the interview with Nuala because it shows how adversity can strengthen love. 'When I get very low, I can't go for a run or have a drink like other people. I just have to work on my inner-self; there's nowhere else to go. It's a bit like being a Tibetan monk without the Himalayas in the background! I used to think I'd lost everything that makes someone feel worthwhile. Where is my dignity when Harry has to carry me to the bath? But I discovered that it is beyond being able to wash yourself. I still feel like a human being because that's what I see reflected when I look into Harry's eyes. He still has the same respect and affection.'

Going back to my client who asked why life is hard, if the evidence of my flying philosopher and Nuala Bingham did not work, I would probably call Dave Stewart from the pop group the Eurythmics. This talented and rich musician once suffered from Paradise Syndrome. He had panic attacks which left him paralysed on the floor, simply because he had nothing to worry about! It seems that humans need problems because pain provides the building blocks for a better tomorrow.

Focusing on ILYB again, here are two casebook examples of reaching for the future, one of them successful and one less successful.

Mark felt lonely after his fifteen-year marriage ended but, despite missing his teenage daughter, he decided to concentrate on the opportunities. 'There were two things I'd always wanted to do: flying and dancing. But I didn't have time for either before and, to be frank, my wife discouraged outside interests. Now I've not only enjoyed the new challenges but met some great people.'

Although Phil had been married for a similar duration and also had children, his story is quite different: 'My friends told me I was better off without my wife. I didn't believe them, but they took me out drinking and I bet you can guess the rest. I started dating the barmaid and the beginning was incredible – such a high. Before long we were talking about living together and planning a holiday in Florida. But I discovered she was seeing someone else too.' Phil took this break-up harder than his wife leaving and sank into depression. Unfortunately he had tried to reach his future life too quickly. Phil thought he had found a woman ready for long-term commitment, whereas she had seen their relationship as a bit of fun.

So how do you avoid the temptation to rush headlong into the future, especially if today seems very bleak?

The First Three Months After a Break-up

- Even if you want to remain friends, give yourself space to end the old-style relationship before starting on the new one.
- Remember you are dealing with grief, so be kind to yourself. Eat well, get plenty of sleep and do not put too much pressure on yourself.
- Disconnecting takes time. At the start of a relationship a couple shares out the jobs. When ending a relationship each partner takes back responsibilities previously given to their ex. Sometimes this unhooking can be the source of joy – especially if your partner, for example, has done all the cooking and you get a chance to rediscover your culinary skills. Sometimes this is a time of growth: for example, your partner took care of all the money issues and you decide it is time to learn yourself.
- For jobs that you cannot do yourself – and have no wish to learn – it is better to ask a friend or hire an expert than to phone your ex-partner. This last option will keep you bound to the old relationship rather than striking out towards the future.

Finding a New Path

- *Go for what you want rather than what you don't want.* Many people in crisis are very aware of what they do not want: for example, to be lonely. However, goals are much better if they are framed in a positive way: for example, 'I want to make new friends.'
- *Be as specific as possible.* The clearer the picture of your new life, the easier it is to spot the first steps on the path. You might think, 'I want to make new friends to go to the theatre with.' This more specific goal would focus the mind towards finding out if any work colleagues were interested in the theatre and turning them from acquaintances to friends or joining a relevant club.

- *When looking for new opportunities, bring new patterns into your life.* If you always do the same things your life will always be the same. So start shaking up your routines – it could be something as simple as taking a new route to work and spotting something that triggers a new interest.
- *Open yourself up to inspiration.* Go for walks or take some exercise – anything that occupies the body but allows the mind to wander will free ideas to pop from your subconscious into your conscious. Other possible sources include: surrounding yourself with beauty (going to an art gallery or attending a concert); surfing the Internet; tidying away the clutter in your home; doing something that makes you laugh; asking a friend for advice.
- *Enjoy the steps on the way.* Sometimes we can be so obsessed with achieving a goal that we forget to stop and smell the flowers on the way. Enjoying the journey also avoids the trap of too-rigid goals and missing out on other options that could also bring happiness.

Obstacles to Healing

- *Anger.* It is perfectly natural to be angry – especially if the relationship ended against your wishes. While expressed anger explodes and disappears, suppressed anger can bubble under the surface for ever.
- *Desire for revenge.* The Internet is full of sites dishing the dirt on ex-lovers and the newspapers full of stories of people who chopped up their ex's clothes, sewed prawns into the hem of the curtains or dumped a precious wine collection on neighbours' doorsteps. While revenge can provide a short-term high, it will backfire in the medium to long term. Firstly, it invites retribution, and secondly, the vengeful are bound by hate into the old relationship rather than thinking about moving on.
- *Children.* When you have had children together, you are bound

together for ever. It is not just when they are small but at their graduation, their wedding and their children's christenings. So accept the inevitable and make the most of it. In the first few months it might be easier to drop the children outside than come in for a cup of tea, but if personal animosity makes being civil impossible seek out a reconciliation service. However much you might hate your ex, please do not express it to your children – remember they will still love both parents – or put pressure on them to take sides.

- *Hoping for reconciliation.* Some people give up too soon and a saveable relationship ends, while others hope for a reconciliation for too long and delay the healing process. So how do you strike a balance? This is very much a personal decision but I would try to journey towards a better independent future – finding new interests – while keeping the door open. If your ex has started a new relationship or left because of an affair, however, it is unlikely that he or she will return while **limerence** is at its height.

- *Timing.* Sometimes circumstances and plain bad luck can prevent someone from moving on. First, take a look at your life: what could be holding you back? Secondly, ask: Is there another way round? Thirdly, be patient. It takes time to recover, and if everything feels like 'pushing water uphill' this may not be the right choice for you now.

- *Have you got the right goal?* Most people just want to be happy. Unfortunately happiness can be very elusive, especially for someone who has been through a relationship breakdown and feels that life has kicked them in the teeth. Although hedonistic pleasures (like a good night out) or sensual ones (a new gadget or new clothes) can bring happiness, they tend to offer only short-term relief. However, if the goal is to grow and become a better person, no experience is wasted. In addition, while happiness can focus attention on what is wrong (and leave someone trapped and dispirited), personal growth focuses on a positive future.

Finding a New Relationship

- *Check that you're really ready.* Divorce is never good for self-esteem and someone, anyone, finding you attractive is bound to go to your head. The giddy excitement of new love will also blow away the blues, so lots of divorcees jump into a new relationship on the rebound. 'It was just going to be a bit of fun,' says Maggie, a thirty-one-year-old personal assistant, 'and we did laugh and I began to feel better and relaxed. That's when he thought I was getting too serious too soon and took off. I came back to earth with a jolt and in fact felt worse than I did before.'

   Tip: Do not overlook the importance of time alone, as this is a chance to find your own individual identity before becoming half of a couple again. As a rule of thumb, we need one year to get through all the difficult dates alone – Christmas, birthday, anniversary – before beginning to heal. So surround yourself with friends or family on these difficult occasions.

- *Don't get stuck on repeat.* Many second-time brides and grooms claim to have married someone completely different from their first partner and have actually gone for the opposite. This means that the same issues are still played out, except from a different position. 'My first husband liked to take charge – to the point of forever telling me what to do and making me feel like a little girl,' says Patsy, a twenty-nine-year-old legal secretary. 'So what I really liked about my second husband was that he was very mild and take-it-as-you-find-it. Except nothing seemed to get done, so I found myself making all the decisions and nagging him. Anybody would have thought I was his mother!' Unfortunately Patsy had not learnt to negotiate properly and find a relationship where responsibility was split evenly.

   Tip: The type of woman or man that you are attracted to

stretches back to your childhood and how you first learnt about relationships: watching your mother and father. The issues they struggled with will be the ones that you are trying to solve too.

- *Don't look too far down the line.* So a year has passed, you are over the worst and back dating again. The temptation now is to think that every new man or new woman is your happy ending. Although this is natural – because it gives us hope that we are not completely useless at relationships – it does not help to fantasise about what breed of dog you will buy together on the second date. 'I always kept the conversation light,' says Jo, thirty-two and divorced for eighteen months, 'but either the men drifted away or became so clinging that it was claustrophobic.' Although Jo was not aware of it, she was giving signals that were putting the right men off.

  Tip: Remember that there are three types of dates: getting to know you dates (first three to five), fun dates (enjoying each other's company) and courting dates. You cannot get to the third type without moving through the first two. Sometimes a fun relationship – in which you can relax and enjoy each other's company – can be very healing and positive, even if it does not lead to a serious long-term relationship. So enjoy the moment.

- *Work out what belongs to the past and what belongs to the present.* When you start a new relationship, do not get angry with your new partner about something that your ex made you angry about. It is easy to read off an old script, particularly when tired or under stress. 'I felt myself freeze when John, my new husband, came into the kitchen and announced that he was stopping decorating because he needed to go off into town for a few bits and pieces,' says Suzanne, thirty-five and a mother of two. 'I snapped at him and he got huffy and we had a terrible row about my attitude. It was only later when I'd calmed down that

I told him how my first husband would use a million excuses –
like not having stuff – to slip out of DIY jobs. But John actually
did need more paint.'

Tip: Become aware of the sensations in your body – heart
beating faster or flushed in the face – so you are aware of the
warning signs of anger. Next, remember to 'check it out' before
flying into a row from the past relationship. For example: 'I'm
sensing that you're using this trip as an excuse – is that right or
wrong?'

- *Don't compare – even in your own head.* However much you
dislike your ex, there will still be things that you particularly
liked: his handiness fixing the dripping tap; her green fingers.
Harping on the past can blind you to your new partner's virtues.
Do not compare yourself to your partner's ex either. 'My second
husband has a cottage in Provence – of course he'd bought it
with his ex but had kept joint custody,' says Gillian, a forty-three-
year-old saleswoman. 'It's great for our combined troop of children, but the holiday was spoilt because he kept mentioning his
ex-wife. How she'd liked this restaurant, about the time they
bought that or did this. All the time I kept thinking, is my cooking
up to standard, did she look better in a bikini?' Although your
new partner will have a natural curiosity about the past after the
first twelve months, don't mention the ex (even in a derogatory
way).

  Tip: Make friends with other couples who have no memory
of either of your first spouses. Only adopting old circles of friends
can trap the relationship in the past.

- *Allow yourself to be vulnerable again.* After being hurt it is
natural to hold something back for fear of being devastated again.
This can also mean that you are not 100 per cent committed to
the new relationship, or alternatively your new partner might feel
that he or she does not really know you. 'A month after the

honeymoon I was in a really strange mood – caged, like an animal,' says Donna, a twenty-six-year-old fitness instructor. 'My husband asked me what was the matter and I was about to push him away with, "Nothing." Instead a small voice said, "I'm frightened." He came over and held me and I cried and cried. At that moment, I'd never felt closer to him.'

Tip: It is impossible to avoid pain; it is part of what makes us human. It is better to accept the ups and downs than take no risks and live life in neutral.

- *Believe in yourself.* If you have gained more self-knowledge, and in particular a greater understanding of your needs, there is no reason why your new relationship should be anything but a great success. 'When I walked into the registry office there were so many friends and family from my first grand wedding,' says Lucy, thirty-one, 'I was fearful they were thinking: here we go again. But deep down I knew this time it was really different.'

 Tip: Surround yourself with people who believe in the power of good relationships, rather than friends who run down potential partners. Ultimately we make good choices and, with love and constructive arguing skills, any obstacle can be overcome.

Summary

- During a major setback, like a relationship breakdown, it feels like the end of the world. However, the dark days could be the springboard for a new, exciting life. The secret is to turn today's bitter lemons into tomorrow's lemonade.
- It takes time to recover from what, after all, has been a personal disaster. So cosset yourself and do not put yourself under extra pressure.
- Allow yourself to be angry but do not take it out on the children or seek revenge, as this will stop them and you recovering.
- With time, self-knowledge and a commitment not to take short cuts, you will reach a better future and fly high again.

Exercises

No matter how positive people choose to be, there are always times when the pain comes crowding back. Normally these destructive thoughts come as pictures or short reels of film. For example, you imagine your ex-partner lying back in the bath with a favourite book and a drink. Meanwhile you still have to cope with the three kids. Alternatively, it might be an event that you regret and your memory keeps playing it over and over. The natural response is to push down these pictures and distract ourselves with something else. Instead try the following exercise. It works best when you're not likely to be interrupted.

Emotional Rescue Package

1 Changing the picture is the best way of reprogramming your brain

to cope with disaster. Give the picture a headline name. Speak it out loud, as this is the first step to distancing yourself from the pain. (For example, you could call the bath picture 'hippo'. A bit of humour always helps diffuse pain.)

2 Where is the picture in your imagination? (Is it straight in front of your eyes or to one side, or perhaps wrapped all round you?) Be specific. Where could you put it and feel better? Try turning the picture into a movie playing on the wall. This can make it seem even further away and therefore less painful. Remember the importance of being specific and again try to speak the results out loud.

3 What colour is the picture? Sometimes changing your picture from black and white to colour, or vice versa, can help you make a memory or your idea of an old partner's new life feel less vivid. It depends on how your imagination works.

4 Is it a moving or a still picture? What can you hear? Once again, changing the form of the picture or changing the voices (turning their volume down, changing the voice to Mickey Mouse-style, etc.) can change the way the memory is stored. Is there a smell or a taste involved? Could you swap a sad sensation for a happier one?

5 Try replaying the movie again. How would you like to change it? (For example, the bath water turns too hot and your ex-partner has to leap out, or the Queen is being shown through his or her bathroom and stops to peer over the tub. She might even ask: Have you come far?) By playing around with your fantasy of their new life you will be reminded that it is only a fantasy. Alternatively, imagine the camera pulling back from the bath and seeing the rest of the house and his or her clothes lying all over the place. Now you can feel relieved that you do not have to pick up after him or her any more.

Finally . . .

In conclusion:

- 'I love you but I'm not in love with you' is the most pressing relationship problem of today. We are no longer prepared to settle for comfortable relationships but expect completely fulfilling ones.
- While love has become the glue that holds relationships together, our culture has treated it as too big or too mystical a subject to be properly pinned down, measured and understood.
- None of our society's myths is stronger than 'Love conquers all'. However, this is only one part of the story – determination, courage and investing time are equally important – but because we shy away from investigating the true nature of **loving attachment** we are blind to its complexity.
- It is impossible to have a fully satisfactory relationship without conflict; avoiding arguments can prevent true loving. The alternative is the hopelessness and powerlessness of, 'Sorry, honey, I fell out of love.'
- ILYB is avoidable and, with a greater knowledge of love and how it changes over time, passion will return along with a truly satisfying relationship.

Appendix

Accentuate the Positive

Below are some possible answers for the exercise in Chapter Eleven:

- Why do I always have to clear up?
  Positive: I'm really grateful when you help me keep the house clean.
  Concrete Goal: It would mean a lot to me if you emptied the bin.

- Will you stop mauling me?
  Positive: I like it when you stroke me gently.
  Concrete Goal: Would you give me a soothing back massage?

- You never initiate sex.
  Positive: I loved it that time that you seduced me.
  Concrete Goal: I'm going to stop asking and wait until you feel ready.

- You're always hanging out with your friends.
  Positive: I love our time together.
  Concrete Goal: Shall we go to the movies on Wednesday?

- I hate it when you avoid me.
  Positive: It's great when you get home early.
  Concrete Goal: Let's meet up after work and go for a drink together.

- You are way too critical.
  Positive: I really appreciated it when you complimented me about . . .
  Concrete Goal: I think we should try to say thank you to each other more often.

- Why can't you lighten up?
  Positive: I really enjoy our fun times together.
  Concrete Goal: Let's do something great this weekend.

- Why didn't you phone me?
  Positive: It's so nice to hear your voice during the day.
  Concrete Goal: Let's try and touch base with each other sometime tomorrow.

- You do nothing with the kids.
  Positive: It means so much to the kids when you do things with them.
  Concrete Goal: Could you take the kids to the park this afternoon?

- Isn't it about time you fixed the hall light?
  Positive: Thank you so much for fixing the sticky drawer, it's made my life so much easier.
  Concrete Goal: Have you any idea when you'll be able to fix the hall light?

Acknowledgements

Thanks for the help, support and advice that have made this book possible: Rosemary Davidson, Mary Davis, Kate Bland, Emily Sweet, Ignacio Jarquin, Chris Taylor, Gail Louw, Jamie Mackay, Sue Quinn, Patrick Walsh, Alan Oliver, Alexandra Pringle, Ruth Logan, Isabella Pereira, Victoria Millar, Lucy Howkins, Jessica Clark, Rosalind Lowe, Nan Parry, Tessa Hilton and Rachel Calder.

NOTE ON THE AUTHOR

Andrew G. Marshall is a marital therapist with twenty years' experience. He works for RELATE, the UK's leading couple-counselling charity, and writes on relationships for *The Times*, the *Observer*, the *Mail on Sunday* and many women's magazines around the world.

www.iloveyoubut.info

A NOTE ON THE TYPE

The text of this book is set in Linotype Sabon, named after the type founder, Jacques Sabon. It was designed by Jan Tschichold and jointly developed by Linotype, Monotype, and Stempel, in response to a need for a typeface to be available in identical form for mechanical hot metal composition and hand composition using foundry type. Tschichold based his design for Sabon roman on a font engraved by Garamond, and Sabon italic on a font by Granjon. It was first used in 1966 and has proved an enduring modern classic.